The Political Economy of Regulation

SUNY Series in Public Administration

Peter Colby, Editor

The Political Economy of Regulation

The Case of Insurance

Kenneth J. Meier

State University of New York Press

Published by
State University of New York Press, Albany

© 1988 State University of New York

For information, address State University of New York
Press, State University Plaza, Albany, N.Y., 12246

Library of Congress Cataloging in Publication Data
Meier, Kenneth J., 1950–
    The political economy of regulation : the case of insurance /
Kenneth J. Meier.
        p.   cm.—(SUNY series in public administration)
    Bibliography: p.
    Includes index.
    ISBN 0-88706-731-X. ISBN 0-88706-732-8 (pbk.)
    1. Insurance—United States—State supervision. 2. Insurance law—Economic
aspects—United States. I. Title. II. Series.
HG8535.M44 1988
368′.973—dc19   87-33769
                                                  CIP

10 9 8 7 6 5 4 3 2 1

To *Alan Clem* who taught me about empirical questions
and *John Fremstad* who taught me about normative questions.

Contents

Tables

Abbreviations

ABA	American Bar Association
ACLI	American Council of Life Insurance
AIPSO	Automobile Insurance Plans Service Office
AMA	American Medical Association
ALR	Adjusted Loss Ratio
ATLA	American Trial Lawyers Association
CAB	Civil Aeronautics Board
CFA	Consumer Federation of America
CLU	Chartered Life Underwriters
CPCU	Chartered Property and Casualty Underwriters
DOD	Department of Defense
DOT	Department of Transportation
DRG	Diagnostic Review Group
EPA	Environmental Protection Agency
ERISA	Employee Retirement Income Security Act
FAA	Federal Aviation Administration
FAIR	Fair access to insurance requirements
FCC	Federal Communications Commission
FCIC	Federal Crop Insurance Corporation
FDA	Food and Drug Administration
FDIC	Federal Deposit Insurance Corporation
FEMA	Federal Emergency Management Administration
FHA	Federal Housing Administration
FIA	Federal Insurance Administration
FSLIC	Federal Savings and Loan Insurance Corporation
FTC	Federal Trade Commission
GAO	General Accounting Office
HCFA	Health Care Financing Administration
HHS	Department of Health and Human Services
HMOs	Health maintenance organizations

ICC	Interstate Commerce Commission
IEA	Insurance Executives Association
IIAA	Independent Insurance Agents of America
INA	Insurance Company of North America
IRAs	Individual retirement accounts
IRS	Internal Revenue Service
ISO	Insurance Services Office
MAP	Marketing assistance plan
NAIC	National Association of Insurance Commissioners
NCUA	National Credit Union Administration
NIC	National Insurance Convention
NICO	National Insurance Consumers Organization
NLRB	National Labor Relations Board
NOW	National Organization of Women
OMB	Office of Management and Budget
OPIC	Overseas Private Investment Corporation
OSHA	Occupational Safety and Health Administration
PAL	Protection against loss
PBGC	Pension Benefit Guaranty Corporation
SBA	Small Business Administration
SEC	Securities and Exchange Commission
SPIC	Securities Investor Protection Corporation
SSA	Social Security Administration
TEFRA	Tax Equity and Fiscal Responsibility Act of 1982
UAW	United Auto Workers
VA	Veterans Administration

Preface

Insurance is a virtually unknown industry to social scientists. Even though the industry's annual sales equal $300 billion, little research covers the political economy of insurance. This book is an attempt to fill that gap by applying the techniques of political economy to the study of insurance regulation.

Other than providing a substantive introduction to the invisible world of insurance regulation, this book has two objectives. First, it seeks to provide an empirical critique of George Stigler's economic theory of regulation. This theory, which contends that regulation is sought by the industry and designed for its own benefit, has been criticized in a variety of other regulatory areas. Insurance regulation, however, is a crucial test. Because insurance issues are generally complex and rarely salient, the insurance industry should have a great advantage over consumer groups, bureaucrats, and political elites. If Stigler's economic theory of regulation works anywhere, it should work in insurance regulation.

Second, the book also seeks to establish a second theory of regulation and subject it to an empirical test. This second theory contends that regulatory policy is a result of a complex interaction of industry, consumers, regulators, political elites, and the environment in which they operate. This theory will be applied to both a historical case study of insurance regulation and a 50-state quantitative analysis of contemporary insurance regulation. The regulatory theory literature is littered with complex theories of regulatory policy that have not been operationalized. This book illustrates that some difficult concepts such as the values of political elites can, in fact, be operationalized in a reasonably efficient manner. Theories that exploit the rich detail possible in case studies can also be used in comparative quantitative analyses. Some readers will recognize that the theory used here has appeared in various forms in my other work (Meier, 1985b; 1987b). I believe the theory can be used to explain a wide variety of regulatory policy.

Three themes permeate this analysis. First, industry groups are rarely unified in pursuing their regulatory objectives. The insurance industry is not one industry but several, each with different policy objectives. Second, the insurance industry has not captured the insurance regulatory policy system. I do not mean to imply that the insurance industry is not the most powerful voice in insurance policy at the state level. It is, particularly in small states without bureaucratic expertise. I contend, rather, that the insurance industry rarely obtains all its goals, that it must make compromises and trade-offs to achieve some of its agenda. As a result, some states have progressive insurance policies that benefit consumers.

Third, simple theories of policy and politics are almost always wrong or incomplete. Regulatory policy must be viewed as a complex interaction between the interests and resources of industry, consumers, regulatory bureaucrats, and other political elites. This study demonstrates that policymakers whether legislators, bureaucrats, or elected chief executives are not neutral arbiters willing to grant the authority of the state to the most powerful group in the interest group process. These policymakers also have policy goals, and they seek to enact them. Their success in this effort varies according to the resources they have and the nature of the political environment.

The Political Economy of Regulation: The Case of Insurance is so titled because the approach used is that of political economy. Both empirical and normative questions are addressed; too often policy analysts avoid addressing normative questions and thus fail to examine public policy fully. The normal distinction between empirical and normative questions is not particularly useful. The second characteristic of a political economy approach is that it is multidisciplinary. Although the techniques of political science and economics are most frequently used in this book, historical analysis also has its role. Technique should not dictate research questions. Because political economy is equally appropriate to quantitative analysis and historical case studies, questions of interest can be addressed regardless of techniques needed to analyze them.

Insurance is a policy area that expands as research examines it. No single book can do justice to all areas of insurance policy, there are simply too many. Priorities were set to restrict the bulk of this book to areas of insurance regulation that had not been addressed before. Social insurance, for example, is discussed only in passing. Volumes already exist on social security, unemployment compensation, and other social insurance programs. In addition, health insurance is treated only peripherally in Chapter 7, and little is included on workers' compensation. Again, the bibliography provides citations for good books in this area. Medical malpractice insurance is also skimmed over; this area is both complex and unique and merits greater treatment than I could give it here.

Ordering the chapters of this book was more difficult a task than I initially thought it would be. Issues at the federal level are difficult to understand without a background in state level regulation. State level regulatory policies similarly are difficult to interpret without information concerning the federal government. In many cases, the reader will be referred to other chapters for more detail about background factors that influence the policy issue being discussed.

Chapter 1 is an introduction to the economic structure of the insurance industry. Because few social scientists have any working knowledge about the industry, its products, and its economics, a substantial introduction was needed. Chapter 2 presents the theory of regulation used to explain insurance regulation. Stigler's theory of economic regulation is subjected to a rigorous theoretical critique, and a multi-interest theory of regulation is presented. Chapter 3 puts insurance regulation in its policy context by describing the activities of the federal and state governments in insurance policy. Again, such background is necessary to understand that regulatory policies are only a portion of the insurance issues that governments influence.

Chapter 4 is a political economy treatment of the history of insurance regulation from colonial times until the late 1970s. Given the separate treatment of lines of insurance by government regulators, providing a smooth flow to this chapter was difficult, although I hope not unsuccessful. Chapter 5 discusses the liability insurance crisis of 1985–1986. This crisis attracted nationwide attention and provided the opportunity to examine the regulatory theory in a contemporary context. Chapter 6 examines five federal insurance issues from the same perspective that the historical review of state regulation took. These five issues—mail-order insurance, flood insurance, no-fault automobile insurance, unisex insurance rating, and taxing insurance companies—are defined as federal issues only because the federal government was a major player in the process not because the states had no role.

Chapter 7 is a quantitative fifty-state analysis of insurance regulatory policies. Using the same theory that drove the discussion of the case study chapters, individual regulatory issues such as regulatory stringency, pricing, regulating access, and taxing insurance policies are examined. Chapter 8 concludes with an assessment of the book's themes and a series of policy recommendations.

Several individuals either assisted or encouraged me in writing this book. I owe them a debt of gratitude. Bill Gormley and Paul Sabatier separately nagged me for years to forget about regulation at the federal level and study it at the state level where all the action is. I would have never started this study had I not taken their advice seriously. Bill also provided an excellent critique of the entire manuscript. Tom Fox, the Wisconsin State Insurance Commissioner, appointed me to his Task Force on Property and

Liability Insurance in 1985. By doing so, he gave me the opportunity to witness the politics of the crisis first hand. I would also like to thank The National Association of Insurance Commissioners (NAIC) and the American Council of Life Insurance (ACLI) for allowing me to use their libraries and badger their librarians. The number of individuals and organizations who responded promptly to requests for data and elaboration are far too numerous to mention. Finally, I would like to thank Peggy Gifford, Peter Colby, and the rest of the persons associated with SUNY Press for encouraging my efforts. Although I would truly like to share the blame with Bill and Paul for any errors I have made in the study, the errors are mine alone.

June 1987
Madison, Wisconsin

Chapter 1

The Insurance Industry

Few industries are as large or as little understood as the insurance industry. In 1985, Americans spent $300 billion to purchase insurance coverages,
an average of $1,257 for every person living in the United States. The indus-
try employs more than two million persons as agents, underwriters, brokers,
or support personnel (Insurance Information Institute, 1986; 12). Americans
routinely insure their lives, their homes, their automobiles, and their health.
Without insurance, goods would not be transported, large construction projects would be impossible, and the overall quality of life would decline
greatly. Despite the importance of insurance in the daily lives of individuals,
people understand the insurance industry about as well as they understand
their homeowners' insurance policy.

If the industry is mysterious, it is no more so than the politics involving
the insurance industry. Even though insurance is the largest state-regulated
industry in the United States, political scientists have ignored the political
economy of insurance regulation. Only one book on insurance has ever been
published by a political scientist and that covered only a minor part of the
industry (regulation of investments; see Orren, 1974). Scholarly articles on
the industry are also sparse.[1]

This chapter presents the reader with a brief overview of the insurance
industry. To provide the background necessary to understand the various
issues of insurance politics, some detail about the industry's structure and
products is necessary.

The Life Insurance Industry

The insurance industry is not one industry but rather several industries
with firms generally specializing in specific lines of insurance. The industry
itself distinguishes between the life insurance and the property and casualty
(PC) insurance industries. The life insurance industry contains not only life

1

insurance but also private health insurance companies.[2] The property and casualty insurance industry consists of the companies that sell all other types of insurance. The distinction between life and health and property and casualty insurance companies was once required by law but now is more tradition than anything else. Most property and casualty companies have life insurance affiliates, and a smaller portion of life insurance companies have property and casualty affiliates.

The 2,600 life and health insurance companies annually collect $156 billion in premiums and earn an additional $78 billion from investments (see Table 1). Unlike most other industries where the profit-making corporation is the norm, many large U. S. life insurance companies are organized as mutuals. Mutual organizations are technically owned by policymakers; purchasing a policy gives an individual an equity share in the company and results in profits returned to the policyholder as dividends. Although only 132 life insurance companies operate as mutuals (the rest are stock companies, the traditional business form), the mutuals control nearly one-half of all life insurance company assets.

The life/health insurance industry offers three basic products—life insurance, annuities, and health insurance. Life insurance comes in a variety of forms including whole life, term, group, and universal life. A life insurance contract essentially builds an estate for an individual, thereby protecting that individual's family from the financial dangers of an untimely death. Annuities are a contract to protect individuals from the financial penalties of old age. An annuity pays an individual a specified income beginning at a certain age and continuing to that person's death. Health insurance, of course, is a contract that obligates the insurance company to pay for health care costs that policyholders incur.

PRODUCT MIX

The mix of products sold by the life insurance industry has varied over time. As Table 1–2 reveals, life insurance was virtually the only product sold by the life insurance industry before 1920. Throughout the last 65 years, the proportion of life insurance company premiums from life insurance has decreased to 38 percent of the total. Annuities and health insurance each contribute approximately 30 percent of these companies' incomes.[3]

Although the insurance industry defines life and health insurance as a single industry, the products have different economic characteristics. Both life insurance and annuities have a long timeframe focus; individuals pay money now for expected future benefits. The contracts are individually based in that benefits to individuals are precisely defined in terms of face value or

Table 1-1
Income Generated by the Insurance Industries (billions)

	Life/Health	Property/Casualty
Premium Income	$156[a]	$144[b]
Investment and Other Income	78	14
Total Income	234	158
Assets	826	311[c]

[a]For 1985, source ACLI, 1986.
[b]For 1985, source *Best's Review,* 1986.
[c]Source, Insurance Information Institute, 1986.

Table 1-2
Premium Income for Life Insurance Companies

	Percent Insurance	Percent Annuities	Percent Health	Total (billions)
1920	99.4%	.6%	0 %	$1.4
1940	90.0	10.0	0	$3.9
1960	69.1	7.7	23.2	$17.4
1970	59.0	10.1	30.9	$36.8
1980	44.0	24.2	31.7	$92.6
1985	38.6	35.6	26.8	$155.9

Source: ACLI, *Life Insurance Fact Book,* annual.

yield. As a result, the cash-flow situation for these products is very positive (that is, income annually exceeds expenses by large amounts; see Table 1-3). Insurance companies issuing these products receive premiums that they are free to invest for many years until the money is needed. Health insurance is much more a pay-as-you-go business for the insurance industry. Health insurance companies annually pay out 66¢ in benefits for every $1 of premiums they collect. Group health insurance is even more short term, the annual benefits to premiums ratio for group insurance is .78 (ACLI, 1985). In addition, health insurance contracts are not individual contracts in the sense that an individual is not limited to collecting a specified amount in benefits.

GROWTH

Life insurance is a rapidly growing industry. According to Table 1-4, the face value (that is, the death benefit) of life insurance in force grew by 71 percent in the five years from 1980 to 1985. Currently, Americans hold life insurance with a face value of $6.1 trillion. Obviously, an industry that expects to pay individuals $6.1 trillion sometime in the future based on an annual premium income of $156 billion is intending to make some money on

Table 1-3
Cash Flow for Life Insurance Companies (millions)

	Benefits Paid	Premiums	Return Rate
Life Insurance[a]	$16,572	$51,274	32.7%
Annuities	17,912	42,859	41.7%
Health Insurance	27,053	40,651	66.5%
All Life Insurance Payments	42,520[b]	51,274	82.9%

[a]Includes death benefits only.
[b]Includes death benefits, surrender values, and dividends.
Source: ACLI, 1985.

Table 1-4
Total U. S. Life Insurance in Force (billions)

1920	$40.5
1940	$115.5
1960	$586.4
1970	$1,402.1
1980	$3,541.0
1985	$6,053.1

Source: ACLI, *Life Insurance Fact Book,* annual.

investments. Life insurance companies are financial intermediaries; they collect savings (that is, premiums) from individuals and invest these savings in the economy. In this sense, they are similar to banks, brokerage firms, or pension funds. Funds invested by life insurance companies are termed *assets*. Life insurance company assets have increased by 72 percent since 1980 and totaled $826 billion in 1985 (see Table 1-5).

The importance of life insurance companies as financial intermediaries is illustrated by Table 1-6. Life insurance companies provide as much money for the U. S. economy as do all the nation's savings and loans associations. Only commercial banks are a larger financial intermediary than life insurance companies. Life insurance companies' assets exceed those of mutual savings banks, credit unions, state and local government pension funds, and all private (that is, noninsurance company run) pension plans.

With large sums of money to invest, decisions made by life insurance companies have ramifications for the national economy. Where life insurance companies invest their money often depends on where the companies feel they can get the best long-term return on investment. Unlike property and casualty companies that must keep a large portion of their investments liquid to pay claims, life insurance companies often do not anticipate paying bene-

Table 1-5
Total Assets of Life Insurance Companies

1920	$7.3
1940	$30.8
1960	$119.6
1970	$207.3
1980	$479.2
1985	$825.9

Source, ACLI, *Life Insurance Fact Book,* annual.

Table 1-6
Assets of Major Financial Intermediaries—1984

Intermediary	Assets (billions)
Life Insurance Companies	$723
Property and Casualty Insurance Companies	264
Savings Associations	724[a]
Commercial Banks	1,056[a]
Credit Unions	108[a]
Private Pension Plans	608[b]
State and Local Government Pension Plans	290[b]

[a]American League of Savings Associations, *Savings Association Fact Book,* 1985.
[b]ACLI, *Pension Facts,* 1985.

fits for 20, 30, 40 or more years in the future. This longer viewpoint allows the insurance company to make longer term investments than can be made by many individuals or by other financial intermediaries.

The distributions of life insurance company investments for 1945, 1975, and 1985 are shown in Table 1-7. Despite the magnitude of their investments, insurance companies move their money to different categories of investments over time. Intracategory movement is even greater. For example, with few domestic investment opportunities and the strong demand for war-related funds, insurance companies invested heavily in government securities in 1945. Over time these securities were sold or redeemed, and investments were made in corporate bonds and mortgages. In recent years, the unattractive rates associated with long-term mortgages have resulted in fewer investments in home mortgages and more investments in other types of assets.

These investment patterns show that life insurance companies are major financial players competing with commercial banks in the corporate bond market and savings associations in the mortgage market. Life insurance companies are not as important in the stock market or in real estate markets because many state laws either have or once had restrictions prohibiting life

Table 1-7
The Distribution in Life Insurance Assets

	1945	1975	1985
Government Securities	50.3%	5.2%	15.0%
Corporate Bonds	22.5	36.6	36.0
Corporate Stocks	2.2	9.7	9.4
Mortgages	14.8	30.8	20.8
Real Estate	1.9	3.3	3.5
Policy Loans	4.4	8.5	6.6
Miscellaneous	3.9	5.9	8.7
Total (billions)	$44.8	$289.3	$825.9

Source: ACLI, *Life Insurance Factbook,* annual.

insurance investments in real estate or stocks (see Chapter 5). Policy loans are, of course, a unique investment for life insurance companies; these assets are loans to policyholders with the cash value of the insurance policies as collateral.[4]

INDUSTRY STRUCTURE

With 2,260 firms nationwide, the life insurance industry has the potential to be a competitive industry. Although companies must be licensed in each state where they sell insurance, many companies sell life insurance in virtually all 50 states. The gigantic size of the industry means that the leading industry firms are by definition large corporations (35 mutuals and 80 stock companies had 1985 assets in excess of $1 billion), but even so the life insurance industry is not especially concentrated compared to other industries. Table 1-8 shows the ten largest life insurance companies ranked according to assets in 1965 and 1985. Although most of these companies quadrupled their assets in the past 20 years and although nine of the top ten companies in 1965 remained there in 1985, industry concentration declined. The percentage of assets controlled by the three largest firms declined from 35.9 percent to 27.1 percent; the portion controlled by the top five firms dropped 11 percentiles, and the portion controlled by the top ten dropped 10 percentiles.

Despite the large size of the industry leaders, the life insurance industry does not have excessive barriers to entry or exit. For the 1980s, between 100 and 150 new life insurance firms were founded annually. The capital requirements to start a new life insurance company vary by state, and in some states capital requirements are modest. (See Chapter 7 on capital requirements.) A life insurance company is prevented by regulation from simply exiting from

Table 1–8
Ten Largest Life Insurance Companies
Assets 1965–1985 (billions)

1985		1965	
Company	*Assets*	*Company*	*Assets*
1. Prudential	$91.1	1. Metropolitan	$22.5
2. Metropolitan	76.5	2. Prudential	22.4
3. Equitable	48.0	3. Equitable	12.2
4. Aetna*	37.9	4. New York Life	8.9
5. New York Life	28.0	5. John Hancock	8.0
6. John Hancock	26.3	6. Aetna*	5.5
7. Travelers*	25.6	7. Northwestern	5.1
8. TIAA*	23.2	8. Travelers*	3.8
9. Conn. General*	22.2	9. Conn. General*	3.3
10. Northwestern	17.9	10. Mass. Mutual	3.3
Assets Held by Top 3	27.1%	1965	35.9%
Assets Held by Top 5	35.4%	1965	46.6%
Assets Held by Top 10	49.9%	1965	59.8%

*Indicates stock company; all others are mutuals.
Source: *Best's Review,* July 1986 and ACLI, *Life Insurance Fact Book,* annual.

the market because individuals purchase life insurance and annuities now with the expectation of future payments. Despite regulatory restrictions, life insurance companies can exit from the industry by selling their policies to another company, merging with another company, or undergoing liquidation by a state regulator. During the 1980s, between 80 and 100 firms annually exited the market; most merged with other life insurance companies.

The Property and Casualty Industries

The property and casualty insurance industry has 3,500 separate companies collecting $144 billion in insurance premiums annually. The property and casualty industry is more heterogeneous than the life insurance industry; it is divided into specialties called "lines of insurance." The major lines of property and casualty insurance, though by no means all lines, are shown in Table 1–10. Each line is, in reality, a separate industry. In the early twentieth century insurance companies generally wrote insurance in only one line (see Chapter 5) because state laws limited companies to specified lines of insurance. Although such restrictions no longer exist and approximately 900 multiline companies operate nationwide, some specialization is still found.

The Political Economy of Regulation

Table 1-9
Entry and Exit of Life Insurance Companies

Year	Total Companies	New Companies	Exits
1980	1958	155	92
1981	1991	137	104
1982	2060	152	83
1983	2117	137	80
1984	2193	166	90
1985	2260	NA	NA

Source: ACLI, 1986.

Table 1-10
Property and Casualty Insurance Lines

Line	1985 Premiums[a] (billions)	Percent	% Growth Since 1976	10-Year ALR
Automobile	61.3	42.5	139%	70.2
Inland Marine	3.7	2.6	154%	58.9
Health and Accident	3.2	2.2	51%	86.6
Workers Compensation	17.0	11.8	126%	72.9
General Liability	11.5	8.0	172%	67.5
Medical Malpractice	2.8	1.9	145%	90.4
Fire and Allied Lines	6.2	4.3	51%	56.6
Homeowners	14.1	9.8	147%	63.3
Commercial Multiple Peril	12.1	8.4	199%	61.4
Ocean Marine	1.2	.8	30%	73.0
Surety	2.3	1.6	285%	40.2
Reinsurance	5.2	3.6	323%	80.6
All other lines	3.6	2.5	—	—
Total	144.2	100.0	138%	68.9

ALR—adjusted loss ratio.
Source: *Best's Aggregates & Averages 1986.*

Insurance companies prefer to write insurance in lines where they have experience. A major automobile insurance company, for example, would be unlikely to offer medical malpractice insurance.

The largest single line of property and casualty insurance is for automobiles; it comprises 42.5 percent of the P/C market. Although the industry further divides automobile insurance into private passenger and commercial insurance *and* into property damage and liability insurance, automobile insurance can be considered a single industry. The marketing mechanisms for private passenger and commercial automobile insurance differ, however. Private passenger automobile insurance has numerous buyers with no single buyer exerting any appreciable influence on the market price. Commercial automobile insurance has large corporate buyers and local governments who are sometimes capable of exerting market power. Commercial automobile insurance policies also can be customized to the buyer while private passenger policies rarely are.[5]

These differences in product result in differences in industry structure. The private passenger automobile insurance market is dominated by direct writers. Direct writers are insurance companies that employ their own sales and claims staffs in contrast with companies that use independent agents to sell and service their policies. Direct writers, because they are more efficient, are able to sell individual insurance policies at a lower price. Direct writers (for example, State Farm, Allstate, Nationwide) control 53 percent of the automobile insurance market and 61 percent of the private passenger market (Wasilewski, 1986b: 14ff). In commercial automobile policies where the mass-marketed, uniform policy is less useful, direct writers have only 21 percent of the market.

Workers' compensation insurance, the second largest property and casualty line, is insurance purchased by industries to pay claims filed by workers injured on the job. Workers' compensation is a complex policy area that merits study by itself (see Chiet, 1961; Williams, 1981; Gersuny, 1981); it will not be covered in this book. One interesting market structure aspect of workers' compensation insurance is that some state government agencies sell workers' compensation insurance in competition with private companies; in other states, the government has reserved a monopoly in workers' compensation insurance for itself.

Homeowners' insurance is a multiple peril type of insurance that covers homeowners for damages from fire, weather (but not flooding), and accidents to visitors among other things. Homeowners' insurance has a marketing structure much like that of private passenger automobile insurance: standard policies can be mass marketed. This $14 billion per year industry is dominated by direct writers who control 46.7 percent of the market.

At one time, commercial insurance as well as homeowners insurance was written only on a single line basis. Business owners had to buy one insurance policy for fire coverage, another for theft, another for broken glass, and another for boilers. The dominant insurance companies at this time were in fire insurance, but with the rise of multiline companies (see Chapter 5), fire insurance and its allied lines has become a minor line of insurance with only 4.3 percent of the market. Fire insurance for business has been replaced by commercial multiple peril insurance which consolidates the various risks. Because a commercial multiple peril policy must in some sense be customized to fit the individual corporation, this line of business must be handled through agents. Direct writers control only 13.3 percent of the market in commercial multiple peril insurance and only 20.2 percent in fire insurance.

General liability insurance is insurance purchased by businesses or professionals to protect themselves from damage claims made by others. Liability insurance for defective products or facilities is a major part of general liability insurance. This line of insurance was the focus of the 1985–1986 liability insurance crisis (see Chapter 6). For many years, medical malpractice insurance was so insignificant that it was included as part of the general liability line. With the rise in litigation in this area (see Meier and Copeland, 1986), it grew to be a separate line comprising almost 2 percent of property and casualty premiums. General liability insurance is another product that must be tailored to individual needs; 83 percent of general liability insurance is written through agents (Freedman, 1986: 33). Medical malpractice insurance went through a major profit crisis in the early 1970s. As a result of this crisis, many insurance companies abandoned the line; and physician-owned mutual insurance companies entered. These "direct writers" write approximately one-half the medical malpractice insurance in the United States (Freedman, 1986: 139).

The remaining lines of property and casualty insurance are fairly minor. Ocean marine insurance protects goods from loss in ocean transport, while inland marine offers the same protection for other modes of transport. Health and accident insurance is the same insurance offered by life insurance companies to protect individuals from medical bills and accidents. Surety insurance covers the financial guarantees needed by certain professionals who require bonding. Specialized lines for aircraft, glass, boilers, wind damages, and so on continue to exist.

Reinsurance is a small, but extremely important, line of insurance. Insurance companies that insure risks with large potential losses seek to minimize their losses somewhat by spreading the risks. They do this by selling a portion of the insurance underwritten to another insurance company. For example, assume a company has agreed to insure a building for $500 million. Because the company does not have the assets to pay off such a claim, it might retain the coverage for the first $100 million for itself and sell coverage on losses of between $100 to $500 million to other insurance companies. Reinsurance companies generally specialize in large risks with low probabilities of occurrence. Lloyds of London is perhaps the most famous reinsurance company. Reinsurance is a vital part of the general liability, medical malpractice, commercial multiple peril, ocean marine, and fire insurance lines.

Property and casualty lines can be divided into long- and short-tail lines. A short-tail line of insurance is one where the losses show up quickly after the insurance is issued. A long-tail line of insurance might not produce a claim for several years after a policy is issued because injured individuals might not immediately realize that they have been harmed (for example, workers exposed to toxic chemicals). Short-tail lines, which include automobile, homeowners, fire, and marine insurance, spend most of their premiums immediately on claims. These companies write a large number of policies and generally have a positive cash flow every year. Long-tail lines often invest premiums for years earning interest before claims come due; general liability, medical malpractice, and reinsurance are long-tail lines. Long-tail lines face less predictable yearly payouts; they often earn a large portion of their income from investments.

The adjusted loss ratios for each line of insurance are also listed in Table 1–10. The adjusted loss ratio is the total claims paid divided by the earned premiums. For short-tail lines, the adjusted loss ratio is a reasonable indicator of financial health (lower ratios indicate more positive cash flow). For long-tail lines, adjusted loss ratios have less meaning because claims paid also include funds set aside in reserves to pay claims that have not yet been made (see Chapter 6).

ASSETS

Because even insurance companies in long-tail lines of property and casualty insurance expect to pay claims sooner than a life insurance company would, the assets acquired by property and casualty companies are substantially less than the assets accumulated by life and health insurance companies. Table 1–11 shows the premium income and the growth of assets for property and casualty companies over time. Property and casualty companies currently have approximately $311 billion in assets. They earned premiums of $144 billion in 1985.

The role that property and casualty insurance companies play in the financial markets is, therefore, substantially less than that played by the life and health insurance companies. Still, $311 billion in assets is not a trivial amount. Historically property and casualty companies had fewer investment restrictions than life insurance companies. Despite the lack of restrictions, property and casualty insurance companies' investments are similar to life and health insurance investments. As Table 1–12 illustrates, property and casualty companies hold more than 60 percent of their assets in government securities; much of that is in tax-free revenue bonds. The major difference between the property and casualty industry and the life industry is the investment in stocks. Without the traditional restrictions that exist in the life insurance industry, and with the need to be more liquid than life insurance companies, property and casualty companies made major investments in

Table 1–11
Property and Casualty Insurance Company Assets and Premiums

Year	Assets (billions)	Premiums[a] (millions)
1940	$5.1	NA
1960	29.4	$14,972
1970	58.6	32,867
1980	197.7	95,568
1984	264.7	118,166
1985	311.6	144,186

[a]Premiums are net premiums written.
Source: Insurance Information Institute, *Insurance Facts*, annual.

Table 1–12
*Percentage Distribution of Property and Casualty
Insurance Company Assets*

Percent of Assets in:	1970	1975	1985
Government Securities	46.0%	53.8%	62.0%
Corporate Bonds	16.8	15.3	12.6
Common Stocks	33.3	26.2	19.2
Preferred Stocks	3.4	4.0	3.8
All Other Investments	.6	.7	2.3

Source: Insurance Information Institute, *Insurance Facts*, annual.

common and preferred stock. Just as life insurance companies' investments change over time to seek higher returns, so do those of property and casualty companies.

INDUSTRY CONCENTRATION

At first glance, the property and casualty industry looks relatively un-concentrated. After all, more than 3,500 insurance companies sell property and casualty insurance. Table 1–13, listing the ten largest property and casualty insurance companies in the United States, appears to confirm this. Although these are large corporations by any measure of the term, the three largest firms have only 18 percent of the market; and the top ten firms have only 39 percent of the market.

Conclusions concerning industry concentration based on Table 1–13 would be misleading, however, because property and casualty insurance is not a single, nationwide market. Many firms offer only a few lines of insur-

Table 1-13
Ten Largest Property and Casualty Insurance Companies

Company	1985 Premiums (millions)
1. State Farm	$14,096
2. Allstate	7,560
3. Aetna	5,718
4. Nationwide	4,436
5. Liberty Mutual	4,161
6. Travelers	4,140
7. Farmers	4,019
8. CIGNA	3,980
9. Hartford Fire	3,627
10. Continental	3,382

Source: *Best's Review,* 1986.

ance, and most companies are not licensed to sell in insurance in all states. Table 1-14 lists the market percentage controlled by the largest three, five, ten, and twenty firms in each major line of insurance. Individual lines of insurance are far more concentrated than the overall P/C market. The top three firms control approximately one-third of the market in private passenger automobile insurance and homeowners' insurance. The concentration percentages for each line are not much different from the life insurance concentration percentages shown in Table 1-8.

The market concentration figures in Table 1-14 are still underestimates, however, because property and casualty insurance lines do not operate as national markets. Because states regulate and license insurance, markets for many insurance lines are statewide at best. Table 1-15 shows the average

Table 1-14
Market Concentration Figures by Property and Casualty Line 1985

Percent of the Market Controlled by the

Line	Top 3	Top 5	Top 10	Top 20
All Property/Casualty Lines	17.9	24.6	39.1	56.5
Automobile Insurance	28.6	35.4	45.6	57.9
Private Passenger Auto	34.5	41.1	50.5	62.1
Medical Malpractice	29.7	36.9	51.0	68.7
General Liability	22.1	30.7	47.4	66.9
Homeowners'	31.1	36.9	45.7	59.1
Commercial Multiple Peril	19.2	28.0	44.5	63.0

Source: *Best's Review,* 1986.

Table 1-15
Three Firm Concentration Percentages*

Line	Nationwide Market	Statewide Markets
All Property/Casualty Lines	17.9	25.8
Automobile Insurance	28.6	36.7
Medical Malpractice	29.7	79.1
General Liability	22.1	26.5
Homeowners	31.1	38.6
Commercial Multiple Peril	19.2	26.9

*Percentage of the market held by the three largest firms.
Source: Calculated by the author from *Best's Review.*

three-firm concentration level for six lines of insurance based on 50-state averages. These figures reveal that statewide markets are more concentrated than national market figures would indicate. Especially sensitive to smaller markets are those lines with aggressive direct writers—automobiles, homeowners, and medical malpractice insurance. Of these only medical malpractice, however, is a highly concentrated industry; the three largest companies on the average control 79 percent of the malpractice insurance market.

ENTRY AND EXIT

Barriers to entry in the property and casualty insurance industry do not appear excessive. Although all states place minimum capital and other restrictions on starting a new property and casualty company, between 26 and 72 new insurance companies have been started annually since 1980. Because the 1980s were not particularly good years for property and casualty companies in general, this rate of entry must be considered reasonable. Exit figures reveal the industry's recent economic difficulties. In the past two years, 46 companies have exited each year. More than one-half the exits were involuntary; that is, firms were forced to exit the industry, in most cases by state insurance regulators. Most exiting firms, however, were small insurance companies. Despite the recent increase in exits, in every year, the number of new firms exceeded the number of exiting firms.

PROFITS

The level of insurance industry profits is a highly controversial issue (see Chapter 6). Insurance is governed by different accounting rules so that indus-

Table 1-16
Entry and Exit of Property and Casualty Firms

Year	Total Firms	Retirements	Involuntary	Liquidation	New Firms
1980	3,345	16	6	6	50
1981	3,361	10	2	2	26
1982	3,391	9	3	3	39
1983	3,411	27	7	0	47
1984	3,456	46	27	3	72
1985	3,468	46	26	5	58

Source: *Best's Review,* annual.

try figures may well underestimate profits compared to profits reported by other industries. Only if the profits are based on relatively similar accounting rules can the figures be compared[6].

One source of reasonably good industrywide profit figures is *Forbes. Forbes* publishes an annual estimate of profits in the insurance industry for life insurance firms, property and casualty insurance firms, and diversified insurance firms (that is, firms that sell both types of insurance). Because *Forbes* also provides an average profit figure for all industries, insurance companies can be compared to some standard. Profit estimates for an 11-year period appear in Table 1-17. A simple scan of the data reveals that insurance industry profits are similar to those in other industries. In seven of the 11 years, property and casualty companies and diversified insurance companies

Table 1-17
Profit Figures for the Insurance Industry
(percentage return on equity)

Year	Life Insurance	P/C Insurance	Diversified Insurance	All Industries
1985	11.9	6.4	9.9	12.7
1984	11.9	6.6	11.8	13.4
1983	13.0	12.4	13.3	12.6
1982	11.0	13.3	15.7	12.7
1981	14.9	17.2	14.9	14.7
1980	13.9	21.5	17.8	16.1
1979	15.0	23.0	20.0	16.7
1978	15.0	25.4	20.8	15.4
1977	13.0	21.3	17.2	13.9
1976	12.3	13.3	12.8	12.9
1975	11.9	10.2	6.2	11.7
11-Year Average	13.1	15.5	14.6	13.9

Source: *Forbes,* annual.

had higher profits than the all-industries figures. In three of 11 years, the life insurance industry had higher profits than the all-industries figure.

The average profit figures for this 11-year period are 13.1 percent for life insurance firms,[7] 15.5 for property and casualty insurance firms, 14.6 percent for diversified firms, and 13.9 percent for the all-industries figure. These averages reveal basically similar long-run profit figures for the insurance industries versus other industries. The one major difference between insurance profits and those of other industries is that insurance industry profits are more variable over time. Particularly in the property and casualty insurance industry, profits fluctuate more than the all-industries' profits because payouts are less predictable.

A second indicator of the insurance industry's financial soundness is stock prices. Since 1975, stock prices for life insurance companies have increased by 278 percent and those for property and casualty companies have increased by 296 percent. These figures compare to the 155 percent increase from 1975 to 1985 in the all stocks index of the New York Stock Exchange.[8] Surprisingly, aggregate stock prices are unrelated to aggregate profits. The correlation between stock prices and profits for the past ten years is -.25 for the life insurance industry and -.51 for the property and casualty industry.

One final note about insurance industry profits is in order. Often, loss ratios are quoted to indicate that the insurance industry is in dire financial straits. Using the ten-year profit figures for property and casualty figures and the loss ratio figures for this industry, the relationship between loss ratios and profits can be estimated. The adjusted loss ratio is the ratio of claims paid (including loss reserves) divided by premiums earned less dividends paid. When this figure is used as the independent variable in a regression on P/C industry profits (Table 1–18), calculations show that the industry breakeven point is an adjusted loss ratio of 81.06. In other words, at adjusted loss ratios of less than 81, the property and casualty insurance industry is profitable.

The combined ratio is the ratio of claims paid plus loss adjustment expenses plus other business expenses divided by the total premiums earned. This figure does not include investment income. The second regression in Table 1–18 shows that the property and casualty insurance industry is profitable at combined ratios of less than 122.08. Combined ratios greater than 100 are profitable simply because the combined ratio does not include investment income or tax rebates. These breakeven points are for the entire industry. Individual lines will have vastly different breakeven points depending on the expenses involved in processing claims and the amount of investment income. Individual firms can also have different breakeven points for the same reason.

Table 1-18
Relationship between Profits and Insurance Loss Ratios

Adjusted Loss Ratio

$$
\begin{aligned}
\text{Profit} &= 95.88 - 1.18 \text{ (Adjusted Loss Ratio)} \\
r^2 &= .84 \\
t &= 6.39 \\
p &= .0002 \\
n &= 10 \\
\text{Breakeven point} &= 81.06
\end{aligned}
$$

Combined Ratio

$$
\begin{aligned}
\text{Profit} &= 106.2 - .86 \text{ (Combined Ratio)} \\
r^2 &= .80 \\
t &= 5.65 \\
p &= .0005 \\
n &= 10 \\
\text{Breakeven point} &= 122.08
\end{aligned}
$$

Summary

Insurance regulation is a widely ignored segment of political economy. Although insurance directly affects virtually every individual in the United States and although the size of the industry dwarfs that of other industries that are frequently studied, social scientists know little about the politics or economics of insurance. This chapter outlines the structure of the insurance industry in the United States.

Insurance is not a single industry but rather several industries. The general grouping of life and health insurance companies into one industry and property and casualty insurance companies into another must be subdivided yet again. Individual lines of insurance have unique characteristics, and therefore, must be studied separately. Overall, these industries, except for medical malpractice insurance, are only moderately concentrated, barriers to entry and exit are generally low, and profits are good but highly variable.

Chapter 2

A Theory of Government Regulation

The study of regulation has spawned several partial theories to explain government policy. Economists prefer their version of capture theory, which predicts that government policy is responsive to the regulated industry. Similarly, some political scientists and consumer advocates also hold dear the idea that regulatory agencies are captured by the industries they are intended to regulate. Both approaches are narrow views of the regulatory process that have outlived their usefulness as accurate predictors of government policy. This chapter presents a synthesized theory of regulatory policy that combines empirical findings in both economics and political science. The theory also incorporates findings from both the quantitative analyses of regulatory policy and the rich case study literature. The result is a theory of the regulatory process that is equally applicable to quantitative cross-sectional analyses and individual case studies.

First, the dominant regulatory theory in economics, George Stigler's (1971) theory of economic regulation is criticized; its shortcomings as well as the shortcomings of other capture theories will be revealed. Second, the case study literature is examined to specify additional actors that must be considered in any adequate regulatory theory. Third, the more recent political science literature that examines regulation both longitudinally and cross-sectionally is presented. Finally, each stream of literature is fused into a comprehensive theory of regulation that is used to explain the political economy of insurance regulation.

Economic Theories of Regulation

The first economist to present an empirical theory of regulation was George Stigler (1971) writing in the *Bell Journal of Economics and Manage-*

ment Science. Prior theories of regulation by economists, often called "public interest theory," were normative, stressing what the purpose of regulation *should* be rather than explaining why regulation produced the policies that it did. Stigler's (1971: 3) central thesis was that "regulation is acquired by the industry and designed and operated primarily for its benefit." He rejected the idea that regulation was designed "for the protection and benefit of the public at large." By postulating regulation's intent to benefit the regulated industry, Stigler contends that regulatory actions are predictable. In support of this contention, Stigler cites airmail subsidies, restrictions on entry by the Civil Aeronautics Board (CAB), the Federal Deposit Insurance Corporation (FDIC), the Interstate Commerce Commission (ICC), and government-sponsored price fixing.[1]

Industry domination of the regulatory process is not perfect, however, because small firms have a disproportionate influence on industry actions,[2] because regulation generates procedural safeguards that impose costs, and because the political process automatically admits powerful outsiders to industry's councils. To illustrate empirically the impact of a regulated industry on regulatory policy, Stigler examined the weight limitations that state governments placed on trucks. To explain variation in state weight limits, Stigler used three independent variables—the number of trucks per 1,000 agricultural employees, the average length of railroad haul for freight traffic, and the percentage of roads with high-quality road service. Although he was able to explain 50 percent of the variation in four-wheel truck weight limits and 24 percent of the variation in six-wheel truck weight limits, these results hardly supported his theory that regulatory interests dominate the regulatory process. None of the indicators relate to the power of the trucking industry. Agriculture trucks relate to farmers' desires to transport goods without regulation; railroad long hauls indicate how profitable competition with railroads might be; what high-quality roads indicate is not clear.[3] Stigler's first empirical example, therefore, demonstrates that nonindustry groups (for example, farmers and railroads) influenced trucking regulation. No evidence is presented that truckers exercised any influence over trucking regulation.[4]

Stigler then discusses the process of political influence. The regulator, he contends, needs political support to stay in office.[5] Industry is willing to supply this political support in exchange for regulations that benefit the industry. What results from this exchange is a situation similar to a market whereby industry has a demand for regulation and regulatory officials can supply it.

The empirical core of Stigler's argument is an analysis of state occupational regulation. Examining state actions to regulate 11 different occupations, Stigler hypothesizes that four variables affect whether a state will regulate a profession. Regulation is more likely if (1) the number of practitioners is large, (2) the per capita income of the practitioners is large, (3) the practitioners are concentrated in urban areas, and (4) no cohesive opposition to licensing is found (Stigler, 1971: 13–14). The first two variables reflect the resources (votes and potential contributions) that an industry has. The urbanization variable, according to Stigler, indicates the amount of contact between group members (greater contact in urban areas).

Stigler's discussion of occupational licensing produces a theory different from his previous discussion of the regulatory process. First, he incorporates the presence of opposition. Regulation cannot be a simple supply-and-demand relationship between the regulated industry and government if the position of other interests must be considered. Stigler implies, but never states, that regulation reflects some equilibrium position acceptable to all groups.

Second, Stigler presents some rudimentary ideas about why one industry might be more effective than another at seeking regulation. Total members, income, and contact between members are the key variables. Although this attempt at a more specific model is laudable, it exposes a contradiction in Stigler's own theory. Size in this example is positively related to impact, but earlier in his free rider discussion he argues that smaller groups are more likely to be influential.[6]

In operationalizing his model, Stigler (1971: 14) actually uses only two variables—the occupation's proportion of the total labor force (the size variable) and the proportion of the occupation that resides in urban areas (the contact variable). Both income and opposition disappear from the model. Using these two variables, Stigler attempts to predict the establishment of regulation by a state. The results must be characterized as disappointing. Only eight of the 22 relationships are statistically significant ($p < .05$), and the model explains only 14 percent of the variation for the average occupation.

Because Stigler's empirical results are widely cited as evidence in support of his thesis that regulation reflects the interests of the industry, they merit closer examination. Essentially, Stigler assumes that regulation reflects the interests of the regulated and then tries to see how well he can predict whether an occupation is regulated given this assumption. The results, 14 percent of the variation explained, would be considered so trivial by political scientists who do state level analysis that they might not even report them. (See Dye, 1966, for the normal level of explanation.) Only for veterinarians does the level of explanation exceed 20 percent.

In addition, Stigler's model may actually explain far less of industry regulation than he claims. The contact variable is the proportion of the occupation residing in urban areas, and this variable is easily the better explanatory variable in Stigler's equations. The variable, however, has a serious limitation. Occupations often have trade associations that exist prior to regulation (see Akers, 1968) so that contact is established regardless of urbanization. Urbanization of an occupation is highly correlated with urbanization of the entire population. This measure, therefore, might be a measure of contact among consumers rather than among producers (Meier, 1987b). If one contends that some regulation might not be in the interests of the regulated occupation, then relationships between urbanization and regulation might indicate a consumer impact. One thing is clear, however: they do not unambiguously indicate that regulation reflects the interests of the regulated (see also Etzioni's 1986 critique of Stigler and Friedland, 1962).

To further support his contention that regulation is in the interests of the regulated, Stigler (1971: 17) presents tabular data that shows (1) licensed occupations have higher incomes than unlicensed occupations, (2) membership in licensed professions is more stable, (3) licensed occupations are less likely to be employed by business enterprises (and thus have opposition to licensing), and (4) occupations with national markets are less likely to be licensed. Because these findings are based on simple tabular data without the benefit of statistical controls, they should be treated with skepticism. A review of the literature (see Meier, 1985b: 184–192) shows that the impact of occupational regulation is not as clear cut as Stigler paints it.

STIGLER: AN EVALUATION

The work of George Stigler has been enthusiastically received by economists and generally ignored by political scientists.[7] Within economics, Stigler's views were a radical departure from the traditional view of regulation. Prior to Stigler, economics was dominated by the "public interest" view of regulation. The purpose of regulation in the public interest view was to correct market failures—monopoly, externalities, imperfect information—that led to inefficient outcomes. Because regulation often failed to correct these market failures, it was deemed a failure.[8] Stigler correctly perceived that if regulation was not attaining the goals that economists prescribed for it, then perhaps regulation had different goals. By presenting his argument that regulation reflected conditions similar to a supply-and-demand situation and that such situations produced regulation in the interests of the regulated rather than efficient allocation, Stigler was asking economists to reject their normative public interest theory for his empirical theory.[9]

Stigler's pioneering work in regulation stimulated a great deal of additional research especially in the area of occupational regulation (see Meier, 1985b: 184–192 for a review). Most economic studies of regulation feel compelled to cite the work even if the perspective is not used. In political science, however, the effort of Stigler is often ignored. Perhaps the reason for this is that Stigler's effort offered political scientists little that they did not already know; political scientists had similar theories, and capture theories had proved at best simplistic and at worst wrong.

To reveal fully the limitations of Stigler's economic theory for political research, a brief synopsis of the theory must be presented again. First, Stigler assumes that regulation reflects the interests of the regulated industry and seeks to explain why. Industries demand regulation because they can economically benefit from regulation; they use regulation to gain the benefits of collusion that they can achieve in no other way. In exchange for regulation, industries can offer political support that "regulators" need to stay in office. The industry and the political system can engage in mutually beneficial exchanges whereby the industry gets protective regulation and the regulator gets resources needed to stay in office. Consumer groups may oppose such regulation, but they are of little consequence because they lack the resources that the industry groups have.

Stigler's main point, therefore, is that regulatory policy reflects the demands of interest groups participating in the political process. Policy is an equilibrium that is acceptable to the active participants. Even though Stigler and other economists denigrate the work of David Truman (1951) as inexact, Stigler presents a simplistic view of pluralism less advanced than the work of Truman and others that was written 20 years earlier. Truman argued policy resulted from the competition between groups. The only addition offered by Stigler was that industry groups have greater resources than consumer groups (not a particularly insightful addition), and therefore, should benefit more from regulation.[10] By the time Stigler's essay was published, pluralism had been rejected by many political scientists for both normative and empirical reasons (Schattschneider, 1960; Pateman, 1970; Bachrach and Baratz, 1970).

The argument that regulation benefits the regulated was hardly new to political science. Pendleton Herring's (1936) examination of several federal regulatory agencies concluded exactly that. Huntington (1952) argued that the poor performance of the ICC reflected this orientation. Marver Bernstein (1955) developed his life cycle theory of regulatory agencies to explain why agencies became captured by the regulated industry. Murray Edelman (1964) found that regulation was often an exercise in symbolic politics; consumers received the symbolic reassurances of regulation while industry received the real benefits. Theodore Lowi (1969) generalized this observation by incorporating it into his concept of interest group liberalism.

Not only was Stigler's view not new to political scientists, but significant empirical evidence suggested that Stigler and other "capture" theorists were incorrect. As early as 1971 evidence suggested that several regulatory agencies were not regulating in the interests of the regulated. The Food and Drug Administration (FDA) was imposing major testing costs on pharmaceutical manufacturers; the Federal Aviation Administration (FAA) required large expenditures for airline safety; the Federal Trade Commission (FTC) had recently become a vigorous consumer advocate. Several agencies had been recently created that showed no signs of being captured—the Environmental Protection Agency (EPA), the National Highway Traffic Safety Administration, the Consumer Product Safety Commission, etc.[11] In time the capture view of regulation was discredited as inaccurate (Sabatier, 1975; Wilson, 1980a; Plumlee and Meier, 1978; Quirk, 1981).

RICHARD POSNER

In an essay entitled "Theories of Economic Regulation," Richard Posner attempted to specify some of the linkages Stigler left implicit. Posner (1974: 337) identifies the limits of economic public interest theory; he argues that what economists term inefficiencies are often policy outputs demanded by interest groups. Rather than blame regulatory agencies for mismanagement, Posner (1974: 339) contends that agencies are asked to do the impossible and some are not able to do so. Posner then terms Bernstein's capture theory "atheoretical,"[12] and criticizes it because it fails to explain why some agencies are captured and others are not.

Posner (1974: 343) modifies Stigler in his interpretation; according to Posner, the theme of Stigler's theory of economic regulation is "regulation serves the private interests of politically effective groups." What attracts Posner to Stigler is the implied assumption that actors in the regulatory process are rational utility maximizers. Using the theory of cartels, Posner (1974: 345) attempts to explain why some groups are able to attain regulatory objectives and others are not. Successful groups are those that share a homogeneous interest, lack the ability to establish a cartel on their own, and are concentrated in a geographic area.[13] Posner deals at length with the relationship of group size to effectiveness. Early in the essay he argues that small size reduces organizational costs and, therefore, should be related to effectiveness (p. 344). Later he argues that members mean votes and, therefore, important resources to offer in exchanges with regulators (p. 347).

Despite his efforts at explication, Posner (1974: 348) is unhappy with the precision of Stigler's theory. He notes that "the economic theory is so spongy that virtually any observations can be reconciled with it. . . . At best it is a list of criteria relevant to predicting whether an industry will obtain favorable legislation. It is not a coherent theory yielding unambiguous and therefore testable hypotheses" (Posner, 1974: 349).

Posner (1974: 351) argues for an equilibrium based regulatory theory, something that is implicit in Stigler but was not stressed. Posner (1974: 351) argues that much regulation is "the product of coalitions between the regulated industry and customer groups, the former obtaining some monopoly profits from regulation, the latter obtaining lower prices (or better service) than they would in an unregulated market—all at the expense of unorganized, mostly consumer, groups." In other words, the organized exploit the unorganized.[14]

Posner recognizes that the theory of economic regulation does not appear to explain several new areas of regulation. Truth in lending, automobile safety, pollution control, and FTC consumer regulation all do not fit the theory (Posner, 1974: 353). In each case, the federal government created new regulations that did not appear to benefit industry. In short, Posner admits that the theory of economic regulation may be irrelevant to the dominant forms of regulation created in the late 1960s and early 1970s.

SAM PELTZMAN

By 1976, the radical arguments of George Stigler had become conventional wisdom to some economists. According to Sam Peltzman (1976: 212), "A common, though not universal, conclusion has become that, as between the two main contending interests in regulatory processes, the producer interest tends to prevail over the consumer interest." Peltzman, however, views the work of Stigler from a different light, arguing that it is really a theory of coalitions rather than a theory of regulation. Producer interests usually triumph over consumer interests because they have greater incentives to organize. Producers are fewer in number than consumers, and benefits to individual producers exceed benefits to individual consumers. As a result, producers are more likely to organize to seek regulation than are consumers.[15]

The conflict between public interest theory and economic regulatory theory is no where near as evident as when Peltzman (1976: 213) declares, "I begin with the presumption that what is basically at stake in regulatory processes is a transfer of wealth." Distributions of income unlike efficiency are phenomena that traditional economic theory is ill-equipped to handle (see Little, 1957).

Similar to Posner and Stigler, Peltzman does not differentiate among regulators. Regulators appear to be a combination of regulatory bureaucrats and legislators; they set regulatory policy and seek to remain in office by attracting votes. Unlike the regulator of Stigler, however, Peltzman (1976: 222) permits the regulator some discretion. He implies that regulators can put together regulatory coalitions and will attempt to bring losing groups into the coalition to maximize support. In fact, Peltzman (1976: 227) feels that consumers will benefit under some conditions more than they will benefit under others. Using price regulation as an example for some formal modeling, Peltzman argues that consumers are more likely to benefit when industry output is expanding rather than contracting, when prices change faster than demand changes, when demand is elastic, and when economies of scale are present. Producers benefit more from regulation when output is contracting, demand changes faster than prices, demand is inelastic, and no economies of scale exist.

Peltzman's effort to specify more detailed hypotheses about who benefits from regulation is commendable. The effort is marred, however, by his emphasis on price regulation. Price regulation is more amenable to economic analysis and the derivation of hypotheses through deductive methods than are other forms of regulation. At the time of publication, regulation at the federal level had begun to shift away from price regulation toward safety, health, and product quality regulation. Within the next several years, the federal government eliminated or restricted price regulation on airlines, trucks, railroads, banks, brokers, and other businesses (see Noll and Owen, 1983). At the state level, insurance regulation had just ended a movement to more competitive pricing. The overwhelming majority of insurance regulatory issues no longer concerned prior approval of prices. To the extent that new forms of regulation differ from traditional price regulation, the hypotheses of Peltzman are less useful. In fact, Peltzman (1976: 240) notes in his conclusions that the utility of his work can only be demonstrated with empirical tests of the model, something he feels is lacking in the literature.

In a brief but insightful aside, Peltzman (1976: 230) notes that industry may seek regulation for reasons other than economic gain. Regulation can be used to reduce uncertainty to a business by structuring part of the business' environment. As such, it reduces the risk to capital by buffering the firm from changes in supply and demand and fluctuations in price and profits.

EXTENSIONS AND MODIFICATIONS OF THE ECONOMIC THEORY

Stigler's review of regulation generated a substantial amount of research particularly in the area of occupational regulation. For the most part, however, Stigler's theory was often just introduced as a way to argue that regulation benefits producers and then the author proceeded to study the policy outputs of regulation. These output studies (see Blair and Rubin, 1980; Rottenberg, 1980) often look for economic rents achieved by professions, barriers to entry, and the impact of regulation on prices. They rarely attempt to examine whether the strength of producer groups or following Posner the strength of all interest groups predict the outcomes of regulatory policy.

The few studies that have explicitly used Stigler's framework have found it wanting or in need of expansion. Richard Ippolito's (1979) study of automobile regulation was undertaken as an attempt to operationalize Stigler's theory for automobile insurance regulation; Ippolito (1979: 86) concludes, "no evidence was uncovered in our study which supports the Stiglerian notion of regulation in the automobile insurance industry." Ippolito feels his study is much more supportive of the competition of interest groups view held by Peltzman (Ippolito, 1979: 87).

Innovative interest group competition studies of regulation have been conducted in state liquor regulation (Smith, 1982) and state consumer protection legislation (Oster, 1980). In a creative effort to explain liquor regulation, Smith postulates that liquor regulations are a function of industry concentration, fundamentalist church membership, the existence of a regulatory agency, and the importance of the tourist industry. In this study, every actor is considered an interest group even the regulatory bureaucracy. Although the industry variable is never a significant predictor of policy (Smith, 1982: 312), her study does provide support for a pluralist view of regulatory policy *if* interest groups are broadly defined.

Oster (1980) attempts to predict the adoption of four individual consumer protection laws at the state level. She uses measures of the strength of industry groups and consumer groups. Unfortunately, Oster lets her data redefine her theory. In part of the analysis, Oster (1980: 50) argues that consumers with high incomes and older than age 65 should oppose drug regulation because they prefer the paternalism of traditional medical practices. This argument is used to justify negative relationships when Oster earlier argues that consumers should favor drug advertising laws because they reduce prices. In other cases, Oster (1980: 49) uses an industry variable (number of retail sales outlets) as a consumer indicator and a consumer indicator (proportion of population in poverty) as an industry pressure indicator. Appleton's (1985) more objective analysis does not find many significant relationships between producer interests and consumer protection legislation (see also Meier, 1987b).

The limitations of Stigler's theory in these cross-sectional state studies are also found in longitudinal case studies. Perhaps the best current application of the economic theory of regulation is Noll and Owen (1983) who present the theory's implications and then examine several areas of federal deregulation. Policy results from the competition of interest groups and "[e]ach group naturally takes positions and makes arguments that it regards as economically beneficial to itself" (Noll and Owen, 1983: 28). Noll and Owen permit all types of interests, but they argue that successful interests are more likely to (1) advocate policies in their own self-interest, (2) have a small number of members, (3) have a large economic stake in the policy, (4) have homogeneous views among its members, and (5) be able to clearly identify the benefits of regulation to the group (Noll and Owen, 1983: 41–45).

Because consumer interests lack many of these characteristics, they will be less successful in attaining their ends than will producer interests. Unfortunately for the Noll and Owen theory, it is contradicted by the case studies that they present. Consumers benefitted greatly from financial deregulation (Carron, 1983) despite their lack of organization in this area. Both surface (Alexis, 1983) and air transportation (Kahn, 1983) were deregulated with some arguable benefits for consumers yet consumer interests were rarely represented in the policy discussions (see Derthick and Quirk, 1985). In short, the recent effort to refloat Stigler's theory fails on the rocks of empirical reality.

Political Theories of Regulation

As economic theories of regulation became more refined, political research directly challenged capture theory. Sabatier (1975) found that air quality regulation in Chicago did not favor industry because a supportive consumer constituency monitored agency actions. Keiser (1980) and Quirk (1980) found a similar constituency acted as a deterrent preventing the FDA from acquiescing to the pharmaceutical industry's demands. Similar discordant findings were found for the Occupational Safety and Health Administration (OSHA) (Kelman, 1981), the FTC (Pertschuk, 1982), the National Highway Traffic Safety Administration (Meier, 1985b), the EPA (Marcus, 1980), and some state utility commissions (Anderson, 1980; Gormley, 1983; Gormley, 1982: 305, 312). These findings were reinforced by a series of economic studies under the guise of "public interest" theory that argued regulation imposed costs on business with few commensurate benefits (Clarkson and Muris, 1981; MacAvoy, 1979; Viscusi, 1983). In sum, these studies found that the regulated industry did not always dominate the regulatory process and at times had to accept regulation that it would have preferred to avoid (see also Kemp, 1981).

These cases of industry losses could not be explained by the existence of a consumer group running roughshod over the industry. Although consumer groups were often active participants, studies of specific industries revealed that regulators did not passively respond to group demands. Regulators played an active role in determining public policy outputs rather than simply ratifying the results of the group process. Professional norms of bureaucrats were related to policy decisions in utility regulation (Berry, 1984: 549), forestry regulation (Culhane, 1981), environmental protection (Melnick, 1983), and occupational safety (Kelman, 1981). Policy values of agency bureaucrats were shown to be significantly different from those of other political elites (Aberbach and Rockman, 1976) and were linked to variations in policy outputs (Kelman, 1980; Mazmanian and Sabatier, 1980). Other bureaucratic resources identified as influencing regulatory policy were legal authority (Welborn and Brown, 1980; Sabatier, 1977), the competence of regulatory staff (Welborn and Brown, 1980; Berry, 1979: 269; Gormley, 1982: 302), the size of the agency's budget and other resources (Mitnick, 1980; Berry, 1984: 526; Lester et al., 1983: 276), the party affiliation of the regulators (Gormley, 1979; Quirk, 1981), and the leadership ability (Behrman, 1980) or lack thereof (Kelman, 1980; Pertschuk, 1982) of regulatory executives.

Political research also dealt harshly with George Stigler's view of a regulator that was somehow a composite of a bureaucrat or a legislator. Political capture theory as enunciated by Bernstein (1955) provided a separate role for political elites; Bernstein attributed the capture of regulatory agencies to the decline in presidential and congressional support for the regulatory agency (see also Plumlee and Meier, 1978; Long, 1962; Rourke, 1984; Freeman, 1956). Recent evidence has found a more forceful role for political elites. Quirk (1980) argued that FDA regulations were sensitive to the political forces involved in drug regulation. Moe (1982; 1984), in quantitative longitudinal studies, revealed a major presidential impact on the National Labor Relations Board (NLRB), the FTC, and the Securities and Exchange Commission (SEC). Cohen (1986) discovered evidence of presidential influence in his similar study of the Federal Communications Commission (FCC) as did Rothenberg (1985) in his study of the ICC.

The role of Congress in first encouraging and then discouraging the consumer protection orientation of the FTC is well documented (Pertschuk, 1982; see Weingast and Moran, 1983 for an alternative interpretation). Major policy innovations in environmental regulation cannot be explained without reference to Congress and key individuals there (Jones, 1975; Rosenbaum, 1984). Rothenberg's (1985) and Cohen's (1985) quantitative studies of regulatory agencies found many strong correlations between legislative variables and policy outputs over time.

Research has also revealed a major role for the courts in establishing regulatory policy (Melnick, 1983). Courts in recent years have been more willing to challenge agency decisions; OSHA in particular has been subjected to rigorous review by the courts (Kelman, 1980). Banking deregulation actually got a major push from the courts when they decided that regulatory agencies did not have the authority to permit interest-bearing checking accounts in 1979. The resulting crisis enabled Congress to pass the Depository Institutions Deregulation and Monetary Control Act of 1980 (Meier, 1985b).

The political literature also suggests that treating the industry as a monolithic interest is incorrect. A substantial number of cases show that industries often fail to present a united front. Airline deregulation, for example, was aided because United Airlines broke ranks and supported deregulation (Behrman, 1980). The 1980's fight over banking deregulation saw large banks supporting deregulation pitted against small banks resisting it (Carron, 1983). The FTC's effort to examine the regulatory practices of physicians was supported by a variety of health care groups including major nurses' associations. Meier's (1987b) study of state consumer protection regulation revealed that portions of the affected industry often supported regulation while other portions opposed it. The regulated industry, therefore, must be viewed as having potentially multidimensional interests.

A Model of Regulatory Policy

Although sophisticated political theories of regulation have been developed (see Mazmanian and Sabatier, 1980; Meier, 1985b; Wilson, 1980b), they are often limited to tests with case studies or single highly specific policy areas. In an effort to develop a theory that can be used to both explain the historical development of insurance regulation over time and a quantitative cross-sectional study of state insurance regulation, a more parsimonious model will be used.[16]

Four key actors have been identified as influencing regulatory policy—industry groups, consumer groups, the regulatory agency, and political elites.[17] Consumer groups are hypothesized to push for greater regulation and, in choices between regulatory policies, to favor regulation that restricts the industry (Berry, 1984: 542). The success of consumer groups should be directly related to their political resources such as the size of consumer groups and their contact with each other. Bureaucratic actors will favor policies consistent with their policy goals (Rourke, 1984; Berry, 1984: 529). Because regulators, similar to other bureaucrats, are likely to identify with the goals of their agency (that is, regulation), bureaucratic actors in general will favor greater regulation (see Downs, 1967; Niskanen, 1971; Rourke, 1984; Miles, 1978).[18] The influence of bureaucratic actors will be positively related to their political resources.

The ability of industry to influence regulation should be a function of their political resources (for example, size, wealth; Rourke, 1984; Stigler, 1971). The impact of the regulated industry on regulation, however, is subject to some dispute. Generally political scientists have assumed that the industry will oppose regulation (see Huntington, 1952), and the reaction of business to regulation of the environment and workplace safety supports this hypothesis (see Vig and Kraft, 1984; Kelman, 1980). Stigler (1971) and others (Kolko, 1965; Posner, 1974; Peltzman, 1976), however, argue that industry strength will be positively correlated with regulation because industry will seek regulation in its own self-interest. Perhaps a more realistic hypothesis is that industry will seek regulation that benefits it and try to avoid regulation that restricts it.

Political elites[19] serve two roles in regulatory politics. First, they mediate among the group pressures; they balance the competition of interests to determine winners and losers. Second, political elites are not neutral arbiters willing to grant the power of government to winners in the interest group process (see Nordlinger, 1981). They also have policy goals of their own (see Kingdon, 1981). This model stresses the second role and explicitly attempts to measure the values held by political elites. Regulatory policy outcomes should be consistent with the values held by political elites. In this case, if political elites favor greater regulation, then the amount of regulation should increase.

The Regulatory Environment

Many scholars have noted that regulatory policy is not characterized by a consistent pattern of politics (Berry, 1979; Mitnick, 1980; Sabatier, 1983). In a perceptive essay, William Gormley (1986) argues that variations in regulatory politics can be explained by variations in the policy environment. Gormley identified two key environmental factors—salience and complexity. A *salient* issue is one characterized by intense conflict of a broad scope. Hazardous waste regulation, regulation of pornography, environmental regulation, and gun control are all salient regulatory issues. A *complex* issue requires specialized knowledge and training to address the factual questions of regulation. Insurance regulation, banking regulation, utility regulation, and drug licensing are complex regulatory areas.

Gormley (1986) contends that salience and complexity determine the actors most likely to have the greatest influence on regulatory policy. Issues that are salient but not complex are made to order for political elites. Salience raises the rewards for acting (that is political elites can gain political support for acting) and the lack of complexity does not prevent political elites from addressing the key questions. Similarly, Gormley feels that consumer or citizen groups are more influential in areas of high salience and low complexity because salience aids organizational efforts and complexity acts as a barrier to participation in the policy process (see also Berry, 1979: 267; Berry, 1984: 555).

Bureaucratic actors thrive on complexity because complexity requires the specialized knowledge of the trained professional for effective regulation. In complex issues that are salient, authority, accordingly to Gormley (1986), flows to upper level bureaucrats. When noncomplex issues are not salient, authority flows to lower level bureaucrats.

The regulated industry will of necessity participate in regulatory policy regardless of whether issues are salient or nonsalient, complex or noncomplex. Because regulated interests have to compete with consumer groups, bureaucratic actors, and politicians when salience is high, the regulated industry will be unable to control the process in this situation. Industry groups have an advantage when salience is low and complexity is high. Under such circumstances, only the regulated industry and the bureaucracy will be able to participate in the policy process in a meaningful manner.

Insurance regulation in general can be characterized as complex but not salient. Complexity can be illustrated by focusing on insurance policies alone; policies are difficult to read and harder to understand. At rate hearings, insurance companies and rate bureaus usually present volumes of statistics to support literally hundreds of different rates. Insurance laws tend to be long and complex, often running hundreds of pages in official statutes.

Despite the large cost of insurance to most individuals, insurance regulation is usually not a salient issue. Few nonindustry people, for example, attend rate hearings. Occasionally an insurance issue will attract some attention for a brief period of time; the no-fault automobile insurance issue in the 1970s comes to mind. After some brief public attention, however, the regulatory subsystem normally reasserts itself. The combination of complexity and lack of salience makes insurance an ideal industry to reexamine Stigler's (1971) theory of regulation. If Stigler's theory works anywhere, it should work in an area with low salience and high complexity (Gormley, 1986). Lack of salience means that political elites have no incentive to intervene in the process; complexity raises the costs of such interventions.

Although the general pattern of low salience and high complexity exists in insurance regulation, at times both dimensions vary somewhat. For an insurance issue usually handled by state government to reach the federal government's agenda, it must become salient. Insurance is not normally perceived as a federal concern so federal actors will be motivated to get involved only when issues become salient. Even state issues can vary in salience and complexity. The property and casualty liability insurance crisis of 1985–1986 and the medical malpractice insurance crisis of the early 1970s are examples of salient issues at the state level. In addition, insurance issues can be more or less complex; the appropriate rate to charge for hazardous waste haulers is incredibly complex for a lay person (or for that matter an actuary) to understand. The general issues of unisex insurance rates, readable policy forms, or no-fault insurance are reasonably simple even if the process of implementing such policies might require some level of expertise.

Summary

This chapter reviews previous theories of regulation and constructs a theory of regulation that is used in Chapters 4 through 7 to study insurance regulation. George Stigler's theory of economic regulation was found to have numerous empirical and theoretical shortcomings. As a result, it was not usable as a complete theory of regulatory politics. Relying on the empirical research in other areas of regulation, a theory was constructed that included the actions of four groups—the industry, consumer groups, regulatory bureaucrats, and political elites. Each group was hypothesized to have specific goals in the regulatory process; the ability of each group to affect policy outcomes depends on the resources that they can mobilize. Stigler's economic theory of regulation is incorporated into this broader theory so that a test of his theory is possible at the same time the broader theory is tested.

Chapter 3

Federal and State Government Roles in Insurance Regulation

Although insurance is regulated primarily by state governments, the federal government is an active participant in the insurance regulatory system. The federalism of shared powers has evolved in a step-by-step process over more than a century. This chapter discusses the different roles federal and state governments play in insurance regulation. Included in the chapter are the federal government's role in creating an economic environment, the minor federal direct role in regulation, the massive federal social insurance programs, and the basic state regulatory system.

Creating an Economic Environment

Because insurance companies are financial intermediaries, the federal government's economic policies are of great concern. Government macroeconomic policies that affect interest rates, inflation, and economic growth influence the insurance industry by determining its costs and ability to raise funds. Interest rates provide an excellent example. Government policies that increase interest rates permit life insurance companies to earn larger returns on their investments; at the same time, increases in interest rates reduce the value of annuities that individuals hold. If high interest rates also affect inflation, they have additional impacts. High inflation rates are reflected in the costs paid by property and liability insurance companies. Automobile repair costs and jury verdict awards appear to be sensitive to inflation.

Government economic policies were, in part, a contributor to the environment that spawned the property and liability insurance crisis of 1985–

1986 (see Chapter 5). In 1978, the Federal Reserve Board (FRB), under the leadership of Paul Volcker, adopted a monetarist economic policy and allowed interest rates to rise hoping that high interest rates would break the back of inflation (Kettl, 1986). As short-term interest rates rose above 20 percent, property and casualty insurance companies made large profits on their investments. Because investments were so profitable, P/C companies engaged in cut-throat competition to sell additional insurance. Even insurance sold at an underwriting loss was profitable because investment income would cover underwriting losses and still provide some profit. When inflation responded to Volcker's policies, interest rates began to fall. Falling interest rates greatly cut into insurance companies' investment income, but underwriting losses continued to mount. The result was the property and liability insurance crisis of 1985–1986 as property and casualty companies began to withdraw from certain high-risk insurance markets.

The federal government also affects the insurance industry's economic environment in more specific ways. Describing the Internal Revenue Service (IRS) as the major federal regulator of insurance would not be inaccurate. Tax policies passed by Congress and implemented by the IRS have greatly influenced insurance companies' profits.

The U. S. federal government has also fostered the growth of private insurance by emphasizing a market system economy. A market system creates uncertainties, and these uncertainties provide opportunities for insurance companies to provide products. Sweden, for example, with its elaborate cradle-to-grave welfare system, has eliminated major markets for life insurance and private pensions (Skogh, 1986). European countries with socialized medicine do not have extensive medical malpractice or product liability insurance lines because injuries are compensated on a "no-fault" basis by the welfare system (see Finsinger and Pauly, 1986). The U. S. economic system, therefore, may well explain why 50.9 percent of all insurance sold worldwide is sold in the United States (Insurance Information Institute, 1986: 15); no other country purchases more than 14.8 percent of the insurance sold.[1]

Under federal tax laws, insurance premiums for businesses are considered business expenses and, therefore, are deductible. Because this principle applies to a business providing health insurance for its employees, it creates an incentive to do so (Dickerson, 1968: 674). Employers can deduct the cost of providing health insurance, and employees can receive health insurance as benefits without paying taxes on these benefits (see below). In 1920, the IRS ruled that group term life insurance provided by an employer was not income subject to taxation (Johnson, 1968: 383; MacAvoy, 1977: 73). Although this rule has been modified several times, it creates an incentive for both employers to offer and employees to accept life insurance as a benefit. Taxing these benefits would raise an estimated $17.6 billion in federal revenues annually (Kosterlitz, 1985: 959).

Private pension plans were given a major push by the Revenue Act of 1942, which offered incentives for businesses to establish pension plans. In addition, life insurance companies manage pension plans for millions of private sector workers. Similarly the Economic Recovery Act of 1981 allowed individuals to establish individual retirement accounts (IRAs), and many of these accounts were opened with insurance companies. The Tax Reform Act of 1986 greatly restricted the use of IRAs (see Chapter 6), and insurance companies opposed this change in the law.

In short, the federal government affects both the general and specific environments of the insurance industry. By actions designed to affect the economy, the federal government manipulates the political economy of the insurance companies. The federal tax code, in turn, has specific and direct impacts on the insurance industry by increasing the value of some products and decreasing the value of others.

Direct Federal Regulation of Insurance

Because insurance is clearly a business conducted in interstate commerce (see Chapter 4), nothing prevents the federal government from directly regulating all or parts of the insurance industry. Some individuals, for example, appealed to the federal government to "solve" the 1985–1986 property and casualty insurance crisis; they advocated passing Senator Robert Kasten's proposed tort reform legislation. Respecting the tradition of state regulation, however, the federal government has limited its regulatory role to addressing specific problems. This limited approach has resulted in several federal agencies regulating some portion of the insurance industry.

The Department of Defense (DOD) regulates the sale of insurance on military installations to protect the interests of military personnel. The SEC regulates securities; stock insurance companies, of course, issue stock; and most life insurance companies invest in securities regulated by the SEC. Despite some major scandals in the securities markets including the Baldwin-United annuity fiasco, the SEC rarely engages in vigorous regulation (Kemp, 1984).[2] Specific events that create risks greater than private insurance companies are willing to underwrite sometimes result in direct legislation to correct the problem. The famous swine flu vaccination program was underwritten only after federal guarantees. Similarly, the Price-Anderson Act limits the liability of nuclear plants for major accidents.

Perhaps the most significant direct limitation is the law separating banking from insurance. The Banking Act of 1933 prohibited national banks in towns of more than 5,000 from selling insurance (Cline, 1982: 78). This act was designed to limit banks to "banking business" only, not to protect insurance companies from competition.[3] In 1956 and 1970, this prohibition was extended to include bank holding companies. Current federal regulations permit national banks to sell only credit life insurance and property and casualty insurance on the collateral accepted by the bank.[4] Banks have recently pressed to eliminate this restriction as part of their efforts to deregulate the banking industry (see Meier, 1985b). Banking in recent years has become similar to insurance by offering a wide variety of financial products and services; banks believe that they can offer some services more efficiently than insurance companies and that such combinations would be highly profitable (MacDonald, 1985: 12–13). The only relaxation of the barrier between insurance and banking was the 1986 legislation that allowed national bank branches (as opposed to bank headquarters) located in towns with fewer than 5,000 people to sell insurance.

Federal Government Insurance Programs

In addition to its major role in creating the economic environment for insurance and its minor role in regulating insurance, the federal government is a major competitor of the insurance industry. The federal government operates a wide variety of programs that are technically insurance programs in that individuals pay premiums to the federal government who in turn protects those individuals from some type of hazard. The mechanisms for offering insurance by the federal government vary; sometimes insurance programs are run through a government corporation chartered for the sole purpose of issuing insurance; other times the federal government operates through private insurance companies.

Determining the dollar volume of federal government insurance activities is difficult because federal government programs are not subject to the same accounting principles that the insurance industry is. Many federal insurance expenditures are "off budget" so that only the annual operating profit or loss is reported. Because the profit or loss is only a small part of the financial transactions that occur, these figures reveal only the tip of the federal insurance iceberg. Notwithstanding these difficulties, the size of the major federal insurance programs is estimated in Table 3-1. These figures show that the federal government's insurance operations are larger than the combined operation of all the life and property and casualty insurance companies in the United States. Although the "premiums" collected by the federal government

Table 3-1
Federal Insurance Programs

Program	Premiums (millions)	# Insured (thousands)	Liability (billions)
Social Insurance			
Social Security			
—Retirement	$162,800	154,000	6,754.0
Social Security			
—Disability	15,657	154,000	790.0
Medicare—Part A	45,475	29,600[a]	48.5
Medicare—Part B	5,180	29,000[a]	25.0
PBGC	252	30,000	608.0
Veterans Life Insurance	118	4,040	28.6
Railroad Retirement Board	2,169	940	NA
Savings and Investments			
FDIC Deposit Insurance	1,440	274,344	1,534.0
FSLIC Deposit Insurance	757	120,500	848.0
NCUA Deposit Insurance	105	39,500	69.0
OPIC	46	NA	11.6
Export-Import Bank	35	NA	18.6
Loan Guarantees			
FHA	1,864	4,758	221.0
VA Housing	152	3,943	108.0
College Student Loans	NA	10,182	39.7
Other Insurance Programs			
Crime Insurance	6	NA	30.0
Flood Insurance	407	2,121	150.0
Crop Insurance	337	700	8.4
ESTIMATED TOTAL	$236,800	857,628	$11,332.4

[a]Beneficiaries.
FHA—Federal Housing Administration.
FSLIC—Federal Savings and Loan Insurance Corporation.
PBGC—Pension Benefit Guaranty Corporation.
NCUA—National Credit Union Administration.
OPIC—Overseas Private Insurance Corporation.
VA—Veterans Administration.

($237 billion) are somewhat smaller than total premiums in the private insurance industry ($300 billion; see Chapter 1), the federal government pays out far more in benefits than the private insurance companies. Because the federal government is not required to keep the massive reserves that state regulators require private insurance companies to maintain, it has less administrative overhead costs and operates more efficiently. In all probability, every living adult in the United States is covered by at least one federal government insurance program. For purposes of discussion, federal insurance programs are divided into four major areas—retirement and aging insurance, savings and investment insurance, loan guarantees, and insurance that fills a private market gap.

RETIREMENT PROGRAMS

The federal government operates a massive social insurance program for the elderly. The largest program is, of course, Social Security or, as it is officially known, Old Age, Survivors', and Dependents' Insurance. Social Security is similar to annuities sold by life insurance companies in that individuals contribute during their working years and are paid a monthly income at retirement. The major difference between Social Security and life insurance is that Social Security is targeted at retirees so that if individuals die before retirement, no death benefits are paid in most instances. The second major difference is that Social Security is compulsory for almost all workers. The compulsory nature allows the system to operate as a transfer-payment system rather than as a true savings system. That is, payments from working individuals are used to pay individuals currently collecting retirement stipends. In private insurance, the individual's premiums are saved as reserves, and these reserves are used to make payments to the individual when he or she requires them. Owing to the different nature of the "savings" system, the Social Security system operates with "reserves" that would provide no more than six months' worth of benefit payments if Social Security taxes ceased (see Myers, 1985; Light, 1985).

The largest single program in the Social Security system is the retirement program. In 1986, 25.6 million retirees collected an average of $463 per month. An additional 7.2 million survivors of Social Security participants also collected benefits. In total, 32.6 million beneficiaries received $162 billion. In 1986, only 3.1 percent of this program's operating budget was allocated to administrative overhead.

The Social Security Administration (SSA) also operates a disability income program as part of Social Security. Individuals who are disabled and unable to work are eligible to collect disability benefits from Social Security. In 1986, 3.8 million individuals received Social Security disability benefits of $19.6 billion. The rapid growth of the disability program has been cause for some concern (Stone, 1984; Scotch, 1984; Mashaw, 1983). A 1980 law required that permanently disabled individuals be reviewed every three years. The Reagan Administration used this law to purge 500,000 recipients from the rolls; nearly one-third of these were restored to the rolls after legal appeals (Cater, 1982: 1512). In 1986, the benefits paid to "premiums" paid ratio was 1.25.

The third major retirement insurance programs is Medicare, which provides health insurance for the aged. Medicare, operated by the Health Care Financing Administration (HCFA) in the Department of Health and Human Services (HHS), is divided into two parts. Part A covers hospitalization costs; individuals pay premiums during their working years and collect benefits after retirement. In 1986, Medicare Part A paid benefits of $48.5 billion to 29.6 million recipients, or 13 percent of the American population (HCFA, 1986). Administrative overhead for this program is approximately 2 percent of costs. Part B of Medicare is optional insurance that individuals can purchase to cover physician payments. In 1986, $24.4 billion in benefits were paid to 29 million recipients. Unlike Part A, the federal government heavily subsidizes Part B. The ratio of benefits to premiums is 4.71. Medicare programs are implemented by private insurance companies and the Blue Cross and Blue Shield Network (Johnson, 1969: 373).[5]

The other major health insurance program, Medicaid, provides for health insurance for indigents. Medicaid is not supported by premium payments by individuals but rather is paid for by general tax revenues. Medicaid, therefore, is considered a welfare program rather than a social insurance program and is not included in this discussion of federal insurance programs.[6]

For individuals with private pension plans, the federal government under the Employee Retirement Income Security Act (ERISA) regulates such plans and provides insurance to guarantee future payments. The program is administered though the Pension Benefit Guaranty Corporation (PBGC). In 1986, PBGC paid $252 million in benefits to 88,000 individuals; it currently insures 30 million persons participating in 110,000 pension plans; approximately 1,000 pension plans have been terminated at an estimated loss of $1.3 billion as of September 1985 (General Accounting Office (GAO), 1986a). Concern about PBGC's potential liability and the number of firms that have terminated pension funds has made this program salient in recent years (Munnell, 1982).

The federal government also insures the retirement, disability, and unemployment programs of railroad workers. This insurance was established in the 1920s as part of a law to extend collective bargaining rights to railroad workers. Because the economic health of railroads has not been good, this program has grown in recent years. Administered by the Railroad Retirement Board, this program in 1986 paid retirement and disability benefits to 940,000 individuals totalling $2.2 billion. An additional $1 billion was paid in unemployment and sickness benefits.

The final set of retirement insurance programs operate in the Veterans Administration (VA). Through arrangements with private companies, the VA has several programs that sell life insurance to veterans. The National Service Life Insurance (NSLI) fund provides life insurance for current service personnel; 3.3 million policies are in effect with a face value of $22.8 billion. The United States Government Life Insurance fund provides life insurance under the War Risk Insurance Act; 58,000 policies have a face value of $227 million. The Veterans Special Life Insurance fund covers veterans that served between 1951 and 1957; it contains 355,000 policies with a face value of $3.04 billion. The Veterans Life Insurance fund provides insurance for veterans of World Wars I and II; 2,951 policies have a face value of $15.5 million. The Service Disabled Veterans Insurance fund sold life insurance to veterans with service disabilities; 184,000 policies have a face value of $1.66 billion. Finally, the Veterans Reopened Insurance fund sold life insurance policies for one year starting in May 1965; this fund has 132,000 policies with a face value of $923 million. Most of these life insurance programs no longer enroll additional policyholders, and the total face value of all policies (approximately $4 billion) is only a minuscule fraction of the face value of all life insurance sold by private companies ($6.1 trillion).

SAVINGS AND INVESTMENTS INSURANCE

The federal government insures a variety of specific savings and investments in the United States. The best-known programs are the deposit insurance programs that insure deposits of up to $100,000 in banks, savings associations, and credit unions. Deposit insurance was born during the Great Depression as part of President Franklin Roosevelt's attempt to restore confidence in the banking industry. The FDIC operates the deposit insurance program for commercial banks. In 1986, the FDIC collected $1.44 billion in premiums to protect more than .25 billion accounts with deposits of more than $1.5 trillion dollars. Well in excess of 99 percent of all commercial banks have their deposits insured with the FDIC. Although bank failures have been more common in recent years than at any time since the Great Depression, the FDIC has accumulated assets of $24.6 billion as reserves against future bank failures.

The Federal Savings and Loan Insurance Corporation (FSLIC), created by the National Housing Act of 1934 (NHA), insures deposits in savings and loans and mutual savings banks. FSLIC provides insurance for 120.5 million accounts in 3,284 savings institutions for a potential liability of $848 billion. In 1986, FSLIC collected premiums of $757 million and had accumulated reserves of $7.8 billion. Defaults in savings associations are running at post-Great Depression highs as a result of deregulating the thrift industry

(Thomas and Pauly, 1986: 51). In fiscal year 1985 alone, FSLIC handled 317 defaults and suffered $4.31 billion in losses. One current estimate has 650 thrift institutions likely to default with losses totalling approximately $33 billion, far in excess of FSLIC reserves (Thomas and Pauly, 1986: 52). Congressional policy discussions center on how to infuse additional capital into FSLIC.

Deposits in credit unions (technically shares) can be insured through the Credit Union Share Insurance fund (created in 1970) operated by the National Credit Union Administration (NCUA). This fund had 1986 premium income of $105.3 million to cover 39.5 million accounts in 15,150 credit unions; total potential liability was $69 billion. Only 70 percent of credit unions are insured by the Credit Union Share Insurance fund. To improve the financial condition of the fund, credit unions must now deposit one percent of their assets with the fund. Interest on these deposits provide the "premiums" for share insurance.

The federal government also encourages other investments by providing insurance for them. The Securities Investor Protection Corporation (SPIC) is a government corporation that insures individual brokerage accounts. Up to $100,000 in assets are insured when investors leave their stocks, bonds, and other investments in the hands of their brokers. SPIC uses an assessment on brokers to maintain a $150 million guaranty fund. Interest earnings from this fund provide operating capital. From 1970 to 1982, SPIC liquidated 161 brokers and paid more than 140,000 claims (GAO, 1983: 38-40).

The Overseas Private Investment Corporation (OPIC) insures the investments of U. S. corporations in foreign nations; this insurance protects these investments from loss due to political risks such as nationalization. In 1986, OPIC collected $45.8 million in premiums to protect foreign investments totaling 11.6 billion. The Export-Import Bank also operates an insurance program to protect certain trade investments. This program collected premiums of $35 million in 1986 and provided protection for $18.6 billion in trade.

Loan Guarantees

Federal loan guarantees are front-page news when special action is taken to underwrite a loan to a major corporation such as Lockheed or Chrysler. Several much larger programs, however, operate without much fanfare. The largest program is the mortgage loan guarantee program. Originally designed to upgrade the quality of the nation's housing, Federal Housing Administration (FHA) loan guarantees support private sector loans for individual mortgages (see Wolman, 1971). With four separate programs for different types of housing, FHA mortgage insurance collected premiums of $1.9 billion in

1986 to protect 5 million home mortgages; the face value of these mortgages was $221.4 billion. The FHA forecloses on approximately 50,000 mortgages per year and has lost $1.6 billion since its inception. A similar mortgage guarantee program is operated by the Veterans Administration (VA) to support home purchases by armed services veterans. The VA has approximately 4 million insured mortgages with a value of $137 billion. Although private mortgage insurance exists, before federal mortgage insurance in 1933, long-term home mortgages were rare.

Perhaps the most newsworthy federal loan guarantee program is the college student loan program. In recent years, the program has made headlines because the default rate for loans (now approximately 11.8 percent) has risen with $3.9 billion worth of loans in default. Approximately 10.2 million persons currently have student loans that are federally guaranteed with a value of $39.7 billion. In 1986 alone, 956,000 new loans were issued.

NONMARKET INSURANCE

In certain circumstances, the federal government perceives a need for property and casualty insurance that is unavailable in the private sector because such insurance cannot be sold at a profit. The largest nonmarket insurance program is the federal flood insurance program. Because flood damage is highly concentrated when it occurs, private insurance companies are unable to spread risks sufficiently to offer insurance at reasonable rates. The Federal Insurance Administration (FIA), an agency in the Federal Emergency Management Administration (FEMA), provides federal flood insurance to individuals who reside in communities that follow federal regulations concerning flood plain management (see Chapter 6). In 1986, FIA collected $407 million in premiums for 2.12 million insurance policies covering an estimated $150 billion in property. This program paid $357 million in losses in 1986, a good year in terms of cash flow; from 1968 through 1986, however, the program had a deficit of $1.5 billion.

The federal riot insurance originated during the urban riots of the 1960s. The federal government, acting through private insurance companies, insured businesses in riot-prone areas against casualty losses from riots. A companion program is the federal crime insurance program for residents of high-crime areas. Both programs are operated by the FIA. In 1983, the Reagan Administration terminated the riot insurance program. The crime insurance program was scheduled to be phased out beginning in 1985. For fiscal year 1986, the crime insurance program collected premiums of $6.2 million and had operating expenses of $29.5 million. These programs have always been small because the programs were offered only where authorized and often private insurance was available (Green, 1978: 361).

The Federal Crop Insurance Corporation (FCIC) provides federal crop insurance to farmers.[7] FCIC insurance is different from most private crop insurance in that it is all-risk insurance (weather, insects, disease); most private crop insurance only protects crops from hail or other storm-related damage (Green, 1978: 359). The FCIC administers its program by subsidizing insurance; the actual policies are serviced by some 50 private insurance companies.

In 1986, the FCIC collected premiums of $337 million and paid subsidies of $103 million to insurance companies. FCIC insurance covered approximately 25 percent of all farmers and insured crops worth $8.4 billion. The FCIC operates at a loss even when subsidies are considered; in 1986, the ratio of losses to premiums was 1.96. Administrative costs paid by the federal government are not included in this ratio. Although the Reagan Administration has proposed to phase out all federal subsidies for crop insurance by 1991, such a goal is optimistic for a program that has lost $938 million since its creation in 1938.

Finally, several other small federal insurance programs exist to supply insurance for markets that are not served by the private sector. The Small Business Administration's (SBA) Surety Bond Program for businesses and the Federal Fidelity Bonding Program for individuals assist people who need bonding to operate certain businesses. The Check Forgery Insurance Fund protects recipients of federal checks from loss due to theft and forgery. The Aviation Insurance Revolving Fund provides insurance for aircraft operating under contract to the DOD or the Department of State (DS). The War Risk Insurance fund exists to provide property insurance for individuals, normally shippers, who support government actions during wartime.

State Regulation of Insurance

Although state governments are the primary regulator of insurance, they also sell insurance just as the federal government does. States operate unemployment insurance funds as the result of a federal "incentive" to do so. Eighteen states sell workers' compensation insurance, and six of those hold a monopoly on the sale of workers' compensation insurance. Other states sell crop insurance or operate title insurance funds (Vaughn, 1982: 124). Maryland, for a period of time, experimented with selling automobile insurance; the experiment turned out to be unprofitable for the state and was abandoned. Wisconsin sells life insurance policies with a face value of $20,000 or less. Although Wisconsin's program provides insurance at an attractive price, state laws prohibiting advertising and hiring agents have limited the program's size.

State government's primary role, however, is regulation. Regulatory laws generally distinguish between domestic companies (those legally domiciled in the state) and foreign companies (those domiciled in other states).[8] State regulatory agencies exert greater control over domestic companies than they do over foreign companies. How closely an insurance company is regulated depends on where it is domiciled. Although regulation varies greatly across states, some commonalities exist. All states license companies to sell insurance, examine insurance companies, and liquidate insolvent companies. Larger states employ large staffs of examiners, while smaller states rely on the National Association of Insurance Commissioners (NAIC), who provides a series of financial ratios for each company to indicate potential financial weaknesses.

Price Regulation

Rate regulation, setting the price of insurance, is perhaps the most visible form of state insurance regulation. Many states assert the right to establish prices for property and casualty insurance. Although states can regulate insurance rates in a variety of ways, in general, two major processes are used. About one-third of the states are considered "competitive" states because the market, rather than the insurance commissioner, determines price (see Chapter 4). California initially established competitive rating in 1947; the most permissive state in this regard is Illinois, who repealed all rate regulation laws in 1969 (see Witt and Miller, 1981).

Two-thirds of the states regulate prices more directly. The predominant form is the prior approval law: companies file rates with the insurance commissioner or a rate-setting board who decides whether to approve them. Rates cannot be used until approved. Although rate filing is complex, in many cases the small companies' task is simplified by rate bureaus. Rate bureaus, trade associations established to share pricing information, can file rate forms for all member companies (Ippolito, 1979: 58). Nonmember companies can either charge the bureau rate or file deviating rates if they wish to charge a different amount.[9] Some states, such as Texas, determine rates by their own calculations rather than on the basis of bureau filings. The general principle advocated by the NAIC in 1921 and adopted by most "noncompetitive" states is that rates should be high enough to yield 5 percent profit on premiums (Joskow, 1973: 94; Lilly, 1976: 106).[10]

The life insurance industry is exempt from direct price regulation; prices in life insurance are indirectly regulated through state requirements that companies use a specified mortality table and keep a given level of reserves to pay future claims. If a state requires higher reserve levels, the price of life insurance to the consumer will increase. Higher reserves also decrease the probability that a life insurance company will be unable to pay its claims.

Private health insurance companies are also free from direct price regulation (Greenspan and Vogel, 1982: 40; Dickerson, 1968: 673). An exception to this regulatory distinction between life and health insurance and property and casualty insurance is the Blue Cross and Blue Shield network. If a state regulates prices in other areas of insurance, it generally regulates prices for the Blues (Greenspan and Vogel, 1982: 40). Such regulation was justified by the argument that the Blues used communitywide rating systems, while the private companies used experienced-based rates. Although this argument once had a basis in fact, currently the Blues also use experience-based rating (Greenspan and Vogel, 1982: 45).

States also regulate policy forms, agents, and trade practices. Although these regulations vary somewhat among states, they have some uniformity because the NAIC has sponsored a wide variety of model laws. As an illustration of uniformity, all 50 states require that fire insurance companies use the New York Standard Fire Policy.

REGULATING ACCESS

States also establish policies to increase access to insurance. In a regulated market, some individuals cannot obtain insurance coverage because no company is willing to provide it at the mandated price. Some states have encouraged, and at times required, universal access to insurance. If an individual cannot obtain insurance in the voluntary market, he or she can be served via an involuntary market. The most common involuntary market mechanism is the shared-risk pool, which most states use for automobile insurance. Agents place an individual in the shared-risk pool if they are unwilling to underwrite the risk at the regulated market price. Each company writing insurance in the state is assigned a number of shared-market risks proportionate to the company's statewide market share (Decker, 1980). Participation in the shared-risk market is considered one of the costs of doing business in the state.

Insurance companies quite predictably prefer to avoid shared-risk systems. The normal proposed alternative to a shared risk pool is a marketing assistance plan (MAP), a voluntary organization that attempts to find companies willingly to underwrite individuals who cannot obtain insurance. MAPs are a popular way to handle insurance availability problems when policyholders are each unique as in the case of business liability insurance.

TAXES

Although not regulation per se, insurance companies pay substantial amounts of state taxes (on federal taxes, see Chapter 6). In addition to licensing fees and other standard business taxes, insurance companies are assessed a premium tax—essentially a sales tax on insurance premiums (Greenspan and Vogel, 1982: 42; Dickerson, 1968: 673). Dating back to 1824 (Lilly, 1976: 100), premium taxes are a significant revenue source for state government; in 1985, premium taxes totaled $4.53 billion (Insurance Information Institute, 1986: 40). Unlike many taxes on other state regulated industries, premium taxes are not used solely to pay the costs of regulation. Only 5 percent of the taxes and fees paid by insurance companies are used to support the expenses of the insurance commissioner.

WHY REGULATE INSURANCE?

The insurance market constitutes what Bailey and Baumol (1984) call a contestable market; it has all the characteristics associated with the perfectly competitive ideal market of microeconomists (see Ippolito, 1979; Joskow, 1973: 391). The number of firms is large, the product offered is fairly uniform (and could be made totally uniform as some European countries have, see Finsinger and Pauly, 1986), and few economies of scale exist. Why should such an industry be regulated?

1. *Solvency.* The primary reason for regulating insurance goes beyond the traditional market failure reasons for regulation to a more basic economic principle. Insurance is a contract; payment is made today for a benefit sometime in the future if certain events occur.[11] Insurance is regulated, therefore, to guarantee that contracts entered into are valid; that is, to guarantee that the insurance company will be around to pay any claims against it. States regulations implementing this goal seek to ensure that insurance companies are solvent.

Although solvency is clearly the reason why states regulate reserves and investments, it is also proposed as a reason for regulating rates. The prevailing regulatory philosophy is that rates should be set high enough to cover expenses and provide for adequate reserves and investments (Kimball, 1969a: 5). Regulators have long raised the specter of destructive competition whereby companies cut rates and insure unwise risks, thereby threatening the firm's solvency (Joskow, 1973: 392).[12] Despite the acceptance of this view by many regulators, no evidence exists that inadequate rates are responsible for failures in the insurance industry (Stelzer and Alpert, 1982: 9; Johnson, 1969: 375; Finsinger and Pauly, 1986).

2. *Fairness.* One market failure that clearly exists in insurance is information asymmetry. Consumers have far less knowledge about insurance than

the individuals who sell it; in fact, several studies show that consumer knowledge is minimal (Formisano, 1982: 23; Joskow, 1973: 404). Because policies are difficult to read and understand by a lay person, consumers may purchase too little (or too much) insurance or may purchase the wrong kind. Critics of the life insurance industry, for example, argue that consumer ignorance is the major reason why people buy whole life insurance, which the critics consider a poor investment (Tobias, 1982; FTC, 1979).

Fairness regulation can take many forms. Some states require that policies be written in less obtuse language. Other states have accepted the legalese and required that policies meet certain minimum standards. More innovative states, such as New York, have even gone so far as to release price and coverage information to consumers (Ippolito, 1979). The Wisconsin Insurance Commissioner provides information concerning the number of consumer complaints that they receive about each insurance company.

3. *Access.* The goal of access holds that insurance should be available to all individuals who need or are required to have it (Stewart, 1969: 25; Stelzer and Alpert, 1982: 8). Access goals are related to price goals because most individuals who advocate greater access mean access at a "reasonable" price. Using three different mechanisms, states have tried to increase access to insurance. One method is for the government to provide insurance directly or to subsidize insurance purchases. Flood and crop insurance are two examples. A second method is to establish some type of shared-risk pool and to require that insurance companies participate in the pool. Automobile insurance and medical malpractice insurance are often handled through shared-risk pools. A final method is simply to ban discrimination on whatever characteristic the companies are using to deny insurance and to monitor the companies for compliance with this ban. Prohibiting discrimination against the blind in life insurance and requiring that New York City be a homogeneous rating territory (Ippolito, 1979: 60) are two examples.[13]

4. *Social Investment.* Solvency, fairness, and access are accepted by most students of insurance as reasonable regulatory goals. Social investment and local protectionism are recognized as goals but subject to much criticism (Kimball, 1969a). Social-investment goals require that insurance companies do something with their capital that they would not otherwise do (see Orren, 1974). Although the days of mandated investments are past, states often provide tax incentives to encourage investment in specified areas such as housing or urban redevelopment. Some states go so far as to adjust the tax rates of companies that invest money within the state (see Chapter 4).

5. *Local Protectionism.* Because domiciled (in-state) insurance companies are more likely to commit a greater portion of their assets to a state than foreign (out-of-state) companies are, many states seek to protect local companies from competition by foreign companies. Although some states

at one time banned foreign companies (Lilly, 1976: 100), the most prominent recent form of protectionism is the use of premium taxes. Many states charged foreign companies a higher premium tax than they charged domestic companies. This discrimination led to a phenomenon known as retaliatory taxes. Under a retaliatory tax system, a state taxes a foreign company at a higher rate if the company's state of domicile charges a higher tax to companies domiciled in the first state. Retaliatory taxes were declared a burden on interstate commerce in 1985 by the U. S. Supreme Court (*Metropolitan Life v. Ward*, 105 S Ct 1676). States that used retaliatory taxes had to pass new laws to continue collecting insurance taxes.

Summary

This chapter provides an outline of the roles played by the federal and state governments in insurance regulation. Although the states are the primary regulators of insurance, the federal government is an active participant. The federal government establishes the economic environment for the insurance industry, directly regulates a minor portion of insurance, and operates a large social insurance program. State governments provide the bulk of the regulatory mechanisms for insurance. Among the areas of state regulation are prices, access to insurance, policy forms, taxes, and agent licensing. In regulating insurance, states have a variety of goals including solvency of insurance companies, fairness of the insurance contract, access to insurance, investments in social goods, and protection of local companies. The early history of state insurance regulation and the development of state regulatory policies is discussed in the next chapter.

Chapter 4

State Regulation of Insurance: From Free Markets to Cartels to Free Markets

Early Regulation of Insurance

Although modern insurance predates the American Republic, little insurance was written in the colonies.[1] Most marine underwriting was done in England, and the colonies had no appreciable market for life or fire insurance, the two other most likely forms (Post, 1976: 39). The earliest recorded mention of insurance appeared in a 1721 Philadelphia newspaper, *American Weekly Mercury,* announcing the establishment of an insurance office (Patterson, 1927: 521). The first formal association of marine underwriters was formed by Thomas Willing in 1757 (Kroos and Blyn, 1970: 14). The earliest fire insurance was offered by the Friendly Society of Mutual Insuring of Homes Against Fire operating in Charleston, South Carolina, from 1735 to 1741 when the Society ceased operations after a major fire (Lilly, 1976: 99). The first successful fire insurance company, the Philadelphia Contributorship for Insurance of Houses from Loss by Fire, was created by the Union Fire Company (organized in part by Benjamin Franklin) in 1752 (Post, 1976: 42). Although life insurance was written as early as 1759 by the Presbyterian Minister's Fund, it was of minor significance until the mid-1800s (Norton, 1973: 1089).[2]

Early insurance in America was essentially unregulated until the corporate form of organization was used to offer insurance. The Philadelphia Contributorship was incorporated as a "mutual" by the Pennsylvania colonial legislature in 1768. The first stock corporation established was the Insurance Company of North America (INA) (still in existence) in 1794 (Patterson, 1927: 523). Corporations at the time had to be established by a special act of

49

a legislature because states did not have general incorporation statutes.

Edwin Patterson (1927: 520), the foremost historian of early insurance regulation, argues that the adoption of the corporate form was the crucial stimulant for insurance regulation. Corporations permitted large-scale insurance operations because they allowed entrepreneurs to accumulate capital from small investors and because they had the longevity to pay future claims. In turn, corporations altered the bargaining power between the policyholder and the insurer. The rise of corporations limited the number of insurers that a policyholder could select from and placed the policyholder at a bargaining disadvantage because the corporation had access to superior information. Thus, Patterson argues that the corporation not only made insurance possible, but also created the demand for regulation.[3]

Although Patterson (1927: 521) argues that the spread of insurance to the common people, rather than wealthy merchants and shipowners, was crucial to establishing regulation in the United States; in fact, regulation preceded this expansion. Regulations were included in the statutes incorporating insurance companies. The legislation creating INA, for example, required that INA capital be invested in specified government bonds and that deposits be made with the Bank of Pennsylvania (Patterson, 1927: 523). Owning real estate for income or speculative purposes was restricted. The first era of regulation, therefore, was regulation of investments by the incorporation legislation (Kimball, 1960: 130).

NINETEENTH-CENTURY REGULATION

Early insurance regulation reflected political patterns that persisted well into the twentieth century. Insurance is essentially two industries. The early property and casualty industry in America was limited primarily to fire insurance, thereby establishing fire insurance in its dominant economic and political position. Most marine underwriting was done by foreign underwriters and only a few American firms before World War I (Innes, 1972: 53). Life insurance was a separate industry with separate incorporation; health insurance, first offered in 1847, was a minor portion of this industry until the mid-twentieth century (Norton, 1973: 1100). Businesses often combined insurance with other enterprises, frequently commercial banking or even individual underwriting by a merchant. Both the life insurance and the fire insurance industries opposed government regulation unless the regulation would somehow benefit the industry. Because the political history of the life insurance and the property and casualty insurance industries developed separately, they merit separate discussions.

EARLY PROPERTY AND CASUALTY INSURANCE REGULATION

State governments, in addition to restricting investments, were also interested in raising revenues and protecting local insurance companies. Because insurance companies produce a high-volume cash flow, they are prime targets for taxation. In 1785, Massachusetts enacted the first insurance tax, requiring that tax stamps be affixed to insurance policies (Kimball, 1960: 251). In 1818, Massachusetts incorporated the Massachusetts Hospital Life Insurance Corporation and required that one-third of its profits go to Massachusetts General Hospital; in exchange, the corporation was granted a life insurance monopoly within Massachusetts (Kimball, 1960: 251). Specific, earmarked insurance taxes gradually gave way to general premium taxes beginning with New York in 1824 (Patterson, 1927: 524, n21).

Because state governments had a financial interest in prosperous local companies, states made serious efforts to protect local companies. Often companies were granted a monopoly within the state's boundaries. As a result of hostility to English companies during the War of 1812, Pennsylvania and South Carolina passed legislation restricting alien[4] insurance companies. A more rational approach, however, was discriminatory taxation because local companies often could not underwrite all the insurance needs in a state (marine underwriting is one example). In 1824, New York enacted a 10 percent premium tax applicable to only foreign and alien insurers (Lilly, 1976: 100). After a major New York City fire in 1835 bankrupted 23 of the 26 New York companies (Vaughn, 1982: 66), the premium tax was reduced to 2 percent to attract foreign companies to New York (Lilly, 1976: 100). Discriminatory insurance taxes were a source of revenue for states until declared unconstitutional by the Supreme Court in 1985 (*Metropolitan v. Ward* 105 S Ct 1676).

The next wave of regulation indirectly targeted the insolvency problem by requiring that insurance companies file reports on their financial status. The theory behind public filing was that individuals could then judge the solidity of the company that wrote their insurance (Patterson, 1927: 525). Massachusetts required some reports as early as 1799 and by 1818 had a general reporting requirement. New York adopted a reporting law in 1828 (Patterson, 1927: 526), and many other states followed suit. Reporting requirements had little impact on the solvency of insurance companies. Policyholders rarely had the expertise to distinguish a solvent company from an insolvent one, and state legislators had little regulatory recourse against an insolvent company.

Of particular threat to solvency were large local fires. In years with few fires, fire insurance underwriting was very profitable. As a result, companies were highly competitive and lowered prices. The agency system exacerbated the competition problems. Having no financial stake in underwriting, agents were under no pressure to avoid bad risks. Because good agents were the key to sales, a form of reverse competition flourished by offering higher agent's commissions (Hanson, Dineen, and Johnson, 1974: 9). When a major fire did occur, many fire companies found themselves without sufficient reserves to pay losses. Legal technicalities in insurance contracts were often used to avoid paying claims. Two approaches to the insolvency problem were undertaken, one by the industry and one by the states.

1. *Industry Efforts*. The industry approach was to collude and restrict competition between companies as well as for agents. Such efforts were not uncommon in the late nineteenth century as trusts were established in a variety of other industries (Markham, 1965: 157). Fire insurance companies established the National Board of Fire Underwriters in 1866 to set fire insurance rates and commissions.[5] The Board was viewed as an effort to regain control of the industry from the agents (Hanson, Dineen, and Johnson, 1974: 13). The Board's domination by large fire insurance companies led the smaller companies to ignore the Board and undercut rates. After the Great Chicago Fire of 1871 and the Boston Fire of 1872, the folly of unrestrained competition was underscored. Of the 4,000 existing fire insurance companies, only 1,000 survived these fires (Kimball and Boyce, 1958: 548). State and local boards were established to set rates in a second effort at collusion (Kimball, 1960: 95; Post, 1976: 94). These developed into regional organizations by 1880 (Kimball and Boyce, 1958: 549). Collusive ratemaking, however, was unsuccessful without government action because barriers to entry were low at this time and new companies were forming all the time. With unrestricted entry, individual companies often cheated on the conspiracy and lowered prices or offered higher commissions (see Armentano, 1982, for a discussion of the limits to collusion).

2. *State Efforts*. State efforts to deal with the fire insurance insolvencies took three forms—establishing an administrative organization, regulating policy forms, and acting against collusive ratemaking. Direct legislative regulation of insurance companies was clearly not effective given the problems in the industry and the massive reports that were submitted to the legislature (but probably not read). The logical response was to create an administrative organization to regulate insurance. Demand for administrative regulation resulted as much from problems in life insurance (see below) as from problems in the fire industry. Elizur Wright, often called the Father of Insurance Regulation, lobbied the Massachusetts legislature to require that life insurance companies maintain policy reserves. Wright had previously developed net valuation tables so that life insurance premiums could be actuarially sound (Buley, 1953: 60). Although the Massachusetts Insurance Commissioner was

to become a national leader in innovative regulation after Wright became commissioner, the first insurance regulatory board was established by New Hampshire in 1851. Massachusetts created an insurance board in 1855 and a single commissioner of insurance in 1866. Other states followed Massachusetts's lead and created first boards and then administrative agencies headed by single commissioners (Patterson, 1927: 534–535).

Early insurance regulation concerned licensing agents, setting reserve requirements, and collecting information concerning company operations. Insurance companies, especially fire insurance companies, were hostile to the idea of state regulation. A common reaction to establishing regulation was threatening to leave the state (Kimball, 1960: 171).[6] Small companies often left, but large ones usually could not afford to withdraw from a major state.

Insurance companies' second reaction was a legal challenge to state regulation. Samuel Paul, a Virginia resident, was an agent for several New York companies. His application for a Virginia license in 1865 was denied because the New York companies he represented had not deposited a bond with the state as required by Virginia statute. Paul solicited business without a license, was arrested, and fined $50. Insurance companies, led by the National Board of Fire Underwriters, used this case to lodge a constitutional challenge against all state regulation (Michelbacher and Roos, 1970: 255). In an appeal that eventually reached the U. S. Supreme Court, the companies argued that insurance of this nature was interstate commerce; under the U. S. Constitution, therefore, only the federal government could regulate interstate commerce. As a result, Virginia's regulation violated the Constitution (Lilly, 1976: 102). The insurance companies favored federal regulation at the time, not because they preferred federal regulation, but because they perceived the federal government would be a weaker regulator than many of the more aggressive states (Kimball and Boyce, 1958: 553).[7]

The Supreme Court in *Paul v. Virginia* [75 U. S. 168 (1968)] rejected the arguments of Paul and the insurance companies. Holding that the issuance of an insurance policy was not commerce, they upheld Virginia's regulation of insurance. The judicial dicta that issuing an insurance policy was not commerce evolved into the principle that the business of insurance was not commerce; this principle protected insurance companies from federal regulation until the *South-Eastern Underwriters* case (see below). The development of state regulation, therefore, owes much to what Jon Hanson (1977: 20) has termed a *judicial accident,* the initial misinterpretation of the Constitution's interstate commerce clause.

After the *Paul v. Virginia* case, the insurance commissioners followed the fire insurance companies' example and formed an organization for cooperation among state regulators. In 1871, the National Insurance Convention

(NIC) was formed; NIC evolved into the National Convention of Insurance Commissioners and then into the National Association of Insurance Commissioners (NAIC) (Lilly, 1976: 114 note 37). Under the direction of New York Superintendent of Insurance George W. Miller, the first convention agreed to adopt a uniform annual statement form, requiring life insurance companies to make deposits to protect policyholders but not requiring deposits from fire insurance companies. In its second session, the NIC drafted a model law on insurance regulation, thereby beginning the NAIC's attention to model laws that continues today.

Ostensibly to protect policyholders, state regulators began to mandate policy forms. The small print in fire insurance policies was often used by unscrupulous companies to avoid paying valid claims. In 1873, Massachusetts passed the first standard fire insurance policy law that was not overturned in court. Most states, however, adopted the New York Standard Fire Policy of 1886.[8] That policy was the work of the New York Insurance Department with the assistance of the New York Board of Fire Underwriters (Lilly, 1976: 106). Most of the work was performed by the Board, and the content of the fire policy reflected its origins. Kimball (1960: 231) argues that the fire policy was designed to favor the industry. "The 1895 standard fire insurance policy [Wisconsin's version of the New York policy] was a harsh contract; notable among its provisions were a number of conditions, breach of any of which rendered the policy void." A 1917 survey revealed that 28 percent of all policies including 55 percent of policies on jointly owned property were void for some breach of moral hazard condition specified in the standard policy form (Kimball, 1960: 232).

The other major innovation in insurance regulation before 1900 was the anticompact law. Designed to prevent insurance companies from meeting to fix prices (as they did with the fire boards), anticompact laws were passed in 23 states by 1913 (Hanson, Dineen, and Johnson, 1974: 14). The statutes were generally ineffective in eliminating collusive rate setting; fire boards simply announced they were in the business of selling "advisory" rate books and offered them to insurance companies (Kimball and Boyce, 1958: 549). Uncontrolled competition, which the anticompact laws were designed to produce, was so feared by the larger insurance companies that rating bureaus continued to operate in states that passed anticompact laws.

The status of insurance regulation in the property and casualty field at the turn of the century was rudimentary. Most insurance commissions were small. Insurance regulation focused on reporting requirements, licensing of agents and companies, and prescribing policy forms. Rate regulation was not exercised by a single state; in fact, the science of ratemaking had only recently developed.

EARLY LIFE INSURANCE REGULATION

Life insurance was the product that popularized the industry and convinced many average Americans to buy insurance for the first time. In the early 1800s, life insurance was in little demand, and few companies offered it (Krooss and Blyn, 1970: 63). Many life insurance companies did business as trust companies and wrote life insurance only as a minor sideline (Krooss and Blyn, 1970: 63). Several innovations changed the industry. In 1846, the agency system was created by Connecticut Mutual Life to increase the size of its sales force; other mutuals quickly followed suit (Krooss and Blyn, 1970: 83). In an era of unregulated capitalism, a variety of marketing excesses occurred. To make policies attractive, dividends were often paid far in excess of the earned surplus. Often, dividends were paid in company script to encourage the policyholder to purchase additional life insurance (Post, 1976: 49). Companies survived in a situation where payouts exceeded premiums only by increasing sales faster than claims were made.

Pressures for growth led to several dubious sales techniques. Some insurance companies allowed individuals to pay only part of the purchase price in cash; the rest was taken as a premium note to be redeemed from policyholder dividends. Hard-sell techniques became common (Post, 1976: 49). Because the emphasis was on expanding sales, successful agents were extremely valuable to companies. Companies engaged in reverse competition by offering individual agents ever increasing commissions without adjusting the price of the insurance policy. Commissions as high as 80 percent of the premium were offered (Miller, 1981: 80).

Perhaps the most successful salesperson of the time was Henry Baldwin Hyde who founded the Equitable Life Assurance Society of the United States (Buley, 1953: 52–53). Hyde resurrected the *tontine principle*. The tontine was invented by Lorenzo Tonti, a Neapolitan banker to Cardinal Mazarin in the mid-seventeenth century. Under a tontine, a group of individuals purchase an interest in a "life insurance" policy together. Dividends are paid at some time in the future (for example, after 5, 10, 15, and 20 years or perhaps only once). Individuals who died before dividends were paid out received nothing; only the survivors collect (Buley, 1953: 16). Essentially, a *tontine* is a wager that an individual will outlive his or her copolicyholders (Kimball, 1960: 164).

Tontines are profitable for insurance companies because they can use large amounts of cash for long periods of time. A high-lapse rate generated even more cash; from 1885 to 1894 $463 million of Equitable Life's $1.4 billion in policies lapsed (Krooss and Blyn, 1970: 110). Using the tontine, Hyde built Equitable into the largest life insurance company in the United

States. Life insurance assets in general increased 25 percent per year from 1860 to 1890.

A second policy innovation was *industrial life,* introduced to the United States in 1875 (Buley, 1953: 107). Regular life insurance was sold predominantly to middle-and upper-class persons who possessed discretionary income. Industrial life was targeted at the working class. Industrial life policies had a small face value (for example, $25) and were sold door-to-door; premiums were collected by the salesperson weekly. In terms of pure insurance, industrial life was expensive because it had high administrative and commission costs. It was popular with insurance companies for just those reasons. Industrial life insurance in force increased from $20 million in 1880 to $1.5 billion in 1900. Prudential Life Insurance, Metropolitan Mutual Life Insurance and John Hancock Insurance became major insurance companies through the sale of industrial life.

As the result of tontines, industrial life, and the replacement of term contracts with whole life contracts,[9] the amount of life insurance in force exploded. In 1840, only $4.65 million in life insurance was in force; by 1870, the face value of life insurance policies was nearly $2 billion. By 1910, Metropolitan alone had $2 billion worth of policies (Post, 1976: 49–51).

The growth in life insurance was not accompanied by a growth in corporate responsibility, however. Companies often erected showy offices that cost more than the company's total assets, dividends were declared that had not been earned, risks were accepted carelessly, and little attention was paid to reserves (Buley, 1953: 93). The financial health of many insurance companies was shaky at best. During the 1870 recessions, numerous life insurance companies collapsed. By 1882, only 55 of the 129 companies in business in 1870 were still operating (Norton, 1973: 1093).

State Regulation. Concern about reserves was the issue that mobilized Elizur Wright to lobby the Massachusetts legislature for insurance regulation. Wright's effort led to the creation of an insurance commission and eventually to reserve requirements. Investment regulations and policy forms were also areas of state regulation in the nineteenth century. Large life insurance companies demonstrated the same hostility toward regulation that the fire insurance companies did. In response to Elizur Wright's aggressive regulation, Massachusetts insurance companies forced Wright out as commissioner in 1867 (Buley, 1953: 63).[10] The overall effect of regulation on life insurance was positive, however. State regulatory requirements that established reserves plus the elimination of weak companies by market forces in the 1870s resulted in an invigorated life insurance industry. By the turn of the century, the face value of life insurance policies had increased to $7.5 billion.

Twentieth Century Insurance Regulation: The Beginning

Insurance regulation at the turn of the century was much like regulation of other industries. Large industries were formally being regulated by state agencies, but the regulatory commissions were generally underfunded and not particularly effective. With the exception of a few states, regulatory agencies were dominated by the insurance interests. The turn of the century, however, marked the beginning of the progressive era in U. S. politics. This was the era of trust busting, muckraking, and regulation. Consumer protection became a serious issue on the national agenda with the passage of the Pure Food and Drug Act of 1906 and the Meat Inspection Act of 1907 (Nadel, 1971; Feldman, 1976). Politics at the time was characterized by investigations that generated publicity and political entrepreneurs that put together pro-consumer coalitions (Wiebe, 1967; Hofstadter, 1955; Goldman, 1952). Insurance regulation was not immune to these political forces.

THE ARMSTRONG COMMITTEE

The major progressive-era reform of the life insurance industry began as an intracompany dispute involving Equitable Life. When founder Henry Hyde died in 1899, control over Equitable Life was intended to pass to his son James Hazen Hyde via a series of trusts. James Hyde had a taste for high living, however, and spent money lavishly even for the time (Post, 1976: 98). This aroused concern among other Equitable Life officers and policyholders about the company's financial security. What began as an internal dispute became public when muckrakers detailed the extravagance of Hyde and his cohorts (Buley, 1953: 200–206). Newspaper stories found evidence of political payoffs for legislation beneficial to Equitable Life. (Kimball, 1960: 55; Buley, 1953: 213).

Responding to the publicity, the New York legislature named a committee to investigate that state's life insurance industry. The New York legislature had previously investigated the insurance industry with major efforts conducted in 1870, 1872, 1877, 1882, and 1885 (Post, 1976: 86). With the public pressure of the progressive era, however, this investigation was to be different. The committee, termed the Armstrong Committee after its chair Senator William Armstrong, recruited Charles Evans Hughes as its chief counsel.[11]

The Armstrong Committee found insurance company abuses in all facets of the life insurance business. Interlocking directorates were common, policyholder control of mutuals was frustrated by management controlled proxies,[12] investments were made in inappropriate businesses, company expenses were not limited, rebating was frequent, excessive first-year premiums were paid, and policy forms and interpretations were biased against policy holders. High surpluses from lapsed policies and deferred dividends paid for lavish headquarters and excessive salaries (Miller, 1982: 81). These economic abuses coexisted with political abuses; life insurance companies were linked to political corruption and influence (Lilly, 1976: 104; Post, 1876: 98). Three companies stood out in the Armstrong Committee investigation as especially abusive—Equitable Life, New York Life, and Mutual of New York.

The Armstrong Committee's 1906 report further raised the salience of life insurance regulation.[13] Salience increased the legislature's willingness to act, and it responded with a series of reform laws titled the New York State Insurance Code. The code required the election of directors by policyholders in mutual companies. Investments were limited to government bonds, secured corporate debt, mortgages, and policyholder loans. Investment in common stocks and real estate (other than temporary ownership of foreclosed mortgage real estate) was eliminated. Political contributions were outlawed, and lobbyists were required to register with the state. Statutes regulated false advertising, bookkeeping, expenses, and other internal operations. Tontines were banned, and four standard life insurance policy forms were approved. To avoid the rapid growth that precipitated many abuses, companies were limited to a certain percentage of growth based on their assets. The New York State Insurance Code, in short, covered most operations of life insurance companies (Post, 1976: 98; Lilly, 1976: 104; Norton, 1973: 1095). Although relatively few criminal indictments resulted from the Armstrong Committee investigation, many insurance company executives were forced to repay company funds; virtually the entire top management of the larger life insurance companies were ousted by policyholders (Post, 1976: 102; Miller, 1982: 83).

The Armstrong Committee had far-reaching effects. Several states conducted investigations similar to the Armstrong Committee, found similar abuses, and passed somewhat similar reforms (Buley, 1953: 300). Perhaps the greatest influence in spreading the impact of the Armstrong Committee reforms was New York Deputy Superintendent of Insurance Henry D. Appleton. Appleton formulated an administrative rule that prohibited foreign life insurance companies (those not domiciled in New York) from conducting business in New York unless they substantially complied with New York law, not only in New York *but also in all other states in which they did business* (Weisbart, 1975: 4; Jackson, 1960).[14] Because the New York market was large, few major insurance companies were willing to forego that market. The result of the Appleton rule was that most insurance contracts were regulated by New York law in every state. As late as 1972, 58.2 percent of all life insurance by volume and 70.7 percent of all group life insurance was issued by companies covered by the Appleton rule (Weisbart, 1975: 5).[15]

The Appleton rule was not popular with other insurance commissioners because it prevented those commissioners from establishing innovative regulation. Any regulatory proposal different from the Appleton rule was immediately opposed by all interstate companies because it might jeopardize New York licenses. The Appleton rule was subsequently enacted as part of the New York State Insurance Code, but recent Superintendents of Insurance have allowed foreign companies to be in "substantial compliance" rather than literal compliance so that conflicts between New York law and those of other states are tolerated.[16]

The Armstrong Committee also contributed to New York's reputation for strict regulation of insurance. According to Weisbart (1975: 26), the Armstrong Committee strongly criticized the New York Insurance Department for allowing life insurance companies to commit the revealed abuses (see also Miller, 1982: 82). The Department's reaction to the criticism led to a bureaucratic norm of strict regulation and literal compliance with the law.

THE MERRITT COMMITTEE

The same year that the New York State Insurance Code was revised following the Armstrong Committee investigation, the great San Francisco Earthquake hit, resulting in damages of $24 million and fire damages of $350 million (equal to about $3.7 billion in current dollars; Insurance Information Institute, 1986: 70, 73). Many fire insurance companies found themselves unable to pay claims and filed bankruptcy. The massive jump in rates by those companies that did survive prompted the New York legislature to constitute a second insurance investigation committee, the Merritt Committee.

Insurance companies testifying before the Merritt Committee blamed their problems on unrestricted competition.[17] Although local and regional rate bureaus existed to set rates in concert, entry into the industry was not difficult; and independent (that is, nonbureau) companies and mutual companies would undercut prices. Short-run profits could be made by undercutting prices because fire insurance was very profitable if no major fires occurred. A price-cutting company was betting that no conflagrations would occur because it cut rates by not building up reserves. Adequate fire insurance protection, the industry concluded, required adequate rates; adequate rates required restrictions on competition.

The Merritt Committee concluded that anticompact legislation had failed and that collaborative ratemaking was needed.[18] Because each individual firm lacked sufficient data to set fire insurance rates, the Merritt Committee concluded that reasonable rates could only be set in concert. It recommended and, in 1911, the New York legislature passed a law that permitted rate bureaus to make rates for fire insurance companies. These rates must then be filed with the Superintendent of Insurance who examines the rates to ensure that they were not unfairly discriminatory (Post, 1976: 95). In practice, the New York Insurance Department administered the law to require prior approval of rates (Hanson, Dineen, and Johnson, 1974: 19). In a sense, New York authorized fire insurance companies to collude to set rates and ratified the practice with the state's official blessing that the rates were not discriminatory. In 1912, casualty insurance was brought under this law, and in 1913, all other forms of property and liability insurance were also included (Michelbacher and Roos, 1970: 264). In 1922, New York also required that the rates be reasonable and adequate (Crane, 1972: 518).

The New York law had an element of price regulation, although Kansas, not New York, was the first state to regulate property and casualty insurance prices. In 1909, the Kansas Insurance Commissioner was authorized to regulate fire insurance rates so that they would be adequate but not excessive. A subsequent decision to decrease fire insurance rates was challenged by the German Alliance Insurance Company. The challenge carried to the U. S. Supreme Court, which held that insurance was an industry "affected with the public interest," and therefore, states could regulate the rates charged by insurance companies [*German Alliance Insurance Company v. Lewis* 233 U. S. 389 (1913)].

New York recommended its fire insurance law to other states via NAIC (or the National Convention of Insurance Commissioners as it was known then). NAIC proposed a group of four model laws in 1914, and several states adopted them. The primary objective of these laws was to recognize rate bureaus; control of rates was an afterthought (Crane, 1972: 514). Many state regulators, as a result, became involved in questions concerning adequate rates and profits. In 1921, the Fire Insurance Committee of NAIC reported that underwriting profit should be defined as the difference between premiums and the sum of losses plus expenses. Investment income was not to be considered in setting rates. A reasonable underwriting profit was deemed to be 5 percent plus 3 percent for conflagrations (any fire with losses in excess of $1 million).

Although collusive rate setting in fire insurance was now the norm in New York and many other states, not all states followed this pattern (see below). In addition, some states allowed collusive rate setting for fire insurance but not for newly developed lines such as automobile insurance (Hanson, Dineen, and Johnson, 1974: 21). Workers' compensation insurance was also price regulated; but in this case, some states offered insurance through the state, and in other states the state reserved a monopoly in workers' compensation for itself. Life insurance had no economic need to go to collusive rate setting because standard mortality tables were available to all life insurance companies. A life insurance company only needed to add its expenses, profits, and rate of return to the pure premium from the mortality table to arrive at a rate. Some credit must be given to state insurance regulators at this time for resisting the urge to regulate the price of life insurance and thereby creating collusion where competition existed.[19]

Regulating Investment Decisions

Perhaps the most interesting aspect of early life insurance regulation involves investment decisions. The investment decisions of life insurance companies are regulated for two reasons. First, life insurance is a contract for future payments; if a life insurance firm goes bankrupt through poor investments, an individual will be unable to collect on his or her premium investment. One purpose in regulating investments, therefore, is solvency. Second, life insurance companies are financial intermediaries. Throughout American history, politicians have been concerned about concentrations of capital. In this regard, restrictions on life insurance companies are no different from restrictions on banks or other financial institutions. The second reason for regulating life insurance investments, therefore, is to prevent economic concentrations of power.

In an excellent overview of the investment regulation policy, Karen Orren (1974: 19ff) discerns three eras of state regulation—mandatory, inducing, and enabling.[20] Life insurance investment regulation began with legislation that incorporated insurance companies in the early years of the republic. INA, for example, was limited by the Commonwealth of Pennsylvania to investments in government bonds. Early legislatures were concerned with concentrations of wealth because most early incorporations limited companies to fire and marine insurance or companies quickly decided to specialize in these areas.[21] Later legislative concern focused on the outflow of capital to eastern states where the large insurance companies were domiciled. States considered and adopted mandatory laws requiring companies doing business in a state to investment a certain portion of their incomes within that state. For example, in 1869, Illinois required an investment of $100,000 in either U. S. securities, Illinois state or municipal securities, or mortgages on Illinois real estate. In the 1850s and 1860s, New Jersey, New York, California, Iowa, Kansas, Kentucky, Ohio, and Wisconsin passed laws that required companies doing business in those states to invest a significant portion of their capital in those states (Orren, 1974: 25).[22]

Even with the mandatory investment laws adopted by several states to limit capital outflows, investment controls on the average nineteenth century life insurance company were fairly limited. Life insurance companies could invest in corporate stocks and speculate in a variety of corporate enterprises. New York's Armstrong Committee investigation revealed that the major life insurance companies had invested in banks, railroads, and other corporations; in many cases the insurance companies' directors also had a financial interest in these corporations. Such investments created the specter of a money trust.

The Armstrong Committee report and the subsequent adoption of reform legislation in New York ushered in the second era of investment regulation, the enabling period. Under enabling regulation, a life insurance company was allowed to invest only in a list of investments approved by the state regulating the company. After the Armstrong Committee investigation, New York life insurance companies were allowed to invest in government bonds, secured corporate debt, mortgage loans with a face value worth 50 percent more than the loan amount, and policyholder loans, (Life Insurance Association of America, 1962: 76). These restrictions limited life insurance companies to conservative investments only. Unlike property and casualty companies, life insurance companies could not invest in corporate stocks. Any real estate acquired through the mortgage business had to be disposed of within five years.

The New York restrictions were applied by the Appleton rule to all companies doing business in New York. Before the Appleton rule, each state regulated companies domiciled in that state. Other states passed similar restrictive legislation, but the degree of restriction varied so that an insurance company could domicile in a state with the most attractive investment laws.[23]

The adoption of enabling investment regulation did not stem the tide of mandatory legislation. In 1907, Texas passed the famed Robertson law, requiring that an insurance company doing business in Texas invest 75 percent of the reserves originating from Texas policies in the state of Texas. Without such investments, a company could not be licensed to do business in Texas (Life Insurance Association of America, 1962: 93). The Robertson law, widely disliked by the industry, remained on the books until it was repealed in 1967 (Orren, 1974: 33).

Enabling investment regulation laws have gradually been liberalized over time. The pattern in New York, the most restrictive state, illustrates this liberalization. In 1928, New York permitted life insurance companies to invest in unsecured corporate debt and preferred stock. In 1934, FHA mortgages were made a permissible investment; in 1938, housing projects. In 1946, as part of the federal government's effort to provide housing for veterans, New York allowed investment in VA mortgages. Not until 1951 did New York permit investments in common stock. In 1958, New York adopted a leeway or basket clause permitting life insurance companies to invest up to

2 percent of their assets in investments not on the approved list. Laws also required that within a category of investments, the actual investments must be spread among a variety of investments. Wisconsin law, for example, allowed no more than 2 percent of assets to be invested in a single issue of secured corporate bonds, and no more than one percent of assets in the corporate stock of a single corporation (McHugh, 1969: 134).

Even though the investment regulations of New York appear strict, they were not a straitjacket. The law permitted investment in various categories up to a certain percentage of assets so that insurance companies could transfer assets from low-yielding investments to high-yielding ones. Table 4-1 reveals that life insurance companies clearly have been able to shift funds to accommodate market or policy shifts. Investment in government securities, for example, peaked at 50.3 percent of assets in 1945, dropped to a low of 4.5 percent in 1973, and rose with the rise in interest rates during the 1980s to 15.0 percent in 1985 (ACLI, 1986: 72).

The enabling legislation, although resisted by insurance companies, clearly has been good for them. The prohibition against ownership of common stock limited the impact that the Great Depression had on life insurance companies. The end result has been sound long-term investments that have permitted life insurance companies to greatly increase their capital bases.

Although the focus here has been on the strict regulation by the New York legislature, other states also regulated investments by firms domiciled in those states (no state has been as aggressive as New York in regulating foreign companies). The strictness of this regulation varies greatly; one illustration is that in 1962 the leeway percentage varied from 2 percent to 75 percent. A 75 percent leeway clause essentially permits a life insurance company to invest in any assets that are not expressly prohibited by law.

The third era of investment regulation is the era of the *inducing statutes*.[24] With insurance companies responding to mandatory investment laws

Table 4-1
Life Insurance Investments in Percent of Assets

	1925	1945	1965	1985
Government Securities	11.3	50.3	7.5	15.0
Corporate Bonds	26.2	22.5	36.7	36.0
Corporate Stocks	.7	2.2	5.7	9.4
Mortgages	41.7	14.8	37.8	20.8
Real Estate	2.3	1.9	3.0	3.5
Policy Loans	12.5	4.4	4.8	6.6
Miscellaneous	5.3	3.9	4.5	8.7

Source: ACLI, 1986: 72.

by refusing to operate in the offending state (Orren, 1974: 36), states began offering incentives to invest in certain state investments. States frequently create incentives for insurance companies to invest in housing, university construction projects, and other "social" investments (Orren, 1974: 24). Other states have tried to attract life insurance investments in any area of the state by creating premium tax inducements. Several states, including Oklahoma, have statutes that reduce the premium tax paid by an insurance company if the company has invested a certain percentage of its assets in the state.

Property and Casualty Insurance
The South-Eastern Underwriters Case

The cozy, cartel nature of the property and casualty insurance industry under the protective eye of state regulators was disrupted in 1944 by the U. S. Supreme Court. The cartel nature of insurance regulation was predicated on an exemption from federal antitrust laws so that companies could share data through rate bureaus and collectively set prices. The antitrust exemption was implied by the *Paul v. Virginia* decision, holding that insurance was not commerce. In *U. S. v. South-Eastern Underwriters Association* (322 U. S. 533, 1944) the Supreme Court held that insurance was commerce and, therefore, subject to federal antitrust restrictions. The *South-Eastern* case and the politics that spawned it reveal much about the relationship between state regulators and insurance companies.

The dispute that eventually produced the *Southern-Eastern* case began in 1922 in Missouri. Missouri, under the typical nature of insurance regulation at this time, regulated the price of insurance. Unlike most regulation, however, Missouri resisted increases in insurance rates. In response, 139 insurance companies filed 137 separate law suits to enjoin the Missouri Superintendent of Insurance and Attorney General from preventing rate increases. A temporary injunction was granted permitting the insurance companies to collect the rate increase but requiring that the rate increase be deposited in a court-controlled account until the final disposition of the cases. Deposits of $10,000,000 were made.

Negotiations over the refund dragged on for several years. In the late 1930s, the Missouri Superintendent of Insurance, Emmett O'Malley, was a member of Pendergast's Kansas City political machine. Because the suits still had not come to trial, O'Malley along with Pendergast and a representative of the insurance companies "negotiated" a settlement. The insurance companies were to receive 80 percent of the paid-in amounts (and, of course, higher rates in the future). The state would accept 20 percent as a settlement. In addition, the insurance companies, acting through Charles R. Street, were to pay Pendergast $750,000 who would, in turn, compensate O'Malley and Street. Pendergast was paid $440,000 of this bribe, and both O'Malley and Street received payoffs (Elmore, 1959: 501). One hundred thirty-four stock fire insurance companies contributed to the bribery fund.

After discovering the conspiracy, in 1939 Missouri Attorney General Roy McKittrick filed suit against the insurance companies that contributed to the bribery fund. His objective was to prevent those companies from doing business in Missouri on the grounds that they had engaged in a conspiracy to defraud policyholders and the State of Missouri. As part of this suit, the Attorney General eventually charged that the companies conspired to fix prices and limit competition. The price-fixing conspiracy, however, was not limited to Missouri. Insurance companies belonged to multistate ratemaking bureaus that gathered information from all member companies. Based on that information, the bureaus determined a "fair" price for insurance. Although prices were maintained by state regulation, the cartel also had its own enforcement mechanisms.[25] Insurance companies that were not part of the bureau (that is, the cartel) were denied access to reinsurance through bureau companies (Lilly, 1976: 106). Some lines of insurance, such as fire insurance, are not feasible without reinsurance. Because a single, large fire can destroy many buildings and because a single company might insure many buildings in a given location, a rational fire insurance company will spread its risks by selling some of its exposure to reinsurance companies. Without access to reinsurance markets, companies had to retain the entire risk. Few companies were large enough to do so without risking insolvency; consequently, the lack of reinsurance eliminated noncartel members from the market.

Recognizing the interstate nature of the insurance cartel, Missouri Attorney General McKittrick requested assistance from U. S. Attorney General Nicholas Biddle. After an investigation by the antitrust division headed by Thurmond Arnold, Biddle authorized grand jury proceedings to investigate criminal violations of federal antitrust laws by the insurance companies. Based on its reputation as one of the more flagrant monopolists, the South-Eastern Underwriters Association in Atlanta was chosen as the target (Elmore, 1959: 507).[26]

The insurance companies' response to the investigation was both legal and political. Their legal tactic was to rely on the *Paul v. Virginia* decision, which held insurance was not commerce and to dispute the jurisdiction of the antitrust division. The political tactic was to use their political resources to convince highly placed politicians that the Justice Department should drop its investigation (Elmore, 1959: 508). The political effort failed.

On November 20, 1942, a grand jury returned criminal indictments against South-Eastern Underwriters Association, 27 individuals who were officers or members of its executive committee, and 198 stock fire insurance companies that did business in Alabama, Florida, Georgia, North Carolina, South Carolina, and Virginia. They were charged with conspiracy to fix and maintain fire insurance rates and monopolization of trade in fire insurance. Cartel members used boycotts, coercion, and intimidation to keep member companies in line (Lilly, 1976: 107).

The legal position of the fire insurance companies was not enviable. In 1941, the defendant companies controlled 90 percent of the fire insurance in the six southeastern states; they collected premium income of $52 million but paid out only $18 million in losses (Elmore, 1959: 510). In the previous ten years, the participating companies collected premiums of $436 million and paid only $197 million in losses (Shenefield, 1982: 14).[27]

The insurance companies faced a decision regarding legal strategy. They could allow the government to present its case and then request a dismissal based on the case law that insurance was not commerce and, therefore, the insurance companies could not be guilty of antitrust violations. The second option was to file a demurrer to the indictment challenging jurisdiction before any evidence was presented. Again, the issue would have been the relevance of *Paul v. Virginia* and similar cases. Initially the Justice Department feared that the insurance companies would opt for the first choice. Under this option, the Department felt sure that the district judge would follow precedent and rule for the companies. Because the Department could not appeal a criminal case without creating double jeopardy, this would end the case without getting a U. S. Supreme Court ruling on whether antitrust applied to insurance companies (Elmore, 1959: 512). The insurance companies selected the second option. Although this was a strategic error, it was not without justification. The companies feared the adverse publicity that the government's presentation would generate.

As expected, the insurance companies won the first battle easily. Judge Underwood of the Federal District Court of the Northern District of Georgia ruled that insurance was not commerce and that the court had no jurisdiction. This decision was immediately appealed to the U. S. Supreme Court under statutory language that permitted the direct appeal of a dismissed indictment to the Supreme Court. The relationship between the insurance companies and state governments is best illustrated by the *amicus curiae* briefs filed before the Supreme Court. Thirty-five states filed briefs opposing the Justice Department's position. Clearly, the dominant partner in the symbiotic relationship between state regulators and the insurance companies was the insurance companies.

The Justice Department's brief made three arguments. First, all prior insurance cases [*Paul v. Virginia, Ducat v. Chicago* (10 Wall. 410, 1870), *Liverpool Insurance Co. v. Massachusetts* (10 Wall. 566, 1870), *Philadelphia Fire Association v. New York* (119 U. S. 110, 1886), *Hooper v. California* (158 U. S. 648, 1895), *New York Life Insurance Co. v. Cravens* (178 U. S. 389, 1900), *Nutting v. Massachusetts* (183 U. S. 553, 1902), and *New York Life Insurance Company v. Deer Lodge County* (231 U. S. 495, 1913)] had involved state legislation not federal legislation. Second, none of the earlier cases had demonstrated the interstate nature of the insurance business because no such evidence had been introduced. Third, all these cases followed the basic fallacy that insurance was not commerce without reconsidering the reasoning (Elmore, 1959: 504).

In a 4-to-3 decision (two justices did not participate), the Supreme Court concluded that a fire insurance company conducting a substantial portion of its business across state lines was engaged in interstate commerce. Writing for the majority, Justice William O. Douglas accepted the government's argument that this case was different from *Paul v. Virginia* because federal law rather than state law was involved (see Kintner, Bauer, and Allen, 1985: 436, note 34). A conspiracy to restrain interstate trade in insurance by fixing arbitrary and noncompetitive insurance rates would be violations of the Sherman Antitrust Act. Although the trial under the Sherman Antitrust Act did not take place, the clear-cut nature of the bureaus as conspiracies to fix prices left no doubt that convictions would be returned.

The McCarran-Ferguson Act

Litigation in the *South-Eastern* case and the court's ruling created an immediate political reaction. Potential concerns with the ruling were raised in Justice Jackson's dissenting opinion when he suggested that the ruling made state regulations and taxes unconstitutional (322 U. S. at 590). Two potential interests were affected by the decision. First, the fire insurance industry, including the defendants in the *South-Eastern* case, now felt the threat of criminal prosecution. Without protection from antitrust laws, these firms believed that competition would drive rates too low to allow a healthy industry. Second, the state insurance regulators were concerned not only about their authority to regulate insurance but also about their ability to collect premium taxes, a substantial contribution to state tax revenues (Kimball and Boyce, 1958: 554). Insurance companies contributed to this fear.[28] Within one year of the ruling, suits contesting premium taxes were filed in 11 states; taxes were paid under protest in 31 states (Lent, 1981: 412). This divergence of interests between insurance companies and state regulators prevented a cohesive coalition and would eventually limit the redress that the industry got from Congress.[29]

The insurance industry did not wait for the *South-Eastern* decision before expanding the scope of the conflict to Congress. In September 1943, bills were introduced in both houses of Congress to exempt insurance completely from the Sherman and Clayton Antitrust Acts (Elmore, 1959: 516). Known as the Walter-Hancock Bill, it was introduced at the request of the stock fire insurance companies. The intent of these proposals was to eliminate the Supreme Court's jurisdiction in the *South-Eastern* case. Insurance companies supported the bills with a grassroots lobby effort; members of Congress received a massive number of letters supporting the legislation.[30] The uniformity of the letters suggested a well-organized, carefully inspired campaign (Elmore, 1959: 517). With the exception of several newspaper editorials, little vocal opposition surfaced initially.

Just 17 days after the Supreme Court decision in the *South-Eastern* case, the Walter-Hancock Bill passed the House by a commanding 283 to 54 majority. The Senate resisted immediate action. The delay allowed a coalition of opponents to mobilize. Attorney General Biddle opposed the bill; in an exercise of bureaucratic discretion, Biddle announced that he would take no action with regard to *South-Eastern* (a trial on the facts had not been held) until the insurance companies had time to adjust their methods of operations and until Congress had time to act (Rose, 1967: 693). Such a moratorium relieved the pressure on the Senate to act immediately. In addition, the Justice Department released a survey of state insurance regulation that revealed about one-half of the states had inadequate provisions for regulating insurance companies; the implication was that policyholders in these states had no protection other than federal antitrust laws.

Further limiting the clout of the industry coalition was its lack of cohesion. The life insurance industry operated without ratemaking bureaus because mortality tables on which rates were based were widely available to all life insurance companies. The life insurance companies did not support the exemption; neither did the casualty companies organized as mutuals rather than stock companies (Weller, 1978: 593; Kintner, *et al.*, 1985: 437, note 41; Rose, 1967: 693). Mutuals had been excluded by the stock companies from the rating bureaus because mutuals could effectively reduce the cost of insurance by increasing dividends (Marryott, 1950: 545). The insurance commissioners, through their organization (NAIC), also opposed a complete exemption. NAIC was more concerned with protecting the states' abilities to regulate and to make sure that state taxing powers were not restricted. The stock fire insurance companies were left in a one-industry coalition.

Despite the defections from the insurance industry coalition, the Walter-

Hancock Bill came close to passage. On September 21, 1944, the Senate passed the Walter-Hancock Bill but then reconsidered the bill and defeated it. Perceived as the most significant reason for the defeat was the opposition of President Franklin Roosevelt who threatened to veto the bill (Weller, 1978: 592, n 34).

With the defeat of the industry bill, the NAIC proposed a bill of its own. Concerned with preserving state taxation and regulation rather than with antitrust, the NAIC bill covered four specific points: (1) declared state regulation and taxation acceptable under the commerce clause of the U. S. Constitution, (2) exempted insurance from the Federal Trade Commission Act, (3) exempted insurance from the Robinson-Patman Act; and (4) limited the insurance exemption from the Sherman and Clayton Acts to cooperative procedures related to statistics, rates, and similar matters (Weller, 1978: 594). When Senators McCarran and Ferguson introduced an amended version of the NAIC bill, the Walter-Hancock Bill was perceived as dead.[31]

Different versions of the McCarran-Ferguson Act passed the House and the Senate. The specific exemptions from individual laws were deleted from both versions. The congressional dispute concerned how to treat conflicts between state regulation and federal antitrust laws. The House favored resolution in favor of state regulation, while the Senate favored resolution in favor of federal antitrust laws (Weller, 1978: 601). A conference committee compromise on this issue resolved the dispute, and the bill passed both houses of Congress. President Roosevelt signed the bill into law on March 9, 1945.[32]

The McCarran-Ferguson Act (also called Public Law 15) has several provisions. Section 1 of the Act declares that continued state regulation and taxation of the insurance industry is in the public interest. Section 2(a) states that the business of insurance shall be subject to state laws in regard to regulation and taxation. Section 2(b) provides that after June 30, 1948, the Sherman Act, the Clayton Act, and the Federal Trade Commission Act shall be applicable to the business of insurance "to the extent that such business is not regulated by State law." Section 3(a) exempts insurance from federal antitrust laws until June 30, 1948; this exemption was designed to give the states time to enact legislation under section 2(b). Section 3(b) states that the Sherman Act prohibitions against agreements to or acts of boycott, coercion, or intimidation shall remain in force. Although section 3(b) covered precisely the behavior of the firms and individuals indicted under the *South-Eastern* case, Attorney General Biddle dropped this case following passage of the Act.

The response to the McCarran-Ferguson Act came in two arenas. In the first, the states adopted new legislation to comply with the provisions of the Act. These laws set the tone for insurance regulation for the next 20 years. The second was the courts; substantial litigation was undertaken to determine what the "exemption" from federal antitrust laws actually meant. The first arena is relatively important to the political economy of insurance regulation; the second arena is often an exercise in legal hairsplitting. Both merit discussion; one for policy reasons and the other because substantial resources are devoted to litigation under the McCarran-Ferguson Act.

THE LITIGATION FRONT

Insurance is an industry that deals with technicalities and relies heavily on litigation to resolve disputes over those technicalities. Possessing substantial legal expertise, the insurance industry probed the McCarran-Ferguson Act for loopholes. The first challenge was to the law itself; if insurance was commerce, then the industry argued only the federal government could regulate insurance. Specifically, this meant that state laws taxing insurance were unconstitutional in that they restrained the interstate trade of insurance. The strength of this case was that the premium taxes of the time were discriminatory. A domestic (in-state) insurance company was charged a lower premium tax than a foreign (out-of-state) company. In *Prudential v. Benjamin* (328 U. S. 408), the U. S. Supreme Court upheld state taxation of insurance premiums including the use of discriminatory taxes. Discriminatory taxes were eventually struck down by the Supreme Court in *Metropolitan Life v. Ward* (105 S Ct 1676) in 1985, but the states' power to tax insurance premiums has remained.

Much litigation has concerned the scope of the antitrust exemption. Insurance companies argue for a broad exemption to place as much of the business of insurance as possible beyond the reach of antitrust laws. The federal government has always taken the position that the exemption is very narrow. President Roosevelt, in signing the legislation, stated, "Congress intended no grant of immunity for monopoly or for boycott, coercion or intimidation. Congress did not intend to permit private rate fixing, which the Anti-trust Act forbids, but was willing to permit actual regulation of rates by affirmative action of the states." (cited in Elmore, 1959: 521).

The Supreme Court has established three requirements for claiming the antitrust exemption. First, the conduct must be within the "business of insurance." Second, the challenged conduct must be "regulated by State law." Third, any agreement to or act of boycott, coercion or intimidation even if within the business of insurance and regulated by state law is prohibited.

The business of insurance has been precisely defined. An act is within the "business of insurance" if "*first,* whether the practice has the effect of transferring or spreading a policyholder's risk; *second,* whether the practice is an integral part of the policy relationship between the insurer and the insured; and *third,* whether the practice is limited to entities within the insurance industry." (*Pireno v. New York State Chiropractic Association* 458 U. S. 119, 1982 at 129). The Supreme Court's view of the business of insurance is a narrow one. Agreements between insurance companies and third parties (not policyholders) are not considered part of the business of insurance. Specifically, various federal courts have held that the "business of insurance" does not include agreements between Blue Cross and hospitals to set payment ceilings, agreements between health maintenance organizations, (HMOs) and drug companies regarding pharmaceutical prices, requirements that medical services be obtained by specified providers, requirements that charges be billed through physicians, and agreements between the insurer and physicians with regard to fees (Kintner, *et al.,* 1985: 450–451). In other cases [*SEC v. National Securities* 393 U. S. 453, (1969)], the Supreme Court refused to exempt mergers from Clayton Act purview even though the merger was approved by state regulators, and it determined that variable annuity contracts were not insurance [*SEC v. Variable Annuity Life Insurance* 359 U. S. 354 (1959)]. The "business of insurance" clause has been interpreted so narrowly that few actions other than rate bureaus and activities related to spreading policyholders' risks are exempt from antitrust. Included in the business of insurance are title insurance, the determination of premium rates, licensing of insurance companies, advertising and sale of policies, and setting agents' fees (Lent, 1981: 413).

While the "business of insurance" clause has been rigidly interpreted by the Supreme Court, the "regulated by State law" clause has received a liberal interpretation. The critical question is whether regulation by the state must be active regulation or if token regulation without enforcement is sufficient to trigger the exemption. In *FTC v. National Casualty Co.* [357 U. S. 560 (1958)], the FTC sought to prohibit false and deceptive advertising by some insurance companies located in Alabama. The FTC argued that because Alabama had never used its enforcement powers under its own deceptive advertising law, that the conduct was not regulated by state law. The Supreme Court held that legislation, even if not enforced, was sufficient to trigger the exemption and, therefore, the FTC had no jurisdiction. The courts have been fairly consistent in this interpretation (Kintner, *et al.,* 1985: 475; see also Hiebert, 1986).

Perhaps the most innovative argument made under the "regulated by state law" clause occurred in *FTC v. Travelers Health Association* [362 U. S. 293 (1960)]. Travelers Health Association was incorporated in Nebraska, which had a deceptive practices act, but was charged with deceptive practices by the FTC in states other than Nebraska that did not have such acts. Travelers contended that regulation in the state of domicile was sufficient to exempt the company from antitrust prosecution in all states. The Supreme Court declined to accept this innovative interpretation of federalism (see Chapter 6).[33]

The "boycott, coercion, and intimidation" clause has been frequently litigated with regard to insurance company actions against agents (Kintner, et al., 1985: 482–485). Such suits are part of a narrow area of the antitrust law that is of little public policy interest. A more interesting area concerns whether insurance companies can agree to boycott policyholders. In Rhode Island in the early 1970s, St. Paul Fire and Marine Insurance, the state's largest medical malpractice insurer, decided to change from an "occurrence" policy, which covers all incidents of malpractice occurring during the policy's life, to a "claims made" policy, which covers only those claims actually made during the policy's life. St. Paul made an agreement with the other three malpractice insurers in Rhode Island that they would refuse to issue any type of malpractice insurance, effectively granting St. Paul a monopoly. The Supreme Court held that such behavior was a boycott under federal antitrust laws [St. Paul Fire & Marine v. Barry, 438 U. S. 531 (1978)].

Although substantial litigation has occurred under the McCarran-Ferguson Act, it has produced little from a public policy perspective. The actions exempted are limited to a narrow definition of insurance; any type of legislation can be interpreted as affirmative regulation by the state; and traditional boycotts, coercive behavior, and intimidation are illegal. Some commentators argue that, given the law's development, the McCarran-Ferguson Act changed the law little from the Parker v. Brown [317 U. S. 341 (1943)] decision that exempted "state action" from antitrust laws (see Lent, 1981: 426; Weller, 1978: 588).

THE STATE LEGISLATION FRONT

The second response to the McCarran-Ferguson Act was the adoption of state insurance regulation laws that would trigger the antitrust exemption. The fire stock companies' contention that free competition would be disastrous for the industry was virtually unchallenged at this time. The specter of an insolvency epidemic loomed as the constitutionality of laws in 50 states came into question.

In retrospect, the reaction to South-Eastern was overblown. Given the state action doctrine of Parker v. Brown and the subsequent interpretations of "regulated by state law" by the courts, Rose (1967: 690) contends that few of the regulatory laws would have been struck down. Only laws that allowed collusion to set rates that were not subsequently approved or disapproved by any state agency were clearly unconstitutional. Only five states had such laws.

Rose's argument raises a second question: to what extent did states regulate property and casualty insurance rates before the *South-Eastern* case? A historical review of insurance laws prior to 1944 found that rate regulation permitting collusion was unusual except in workers' compensation insurance. Thirty-six states had rate regulation for workers' compensation insurance. Even fire insurance was often regulated in other ways; only 18 states regulated rates. In other fields, rate regulation was the exception; seven states had rate laws for automobile insurance and only two for general liability insurance (Marryott, 1950: 543).[34] In automobile insurance less than one-half the insurance written nationwide was by bureau-affiliated companies (Mosher, 1950: 527).

The rate regulation that did exist was primitive. Most laws did little other than recognize or prohibit rate bureaus. States could reject rates that were unfairly discriminatory, but few had powers over the actual rate levels (Crane, 1972: 512). Although fire insurance rates had to be filed in 31 states in 1942, only nine states required state approval of rates (Crane, 1972: 512). In addition, rate filings did not have to include supporting data, thus limiting any potential action by insurance commissioners. New York was one of only a few states with a strict prior approval law to regulate rates in most property and casualty lines (Crane, 1972: 513).

The pre-1944 status of insurance regulation is not nearly so collusive as commonly viewed. Property and casualty insurance was generally characterized by competition rather than collusion (Mosher, 1950: 526). Even in areas dominated by bureaus such as fire insurance, some independent companies set deviant rates. Only in workers' compensation insurance was collective rate setting the norm in all states.[35]

After the passage of the McCarran-Ferguson Act, the insurance commissioners, acting through NAIC began efforts to establish state regulation of insurance rates. In a sense, the McCarran-Ferguson Act was an opportunity to use the crisis created by the *South-Eastern* case to augment the commissioners' regulatory powers. The leading force in the NAIC effort was New York Superintendent of Insurance Robert Dineen, who supported the desires of the major New York rate bureau companies to be shielded from competition.[36]

The NAIC built support for their regulatory imperialism by co-opting the insurance industry. NAIC's Federal Legislation Committee asked industry members to form a committee to propose new state legislation. The resulting All-Industry Committee was composed of 19 organizations representing most interests in the insurance industry. The committee's composition had a significant impact on the final product (Rose, 1967: 697; Brook, 1950: 608). Six committee members had little interest in rating because they represented lines of insurance such as life insurance that neither had nor desired rate regulation. Four other organizations represented brokers or agents; two of these organizations opposed rate regulation. Three other organizations represented mutual insurance companies; mutuals would benefit from strict rate regulation because they could charge the same front-end price as the stock companies but undercut these prices by increasing dividends. The remaining six organizations represented companies that had been collusively fixing prices before 1944 (Brook, 1950: 610). The Committee, therefore, had nine members for rate regulation, two opposed, and eight neutral (Rose, 1967: 698).

Although the public view was that the industry dominated the drafting (see Rose, 1967: 698), in reality Dineen and the NAIC manipulated a divided industry into accepting stronger regulation. Mutual companies wanted strict rate regulation so that they could compete by increasing dividends. Independents felt that their rates need not be regulated because they did not conspire to set them. Stock companies wanted the right to set and enforce rates, but they did not want too much state "interference" in what rates were set (Crane, 1972: 530–531). The key issue became "prior approval": would insurance commissioners have the power to approve rates prior to use? To the stock fire insurance companies, prior approval was not needed under the McCarran-Ferguson Act; a file-and-use system was preferred (Crane, 1972: 523).[37]

On March 10, 1945, five months before the first meeting of the All-Industry Committee, the NAIC Committee on Rates and Rating Organizations gave preliminary approval to a prior approval rating bill but did not release the bill to the public (Crane 1972: 524). The NAIC's position on regulation, therefore, appeared to have been determined before the All-Industry Committee met. The All-Industry Committee had trouble resolving intraindustry disputes particularly on the prior approval versus file and use issue. Impatient with the lack of progress by the All-Industry Committee by late in the year, the NAIC applied pressure to the Committee. The mutuals and the small agents favored the NAIC's now-public proposal while the stock companies, the larger agents, and the independents favored the file-and-use system (Crane, 1972: 527). Faced with the NAIC's willingness to act with the support it already had, the fire stock companies accepted a compromise. Rather than allowing prior approval, companies were to file rates but could not use them for 15 days. The commissioner had 15 days to disapprove the rates. Although stock companies claimed victory, in fact, "subsequent disapproval" and "prior approval" are identical (Crane, 1972: 528).

By acting early and creating pressure on a divided industry, Dineen and the NAIC were able to impose stronger price regulation than the industry wanted. A divided industry was unable to successfully oppose the commissioners. By agreeing to the industry offered "compromise," the insurance commissioners gained industry support for their efforts to pass new state laws. The insurance commissioners emerged the big winners.

The joint NAIC and All-Industry Committee effort produced two model rate regulatory laws, one for fire, marine, and inland marine, and one for casualty and surety. Collectively referred to as the "All-Industry Bills," they are similar in content. Rates were to be established by state regulation and could not be "inadequate, excessive, or unfairly discriminatory." Rates must be filed with the insurance commissioner before they could be used, but a filing was deemed to be approved if the commissioner had not disapproved it in 15 days (the prior approval concept). Any disapproval required that the commissioner hold a rate hearing. Rating organizations were to be licensed by the state; these organizations could file rates for all member organizations and had to permit nonmembers to subscribe to its services without discrimination.[38] Finally, deviations from bureau rates could be granted only if the individual company made a separate filing and defended a separate rate.

The All-Industry/NAIC Bills were not the only options proposed for consideration; Rose (1967: 701-703) noted five additional proposals. First, the Justice Department proposed that property and casualty insurers be allowed to pool their loss data and that "pure" premiums be calculated based on this data. *Pure premiums* are premiums without any expenses added. These figures would be given to all insurers; and each company could then set its own price based on its cost of sales, overhead, and loss adjustment. Such a process is similar to life insurance pricing, because mortality tables can be used to calculate pure premiums.

Second, the brokers proposed that the All-Industry Bills be considered the maximum amount of state regulation. They favored a file-and-use system whereby rates could be used as soon as they were filed; commissioners would be empowered to suspend rates that did not meet appropriate standards after an administrative hearing. Third, one proposal suggested that rates need not be filed at all, that the commissioner merely be empowered to investigate rates and issue "cease and desist" orders if rates were inappropriate. Fourth, an association of insurance buyers for large firms proposed that bureau-collected data be made available to all interested parties so that consumers would have the same information as insurance companies.

Fifth and most interesting is what has been termed the California plan. Under the California plan, bureaus are legal but are not allowed to fix rates. Individual companies can file and charge whatever rates they wish. Essentially, the California plan uses the market to regulate rates and limits collusion among companies.

In 1946, the NAIC proposed its two model laws to state legislatures for adoption. Few innovations have been diffused as rapidly as the All-Industry Rating Laws. Although agents and some insurers opposed the All-Industry Rating Laws, within a year, 37 states had adopted versions of these laws; by 1951, all states had adopted new rate regulation laws (Hanson, Dineen, and Johnson, 1974: 29).

Not all new laws were identical, however. Some states required mandatory bureau membership. Texas empowered the state insurance commissioner to gather loss data and calculate rates independently of industry. California adopted the California plan, forbade agreements to charge bureau rates, and relied on market competition to regulate rates. Fifteen years later, California was used as an example when several states rejected collusive rate setting and moved to a market-oriented system (see below).

Several insurance lines avoided rate regulation altogether. The life and health insurance industry had not colluded to set rates in the past and saw no reason to do so in the future; competition would be used to keep rates in line (Dickerson, 1968: 684). The other major exception to the imposition of rate regulation after the McCarran-Ferguson Act was marine insurance. The marine insurance industry had a specific exemption from the antitrust laws dating from World War I. Some marine insurers set rates collectively with the American Hull Insurance Syndicate while others rated risks independently. Marine rates set in this manner were not subject to state rate regulation (Innes, 1972: 53).

Flushed with the success of the All-Industry Bills designed to protect industry in its ratemaking activities, the NAIC turned to the other federal antitrust threat, the FTC, who polices unfair and deceptive competitive practices. In 1947, the NAIC proposed a model Unfair Competition Act that listed a series of illegal actions. This model was clearly intended to eliminate the FTC's jurisdiction over insurance marketing practices (Lilly, 1976: 108). Every state eventually adopted this model act. In addition, 22 states also adopted a later NAIC model "Little Clayton" Act intended to shift Clayton Act regulation from the federal government to state governments.

THE ALL-INDUSTRY BILLS: A BRIEF EVALUATION

Although the All-Industry Bills were popular with both the insurance industry and state governments, they contained some serious flaws. Herbert Brook (1950: 611), a contemporary critic, contended,

> The obvious purpose was to destroy competition and to make the entire industry conform to the standards of those operating in concert. . . . In one generation laws were passed to protect the public from insurers fixing rates in concert

[the anticompact laws]; in this generation those same insurers obtained the passage of laws to protect themselves from competition!

Essentially, Brook is arguing that competitive industries such as automobile insurance were made noncompetitive by forcing the collusive pattern of fire insurance on all property and casualty insurance lines.

In the long run, the attempt to restrict competition in insurance lines that were potentially competitive was doomed to fail. The laws contained loopholes that allowed competition. A rational insurance company will seek to underwrite the best risks and offer a lower, but still profitable premium to do so. After the passage of the All-Industry Bills, direct writers (companies that sell direct to customers and do not use agents) with their lower costs (Joskow, 1973: 388) came to dominate the automobile and homeowners' insurance market. As Dominick Armentano (1982) argues, cartels are inherently unstable. If cartel members can cheat on the cartel, they will. Without some supporting government coercion, then, price fixing is doomed to failure.[39]

The Growth of Competition

The enactment of the All-Industry Bills has been interpreted by some as the establishment of government-sponsored cartels in the property and casualty insurance industry (see, for example, Joskow, 1973). Rather than the beginning of cartel dominance, however, the adoption of the All-Industry Bills marked the beginning of the decline of cartels and the movement to greater competition in insurance. Initially, cartels made some progress in establishing monopolies, but loopholes in the All-Industry Bills undercut such efforts.

One indicator of cartel strength after the All-Industry Bills was the consolidation of the ratemaking bureaus. The local and regional fire bureaus began consolidating so that by 1960 statistical collection had been centralized in the National Insurance Actuarial and Statistical Association (for stock companies) with rates being made by local organizations (Trupin, 1978: 256). In casualty insurance, two rating organizations emerged dominant—the National Bureau of Casualty Underwriters for stock companies and the Mutual Insurance Rating Bureau for mutuals. In 1967 the National Bureau of Casualty Underwriters merged with the National Automobile Underwriters Association to become the Insurance Rating Board (Trupin, 1967: 256). In 1971, six national rating bureaus for individual lines of insurance merged to form the Insurance Services Office, a statistical bureau for all lines of insurance (Trupin, 1967: 256). At this point consolidation into a single nationwide bureau for statistical purposes was complete.

ALL-INDUSTRY LOOPHOLES

By the time rate bureaus had been consolidated into the Insurance Services Office, the rate bureaus' power had been broken. Insurance is an industry where profits are often a secondary goal; growth has been a primary goal
of insurance companies at least since the mid-1800s and the rise of the large
life insurance companies. Size is considered a better indicator of financial
security than short-term profits. Several types of insurance companies sought
faster growth and thus had an incentive to underprice the cartel to attract
more business. Independent insurance companies were never part of the cartel and, except in states with mandatory bureau membership, were still outside the conspiracy. Mutual companies were never cartel members and could
use dividends to cut prices below posted rates. Several large companies, such
as INA, desired greater growth and had the economic resources to strike out
alone. Finally, new competitors attracted by the profits in the insurance business entered the market or dramatically expanded their market share. Five
factors led to greater competition in the insurance industry–installment premiums, use of deviations, partial subscribership, the restriction of the
aggrieved-person doctrine, and the growth of direct writers.

1. *Installment Premiums.* In the late 1940s, INA attempted to introduce a
pricing innovation called the *installment premium endorsement.* Paying insurance premiums in installments allowed the insured to use insurance company
financing. The insured got somewhat lower fire insurance rates while the
insurance company made some profit by charging interest. The bureau reaction to the INA proposal was negative; the proposed rate filing was rejected
by the rate bureaus. INA then filed the installment premium endorsement rate
as an independent filing; most insurance commissioners approved the installment premium innovation although in some cases litigation was necessary
(Hanson, Dineen, and Johnson, 1974: 36). A company without INA's resources, however, could not have borne the expense of independent filings in
numerous states. The successful fight to establish an independent rate encouraged large insurance companies to become less attached to bureau rates.

2. *The Increase in Deviations.* Under the All-Industry Rating Laws companies belonging to the rate bureau could file for deviations from bureau
rates. Because deviations were a way to undercut the stability of cartel pricing, bureaus vigorously resisted deviations (Trupin, 1978: 256; Hanson,
Dineen, and Johnson, 1974: 36). When a deviation was filed, the bureau
would challenge the rate and demand a hearing. If the hearing failed to re-
scind the rate, legal action would be commenced. An effort was made to
make deviations expensive and time consuming.

Many insurance commissioners, however, encouraged deviations. In
what is perceived to be a landmark case, in 1959 Allstate filed an indepen-

dent rate to enter the New York fire insurance market for the first time and to charge rates 20 percent below bureau rates. As a first time entrant, Allstate could hardly have had massive data on New York fire risks. The filing was challenged by the New York Fire Insurance Rating Bureau (the rate bureau). After a hearing, the Superintendent of Insurance approved the entry of All-state and allowed a rate 15 percent below the bureau-approved rate. A subsequent court challenge upheld the Superintendent's action (Trupin, 1978: 258; Hanson, Dineen, and Johnson, 1974: 36). Similar fights in New York and other states resulted in additional deviations. By the mid-1960s, more than 20 percent of New York insurance coverage for homes, automobiles, and general liability was written at prices deviating from bureau rates (Franson, 1969: 1108).

3. *Partial Subscribership.* The obstacles and limitations bureaus created for companies led several companies to resign from bureaus and become independents. Because the bureaus' statistical services were valuable and because some risks will still be priced at the bureau rate, several New York insurers attempted to resign from the New York Fire Insurance Rating Bureau for most dwelling classes but at the same time remain bureau members for other dwelling classes and commercial risks (Hanson, Dineen, and Johnson, 1974: 37). The bureau challenged this partial subscribership contending that such action violated the bureau's property rights. The New York Insurance Department upheld the concept of partial subscribership, and its decision was subsequently upheld by the New York Supreme Court (Hanson, Dineen, and Johnson, 1974: 37; Trupin, 1978: 259). Partial subscribership provided greater competition not only by allowing independent filings for partial subscribers but also because it created a situation whereby some companies could become partial independents without the risk of being independents in all cases. Such companies then did not have to use the cumbersome deviation filing procedure for bureau members (Trupin, 1978: 259).

4. *Aggrieved-Person Doctrine.* Any company desiring to file a deviation or to file an independent rate could be opposed by any "aggrieved person." Competing companies, as well as rate bureaus, contended that they were aggrieved persons and, therefore, had standing to intervene in rate cases. This intervention created delays and increased the costs of filing rates different from rate bureau rates. Eventually, legislative bodies at the insurance commissioners' recommendation eliminated the right of bureaus to intervene as aggrieved parties. Without the ability to intervene, bureaus could no longer delay deviations from their rates (Trupin, 1978: 259; Hanson, Dineen, and Johnson, 1974: 39).

5. *Direct Writers.* Direct writers are insurance companies that do not use agents to sell and service their insurance policies. Direct writers hire their own employees for such functions; as a result, direct writers have lower

operating costs (Joskow, 1979: 388). With lower operating costs, the rational direct writer will price its insurance below the market price in an attempt to increase its market share. Direct writers such as Allstate, State Farm, and Nationwide have pursued aggressive tactics to increase market share; these companies are large enough to file independent rates. Between 1949 and 1959, direct writers increased their premium income by 463 percent compared to an average of 175 percent for stock companies (Post, 1976: 57). By 1985, direct writers controlled 40 percent of the market for all property and casualty lines and a significantly larger share of homeowners' and automobile insurance. They are widely credited with being a major force for increasing competition in certain lines of insurance.

6. *Conclusion.* The sum of these innovations—installment premiums, deviations, partial subscribership, elimination of aggrieved-person status, and direct writers—all increased competition in the insurance industry under the All-Industry Rating Laws. Few companies were immune to this competition. Bureau members who were prohibited from cutting prices to meet competition used differences in coverage or services to compete. Mutual companies competed by increasing their dividends so that the actual price of insurance was reduced. Mutuals in this manner were able to quadruple their fire insurance market share to 18 percent by 1962 (Sichel, 1966: 95).

THE GROWTH OF MULTILINE INSURANCE

In addition to the changes in rate filing as a result of the All-Industry Rating Laws, a change in the insurance industry's structure was taking place that further increased competition. Insurance companies were changing their product mix and becoming multiline companies, offering insurance in all property and casualty lines. The development of the multiline insurance company and its contribution to greater competition merits in-depth discussion.

In the United States, insurance operated for almost two centuries with what was called the *American system.* Unlike the English system, the American system required insurance companies to specialize in a given line of insurance.[40] In general, liability companies did not write marine insurance, fire companies did not write automobile property damage insurance, and property and casualty companies never wrote life or health insurance. Mono-line insurance developed after the industry was created. The initial incorporating laws for companies such as INA and Aetna permitted multiline underwriting, but these companies allowed their life insurance powers to atrophy (Bickelhaupt, 1961: 14). The general preference for insurance companies to specialize in a single line of insurance was formally recognized and then required by the New York incorporation law for insurance companies.

Life and health insurance were made distinct lines of business, as was fire insurance (Lilly, 1976: 101).

The requirement for monoline insurance companies was not without reason. Legislators felt that monoline insurance allowed companies to specialize in the technical problems of a single type of insurance, thereby improving performance. They also believed that monoline companies would permit more accurate appraisals of the financial requirements needed to operate in a given line and more specific regulations could be tailored to the needs of a given line (Michelbacher and Roos, 1970: 2). A second-order consequence of monoline legislation was that it protected fire insurance companies from competition by casualty companies.

At the second meeting of the NAIC (then the National Convention of Insurance Commissioners), model legislation was proposed to require separate life insurance companies (Pugh, 1969: 244). The greatest influence on creating a monoline system, however, was the famed Appleton rule. Because New York required monoline companies and the Appleton rule required all companies licensed in New York to observe New York laws both in New York and other states, the Appleton rule effectively established monoline insurance for all the major insurance companies (Bickelhaupt, 1961: 17).[41]

Monoline insurance had severe limitations in dealing with new products. The automobile, for example, did not fit within given lines of insurance. Under monoline principles, an automobile owner had to purchase separate insurance policies from separate companies to cover property damage and liability. Similarly, a homeowner needed separate policies for fire, theft, and liability.

The inconvenience of monoline insurance led to agitation to eliminate monoline restrictions. As early as 1922, the NAIC was on record in favor of abolishing the American system except for life insurance (Pugh, 1969: 245). Any attempt to change the monoline system, however, was effectively stalled by the Insurance Executives Association (IEA), a major trade association. The IEA was controlled by a committee of 15 who were the chief executives of the largest fire insurance companies in the United States. Fire insurance companies, fighting to keep the cartel nature of fire insurance established after the Merritt Committee, resisted multiline legislation. With strong opposition from the industry, multiline legislation was suppressed (Pugh, 1969: 246).

Although formal recognition of multiline insurance was not adopted, several ways around the monoline restrictions were discovered in the 1930s and 1940s. First, insurance companies grouped in fleets joined by common stock ownership; this permitted a fleet to operate as a multiline company by combining a series of monoline companies (Bickelhaupt, 1961: 28).[42] Second, inland marine insurance, originally designed to cover transportation of goods, had few restrictions on what it could cover. Creative inland marine companies developed personal property and automobile floaters that essentially covered several lines of insurance (Michelbacher and Roos, 1970: 4).

The leak in the monoline concept resulted in the NAIC's appointing a committee to study the monoline problem. Called the Diemand Committee, it was comprised of insurance executives but had no representatives from fire insurance companies. Although the Committee appeared to favor full multiline insurance, it recommended a limited multiline law. The proposed law allowed companies to write multiline insurance in any foreign country, to operate on a multiline basis in reinsurance, and to write some multiline policies in automobile, aircraft, and personal property insurance (Michelbacher and Roos, 1970: 6).

The key arena for the multiline proposal was, of course, New York because the Appleton rule had an impact over and above the actual size of the New York market. New York adopted the NAIC model laws in two parts, the latter effective in 1948. New York insurance companies supported multiline powers because they were handicapped in competing for business outside of New York where non-New York companies could operate as multiline enterprises. Although the fire insurance companies were opposed, New York adopted a full multiline law in 1949. By 1951, only four states prohibited multiline insurance companies (Bickelhaupt, 1961: 37).

The creation of multiline insurance companies is a force for greater competition because multiline companies have administrative economies of scale. They can, as a result, charge lower prices for combined coverage. In New York alone, the number of multiline companies expanded from 48 in 1949 to 360 in 1957 (Post, 1976: 56). The battle was not finished, however, because existing rate bureaus opposed multiline rate filings under the All-Industry Laws. In the spring of 1951, Aetna, INA, and ten other large insurance companies formed a multiline rating bureau to support their new homeowners' policies (Pugh, 1969: 253). The fire insurance companies' resistance was broken when several large insurance companies threatened to withdraw from the fire rating bureau unless the companies were given more flexibility. Already weakened by partial subscribership, the fire rate bureaus conceded. Multiline insurance policies became an accepted insurance industry product. To illustrate their impact on competition, New York regulations priced multiline policies at 15 percent less than the combined cost of monoline policies (Franson, 1969). Price competition from the multiline companies in conjunction with loopholes in the All-Industry Laws greatly stimulated more price competition in the insurance industry.

OPEN RATING LAWS

If creative implementation of the All-Industry Laws generated environments that fostered competition, insurance regulators then had to face the question, why regulate the price of insurance at all? California had allowed the market to set insurance prices since 1947 with no apparent ill effects. Gradually, insurance commissioners recognized the merit of moving toward more competitive rating systems.

One indicator of willingness to consider alternative price regulatory mechanisms was a 1966 survey by the NAIC's Subcommittee on Rates and Rating Organizations; it found that about one-half of the regulators felt that the All-Industry Laws were no longer appropriate. These attitudes did not translate into support for greater competition at this time, however, because only a small number of commissioners favored no-file or file-and-use systems (Williams, 1969: 208).

In 1966, Wisconsin began a study to revise its insurance laws under the direction of Spencer Kimball (1969a). The Kimball task force surveyed insurance companies and found that they had the least problems with California's no-file system of regulation; fewer than one-sixth of all insurance companies (even in fire insurance) favored the continued use of the model All-Industry Laws (Williams, 1969: 212). Most insurance companies favored no-file or file-and-use laws. Arguments that prior-approval rate laws protected company solvency were discounted by noting that rarely were rates disapproved for being too low and that unregulated companies had no worse solvency records than regulated insurance companies (McHugh, 1969: 201). Also, in 1967, Florida and Georgia adopted no-file statutes in place of their previous All-Industry Laws.

The Wisconsin study strongly endorsed more competitive ratemaking laws. In October 1968 New York Superintendent of Insurance Richard Stewart supported an effort to pass a competitive rate law in New York. The endorsement of New York, the home of strict rate regulation, could not but have assisted the proponents of greater competition in insurance rating (Williams, 1969: 217). In December, the NAIC Subcommittee on Rates and Rating Organizations recommended that the NAIC model rate law be changed and that "where appropriate, reliance be placed upon fair and open competition to produce and maintain reasonable and competitive prices for insurance coverage" (Williams, 1969: 215).

With the NAIC and New York both favoring increased competition, competitive rate laws passed in more states. New York adopted its competitive rate law in April 1969; by July 1969, 19 states had adopted a California-style rate regulation law for some lines of property and casualty insurance (Williams, 1969: 219). Illinois even permitted its rate filing law to expire and did not adopt a replacement, thereby producing a free market for insurance rates.

The movement to more competitive ratemaking laws came to a stop only a few years later. With increased inflation in the 1970s, especially in construction costs and automobile repair costs, rates rose rapidly. Consumer groups appeared before insurance commissioners and legislatures to protest such rate increases. In those states with competitive rate laws, state regulators could do little to contain the rising prices; the competitive laws were blamed for higher prices. In states with prior approval laws, insurance commissioners held down rate increases for a period of time (making insurance unavailable in some cases). The trend toward greater competition in ratemaking laws, therefore, died at the hands of inflation and the increased salience of insurance rates to consumers (Hartman, 1971; 1972: 161).

The 1970s also saw states adopting various approaches to competitive rating within different lines of insurance. With the adoption of no-fault automobile insurance as a perceived cost saver, New York reinstituted rate regulation on automobile insurance to ensure savings were passed on to consumers (Hartman, 1972). As part of the malpractice insurance crisis of the mid-1970s, California, the home of open competition, established rate regulation for medical malpractice insurance.

A Theoretical Recapitulation

This chapter examines the political economy of insurance regulation from its inception to the mid-1970s. The political economy of insurance regulation fits the theory presented in Chapter 2 fairly well. At several points in the history of insurance regulation, the increased political salience of insurance resulted in broader forces entering insurance politics to the detriment of the insurance industry. Although the industry often was unable to get action when issues were not salient, they lost control of the agenda when they became salient.

The Armstrong Committee deliberations produced major reforms in the life insurance industry. After salience was raised by muckrakers and the internal fights among Equitable stockholders, political elites altered life insurance operations in fundamental ways. When the pattern repeated itself after the San Francisco Earthquake and the Merritt Committee, the insurance industry was able to exploit salience for its own end. Property and casualty companies fared better under the Merritt Committee reforms than the life insurance industry did under the Armstrong Committee. The reason is that the Merritt Committee asked reasons why fire insurance companies failed and the Armstrong Committee addressed political and economic abuses by the life insurance industry. The former, dealing with adequate rates and other technical issues, is more complex than the latter. The insurance industry was able to improve its position with the Merritt Committee because it was able to control information in a complex issue area.

The importance of issue salience is evident in the passage of the McCarran-Ferguson Act and the All-Industry Bills. In this case, the salience was created by the *South-Eastern* case and the potential elimination of the fire insurance cartel. When this issue became salient, the property and casualty insurance industry was able to get a resolution, but not nearly the resolution that it wanted. The industry preferred the Walter-Hancock Bill to McCarran-Ferguson and preferred file-and-use laws to prior approval laws. Salience increased the activities of political elites who produced a result somewhat different from industry objectives.

This historical review of insurance regulation also illustrates how rarely the insurance industry acts as a unified entity. Although the industry opposed regulation early in this century, New York dealt with the life insurance and the property and casualty insurance industries separately. Because the industries had different interests, the legislature was able to divide and conquer. Lack of industry cohesion is also evident in the industry's responses to the *South-Eastern* case. Not only were the fire insurance companies unable to get support from the life insurance companies; but even within property and casualty insurance, the fire companies' proposals were opposed by mutuals and independents.

Perhaps the best illustration of the nonmonolithic nature of the insurance industry is the rise in competition during the 1950s and 1960s under the All-Industry Laws. A monolithic industry does not look for loopholes to undercut the cartel. Firms in the industry, however, were innovative in introducing more competition into the insurance market. INA was instrumental in exploiting the installment premium; large companies demanded and got partial subscribership to bureaus; direct writers filed deviations and undercut the cartel's prices; multiline companies put together packages of insurance that were much cheaper than monoline insurance. The self-interests of the various components of the insurance industry are the strongest force preventing the insurance industry from presenting a unified front. Without unity, industry dominance of the regulatory process is difficult.

This chapter also revealed the role that insurance regulators and other bureaucrats play in the creation of regulatory policy. The response of the New York Insurance Department to the criticisms of the Armstrong Committee resulted in strict insurance regulation in New York and via the Appleton rule in many other states as well. During the aftermath of the *South-Eastern* case, the insurance regulators took positions different from the industry's. In both the McCarran-Ferguson Act and the All-Industry Bills, the insurance commissioners were able to impose their proposals on a divided industry. The industry was unable to get a complete exemption from federal antitrust laws, and it had to settle for prior approval laws rather than more liberal pricing laws. Bureaucratic values clearly came into play here because insurance commissioners were interested in protecting both their ability to collect premium taxes and their jobs as regulators. Finally, insurance commissioners were active in the repeal of the aggrieved-person doctrine and the multiline effort. In both cases, the insurance commissioners, or at least those from the larger, more progressive states, were able to increase competition in the insurance market.

Other bureaucrats were also involved at various times in setting insurance policy. The decision to file an antitrust suit against South-Eastern Underwriters was made in the U. S. Justice Department by individuals who were more interested in antitrust policy than in insurance. The trustbusting reputation of Thurmond Arnold most likely influenced individual lawyers to take a strong position in this matter. Attorney General Biddle's opposition to the Walter-Hancock Bill and his delay of prosecution in the *South-Eastern* case provided additional time so that an NAIC-backed bill could be passed.

Political elites were active throughout this era of insurance regulation particularly during times of high salience. The Armstrong and Merritt Committees were legislative committees. The courts and the Justice Department created the *South-Eastern* crisis that resulted in major changes in insurance regulation and set the stage for greater competition under the All-Industry laws. The withdrawal of McCarran's and Ferguson's support from the industry-sponsored bill was instrumental in its eventual failure. Even the president played a small role; President Roosevelt's threat to veto the Walter-Hancock Bill made Congress reassess its approach and produce a much different antitrust exemption.

Although consumer groups were not particularly active in early insurance regulation, they were not without a role. The growth in competitive rate laws in the 1970s was brought to a close by consumer opposition. The rise in inflation made insurance costs a salient issue at a time when consumer groups had gained strength from a series of other issues.

In sum, the theoretical framework presented in Chapter 2 works fairly well in explaining the development of insurance regulatory policy to the late 1970s. The Stiglerian view that industry dominates the regulatory process is simply inconsistent with the facts. Industry had to accept less than it wanted in the Armstrong reforms, the McCarran-Ferguson Act, the All-Industry Bills, and the rise of competition in the industry. If insurance companies dominated the political economy of insurance regulation, there would have been no Armstrong Committee investigation, the *South-Eastern* case would never have been filed, and state government regulators today would be enforcing cartel-established insurance prices. The insurance industry may have been the most powerful actor in this policy arena, but it clearly did not dominate the arena at all times.

Chapter 5

The Liability Insurance Crisis of 1985–1986

In 1985, the insurance regulatory system was shaken by the most salient insurance issue since no-fault, the liability crisis.[1] The property and casualty insurance industry often operates at a net underwriting loss with profits coming from investment income and favorable tax credits. Between 1980 and 1984 (the last years with reliable data before the crisis), the property and casualty industry's overall operating ratio increased from 95.9 to 107.4. The overall operating ratio is the ratio of income from all sources other than capital gains and tax credits divided into the total costs of the industry. An overall operating ratio of 107.4 means that the property and casualty portion of the insurance industry had $1.07 in costs for every $1 in income.[2]

Translated into dollar terms, this meant a $3.8 billion loss for the industry, which created some concern among industry management. A closer look at the operating ratios by line of insurance revealed that not all lines of property and casualty insurance were unprofitable. Table 5–1 shows the overall operating ratios for several selected lines of property and casualty insurance. The first four lines listed are among the lines termed *personal lines*. The personal lines of insurance, while not lucrative by industry figures, were not serious problems; operating ratios clustered around 100. The concern focused on the commercial lines of insurance—commercial automobile insurance, commercial multiple peril, general liability, and medical malpractice. These lines showed loss ratios as high as 130.8.

Commercial lines of property and casualty insurance have a different economic structure than the personal lines. In personal lines, such as automobile insurance, companies can cover such a large number of risks that yearly cash flow for the more efficient companies is always positive. This means that a successful personal automobile or homeowners' insurance com-

Table 5-1
Overall Operating Ratios for Property and Casualty Insurance By Line

Line	1984	1980–84
Private Passenger Auto Liability	103.9	101.5
Private Passenger Auto Physical Damage	98.9	97.2
Homeowners'	101.8	100.3
Group Accident & Health	92.6	97.3
Commercial Auto Liability	130.8	115.7
Commercial Auto Physical Damage	108.5	101.9
Commercial Multiple Peril	125.1	109.2
General Liability	125.1	106.7
Medical Malpractice	118.3	108.4
Reinsurance	122.2	104.7

Source: *Best's Aggregates and Averages*, 1985: 78–79.
N.B. Overall Operating ratio includes investment income but excludes capital gains and tax credits.

pany could technically operate without any capital because yearly income would exceed yearly expenses.

In commercial lines, insurance risks are often characterized by what is referred to as a *long tail*. Physical damage automobile claims are made almost immediately and usually settled quickly. Liability problems, particularly in terms of product liability and medical malpractice, often do not reveal themselves until years later. Liability claims against a manufacturer might be filed two, three, four, or 20 years after the product was manufactured. This long tail requires that commercial insurers have large capital and surplus reserves to pay for future claims. Normally, the commercial and personal lines followed similar economic patterns. In the 1980s, the patterns diverged; and the overall ratio for commercial lines was 9.2 percent higher than that for personal lines, a situation unprecedented in underwriting history (Nichols and Smith, 1985: 45).

The higher losses and the longer term focus of commercial insurance lines requires that commercial insurance companies set aside greater reserves to pay future claims. These reserves must come from policyholder surplus or from infusions of new capital. The reduction of capital and surplus for reserve purposes in turn reduces the insurance companies' ability to write insurance in subsequent years. Conservative insurance companies write at approximately a 2-to-1 premiums-to-surplus ratio although many companies write at 3-to-1 or higher ratios. This restricted ability to write new insurance became known as the *capacity crunch*. The Insurance Services Office estimated that the property and casualty insurance industry faced a three-year

$62 billion shortfall in needed capital as a result of poor underwriting results (McNamara, 1985: 3; Bradford, 1985b).[3]

Causes of the Crisis

The large losses in the commercial lines of the property and casualty industry were attributed by the industry to three causes—cash-flow underwriting, an availability crisis in reinsurance, and an explosion of litigation. Each cause had a different culprit. Cash-flow underwriting could be blamed on the insurance companies. Reinsurance problems could be blamed on inexperienced underwriters in the reinsurance industry. The explosion in litigation, of course, was the fault of creative judges and the large number of attorneys.

CASH-FLOW UNDERWRITING

Significant investment income is a recent phenomenon in the property and casualty insurance industry. Until the 1960s, investment income for property and casualty companies was small so that it could be ignored in corporate decisions concerning the pricing of risks. Insurance companies made money on underwriting; investments were merely a way to protect capital and surplus from inflation. Until 1974–1975 the property and casualty industry basically invested in blue chip stocks on a long-term basis (Nichols and Smith, 1985: 45).

During the mid-to late 1970s, short-term interest rates skyrocketed. Property and casualty companies began investing in short-term money markets and in the process were able to increase annual investment yields. When the prime rate reached 20 percent during Paul Volcker's effort to break inflation, property and casualty companies aggressively sought additional funds to invest at favorable short-term rates. To accumulate more investment funds, insurance companies reduced their underwriting rates. The strategy was to increase premium income as much as possible with little concern as to risk with the idea of making large profits on the investment side of the ledger (Moore, 1985). Actuarial advice was ignored (Morais, 1985: 104). In effect, the investment tail was wagging the underwriting dog.

Not all lines of insurance were amenable to cash-flow underwriting. Personal lines of insurance were highly competitive and had short payment tails so that a surplus of investment was not found in the personal lines market.[4] The liability lines with tails of five or more years were the most lucrative area for cash-flow underwriting. Premiums in some commercial lines dropped by 50 percent and more from 1979 to 1982 (Nichols and

Smith, 1985: 44). Perhaps the most extreme example of cash-flow underwriting occurred when an insurance company agreed to insure the MGM Hotel in Las Vegas, Nevada, for fire claims resulting from their major fire after the fact. For $30 million in premiums, the company felt that it could make a profit by investing the money and paying claims as they came due (Millus, 1985: 36).

The weakness of cash-flow underwriting is that it requires high interest rates to compensate for the underwriting losses that result from accepting poor risks. At a prime rate of 20 percent many poor risks become long-term money makers. In 1982, for example, property and casualty companies lost approximately $7.9 billion on the underwriting portion of their business, but with their investment income managed to break even. When the prime rate drops to 10 percent or less, however, companies that engaged in cash-flow underwriting are in trouble. They still have the long tail of the poor risks they accepted, but they no longer have the booming investment income necessary to offset those risks. The result was major operating losses in the insurance industry.

THE REINSURANCE CRISIS

Problems in the reinsurance market exacerbated the problems caused by cash-flow underwriting. The liability insurance lines have always relied on the reinsurance market to spread some of their risks. By reinsuring a portion of its risk with another company, the primary insurer can use its surplus to write additional insurance and also limit potential losses from its current risks. Reinsurance by one estimate covers 10 percent of the risks in the property and casualty industry at annual premiums of $11.3 billion (Farrel and Ehrlich, 1985: 128).

The reinsurance industry is a unique part of the property and casualty insurance market. Reinsurance companies specialize in taking risks with low probabilities but large potential payouts. For example, if a liability insurance company agreed to insure a chemical company for claims up to $300 million, the liability company would probably reinsure any losses from $100 million to $300 million with a reinsurance company. Reinsurance companies, including the most famous one, Lloyds of London, often underwrite unusual risks such as a magician's hands or a professional athlete's legs.

Reinsurance companies generally have low operating costs and access to funds for long periods of time. Reinsurance companies do not use agents; other insurance companies contact them. Because reinsurance companies specialize in low probability, high payout areas, the cost of processing claims is relatively small. With a specialty in long-tail liability areas, reinsurance companies have access to their premiums for long periods of time. The Reinsurance Association of America revealed that reinsurance companies know only 48 percent of their losses at the end of five years and only 62 percent at the end of nine years (Fenske, 1985b).

Perhaps the most unique aspect of the reinsurance industry is that it is virtually unregulated (Adams, 1986). Most states permit unauthorized reinsurance companies to reinsure risks through licensed companies. Entry to the industry is easy; one only needs access to a small amount of cash or investors with funds to pledge to establish a Lloyds-type company. Regulations regarding investments, reserves, and solidity are for the most part absent. Fraud is not unknown in this environment (see Adams, 1986).

The explosion in high-risk underwriting taking place under cash-flow underwriting meant that the demand for reinsurance was high. Without any significant barriers to entry, capital flowed into the reinsurance market. From 1979 to 1982, the number of domestic reinsurance companies doubled to 137 with a influx of $400 million in new capital (Heap, 1985: 24). Many new entrants in the reinsurance business, however, had little underwriting knowledge. They were attracted by the industry's traditionally high profits and had money to invest but little experience. Some major U. S. corporations were among the new entrants. Armco, Inc., a steel company, lost $65 million writing reinsurance in one quarter and quit the business. Phillips Petroleum lost $73 million between 1982 and 1984 with its reinsurance subsidiary. Dana Corporation founded Cherokee Insurance, which was in rehabilitation by 1985 (Clifford, 1985: 218).

Other reinsurers fared no better. Approximately one-half the reinsurance companies left the market, with perhaps one-half of those being insolvent (Farrell and Ehrlich, 1985: 129). The industry as a whole in 1984 had $1.22 in expenses for every $1 in income it produced. Without the significant investment income gains, the operating ratio would have been a dismal 140.9 (*Best's Aggregates*, 1985: 79).

The contraction of the reinsurance market was exacerbated by the withdrawal of Lloyds of London from the American market. In 1985, Lloyds announced its 1982 underwriting results; Lloyds lost a total of $304 million. Although only 12 percent of Lloyds' premiums were from the United States, virtually all of its losses were (Moore, 1985).[5] As the reinsurance market contracted, pressure was placed on primary insurers. They had to carry a larger proportion of the risks they underwrote, especially the poor risks taken during the cash-flows underwriting period. The default of reinsurers also meant that the primary insurer had to pay the claims that were supposed to be covered by reinsurers. The financial conditions of the primary liability insurance carriers were such, however, that they could neither reabsorb reinsurance risks nor assume any additional risks without some changes in underwriting conditions.

THE LITIGATION EXPLOSION

Both primary insurers and reinsurers laid part of the blame for the insurance crisis on a perceived growth in litigation. Legal doctrines in liability cases had changed dramatically. In medical malpractice, the elimination of the locality rule, the imposition of the *res ipsa* doctrine, the use of the discovery rule, and other legal changes made medical malpractice suits feasible in the early 1970s (Meier and Copeland, 1986). In product liability, courts in many states began applying the doctrine of strict liability; under strict liability, a product only needs to be shown to be improperly designed or manufactured or to have an inadequate warning. Strict liability replaced a negligence standard that required the plaintiff to show that a manufacturer had been guilty of negligence [see *Escola v. Coca Cola Bottling Co.* 150 P. 2d 436 (1944)]. Further complicating the defense of product liability suits was *Beshada v. Johns-Manville* [447 A. 2d 539 (1982)]. Johns-Manville, a manufacturer of asbestos products, argued that its safety standards met industry standards at the time the product was manufactured. When this "state of the art" defense was disallowed, suits based on current safety knowledge rather than knowledge at the time of manufacture became feasible.[6] Similar changes in legal doctrine were made in municipal liability. The old doctrine of sovereign immunity was being swept away, and government agencies were held responsible for civil rights violations[7] and for contributing to dangerous conditions that resulted in accidents (Blodgett, 1986; Goldberg, 1986). In 1983 alone, 19,553 civil rights suits were filed in federal courts against state and local governments or officials (Blodgett, 1986: 48).

That legal doctrines were changing rapidly was irrefutable. The insurance industry claimed that the volume of litigation had also increased dramatically. Lawsuits in state courts increased by 22 percent from 1977 to 1981; federal courts heard 13 percent more civil suits in 1982 than in 1981. In 1962, only one $1 million verdict was returned; in 1982, 251 such awards were returned (Nutter, 1985: 5). Whatever the volume of litigation, legal expenses were taking a larger portion of the insurance industry's operating budget. In the commercial general liability line, the industry paid $2.9 billion for legal defense or about 25 percent of premium income (Work, Thornton, and Maynard, 1985: 57). This figure had increased from 5 percent in 1960.[8]

Industry Internal Responses to the Crisis

The insurance industry thinks of itself as a risk-spreading conduit. It collects premiums and pays claims; the actual level of the premiums and claims is unimportant as long as the premiums are sufficient to cover the claims.[9] The rational economic response to large insurance losses would be to either increase income or reduce losses. The insurance industry pursued both strategies.

After several years of declining premiums, in 1985 the insurance industry began to raise rates on unprofitable lines of insurance. Reports of staggering increases in insurance premiums made front page news. Premiums for operating buses increased by 300 percent to 1,200 percent; an oral surgeon had his rates increased from $10,000 to $28,000; day care rates increased by 300 percent to 500 percent (Work, et al., 1985: 56–57; Kocolowski, 1985). Especially hard hit were small manufacturers and city governments.

In one sense, individuals who received large premium increases were lucky; in an effort to reduce losses, insurance companies began to drop certain high-risk lines of business. As a result of high claims, Utica Mutual Insurance cancelled the insurance of 250 Ohio school districts (Work, et al., 1985: 56); Aetna dropped insurance coverage for 400 cities (Consumer Reports, 1986: 544). Industries that manufactured asbestos products and local firms that removed asbestos from buildings found insurance unavailable at any price. More than 35,000 lawsuits had been filed concerning asbestos, a figure growing at the rate of 500 per month; court judgments totalling $1 billion had already occurred (Kuntz, 1985). Day care centers became a high-risk category after news stories reported cases of sexual abuse of children. Those insurance companies that did not drop day care centers altogether increased rates dramatically (Pave, 1985: 114). Pollution liability insurance became unobtainable. Traditionally, the insurance industry insured companies against sudden and accident pollution discharges, but when a court held an insurance company liable for a long-term pollution leakage [*Jackson Township v. Hartford Accident and Indemnity*, 451 A.2d 999 (1982)], pollution insurance became impossible to obtain (Faron, 1985: 21).[10] Finally, numerous municipalities had their insurance cancelled or had their insurance rates skyrocket for much reduced coverage. These cities then closed playgrounds and cancelled events to reduce their risk exposure. In New York alone, 11,296 lawsuits were pending against cities other than New York City asking for $26 billion in damages (King, 1985: 72–73).[11]

A second strategy adopted by insurance companies to reduce their risk was to change policy forms. Although courts had often interpreted policies to be more liberal than they were intended to be, policy restrictions are one way to limit an insurance company's risk. The Insurance Services Office developed a new commercial general liability policy form that made three specific changes. First, the policy was a *claims made* form rather than an *occurrence* form. Occurrence forms cover the policyholder for all claims that occur during the life of the policy. Claims made forms cover only those claims actually made during the life of the policy. Introduced in many states during the medical malpractice crisis of the mid-1970s, the claims made policy is an attempt to eliminate the long tail facing the insurance companies.

Second, the policy form put a total dollar limit on the claims that the policy would pay. Rather than being restricted to a certain amount per incident, the form restricted all claims paid to a set figure. Third, pollution damage was expressly excluded. The Insurance Services Office, in its role as a rate bureau, filed the form in all states. By November 1985, it had been approved in 20 states and rejected in only 5. Starting January 1, 1986, most general commercial liability was written on a claims made basis in most states.

External Demands on the Political System

The insurance industry did not believe that it could accomplish sufficient change by itself to return the industry to profitability. Accordingly, it began to organize political coalitions to support changes in insurance regulatory laws to increase certainty or decrease risk. Putting together a coalition was fairly easy. The industry presented its case to those individuals who had their insurance cancelled or their premiums increased. Together, the industry suggested, they could solve the underlying problems. The tort liability system became the reform target of a coalition of insurance companies, physicians, municipalities, day care centers, small businesses, and commercial truckers.[12] In an effort to influence public opinion, the Insurance Information Institute began a $6.5 million media campaign linking the litigation crisis to problems with scholastic sports, obstetrics, cities, and even clergy (Marcotte, 1986: 19; Wasilewski, 1986: 14).

The insurance industry coalition had a specific agenda. The Alliance of American Insurers (Nutter, 1985) proposed the following reforms: (1) mandatory and binding arbitration should be used to settle small claims; (2) class-action suits should be limited by assessing the plaintiff part of the notice costs; (3) the standard of negligence should be modified comparative negligence;[13] (4) the doctrine of joint and several liability should be repealed,[14] (5) discovery must be shortened and limited, (6) lawyers' contingency fees should be reduced and placed on a sliding scale; (7) jury instructions should be made uniform among all jurisdictions; (8) assessing interest on judgments made should be prohibited; (9) awards for pain and suffering (as opposed to medical bills or economic damages) should be limited ($250,000 and $100,000 were the most commonly proposed figures); (10) the federal government should adopt a uniform product liability law; *and,* (11) punitive damages should be abolished (Nutter, 1985: 11–19).

These far-reaching proposed reforms, which are basically similar to the American Medical Association's (AMA) medical malpractice reforms (Browning, 1986: 39), would have made it more costly to bring a liability suit and easier to defend one. The clear objective was to reduce legal costs.[15]

Whether the changes the industry sought would have alleviated any long-term problems is open to question. The industry has some structural economic constraints that make long-term efforts to increase profits difficult. First, economic barriers to entry in the property and casualty insurance lines are few; and barriers to entry into reinsurance are nonexistent. Numerous new firms start every year (see Chapter 1). Second, serious barriers to exit exist. A property and casualty company cannot simply cease to exist; it must make provisions to service or sell its remaining policies. Given the economies of scale in insurance, phasing out a line of insurance is expensive. Third, substitutes for insurance are available. Large companies can self-insure; groups of professionals can establish captive insurance companies.[16] Distressed customers can always opt for substitutes. Unlike the policyholders in the personal lines, those in the commercial lines can bargain with insurance companies as equals. Long-term prospects in the property and casualty industry, therefore, were not bright even if the tort reforms were adopted.

The Opposing Coalition

Changing the tort laws requires a political effort to persuade lawmakers to act. The insurance industry's efforts were opposed by a small, but well-organized coalition. Most prominent in the coalition was the American Trial Lawyers Association (ATLA) or its state-level affiliates. Trial attorneys, unlike most attorneys, earn their living on litigation, particularly liability suits. Efforts to change the litigation rules as proposed by the Alliance of American Insurers are perceived by this group as a direct threat to their livelihood. The trial attorneys often presented well-organized statements by effective speakers such as 1986 ATLA President Elect Robert Habush. Joining the trial attorneys was the National Insurance Consumers Organization (NICO), led by former Federal Insurance Administrator J. Robert Hunter. Hunter had been a long-time critic of the insurance industry dating back to his decision to remove private insurance companies from the federal flood insurance program. Given Hunter's ties to consumer advocate Ralph Nader, a variety of other consumer groups joined the coalition. Although consumer organizations and trial attorneys might be perceived as strange coalition partners, many of the major laws governing consumer protection are enforced by litigation.[17] Occasionally, this group also contained labor unions or other local groups (Geisel,

1985: Felter, 1985). The coalition formed a national umbrella group called the Coalition for Consumer Justice comprising 35 organizations (Marcotte, 1986: 19).

The opposition coalition had two counter arguments to the insurance industry's proposed civil liability changes. First, they argued that the solution to the problem was stronger insurance regulation so that insurance companies could not engage in dangerous cash-flow underwriting. Among the proposals for stricter regulation was a demand to adopt a prior approval rate laws.[18] Hunter and NICO were especially critical of state insurance regulation; Hunter noted, for example, that state regulators employed only 62 of the 7,000 actuaries in the United States.[19] One-half of the states employed no actuaries, an essential profession needed to monitor the claims of insurance companies (Felter, 1985; Hunter, 1985a; 1985b).

The second tactic of this coalition was to challenge the data presented by the insurance industry. Rather than a 1985 operating loss of $5.5 billion that the insurance industry claimed, Hunter argued that one needed to offset this loss by a capital gain of $6.5 billion, federal tax credits of $3.5 billion and dividends of $2.1 billion for a profit of $6.6 billion (Wish, 1985; Washington Correspondent, 1985). State legislators were subjected to a version of dueling statistics with each side presenting numbers that best illustrated its point of view. For example, the insurance industry coalition argued that the average product liability jury award was $1 million. The lawyers' coalition responded that such figures were distorted by a few large awards; the median award was only $271,000. In addition, jury awards are not the final step in the litigation process; of the 26 largest jury awards the previous year, seven were reduced by judges (one award was reduced by 98.5 percent), four were settled for lesser amounts (from 73 percent to .1 percent of the award), and six were settled (obviously for lower amounts) but no figures were released (Greene, 1986: 79).[20] Rational choice in such a situation was limited because insurance companies often did not keep statistics in the ways needed to determine the actual patterns.[21]

As the deliberation of state governments over the insurance crisis continued, the evidence supporting a litigation crisis was challenged. In a widely cited article, Marc Galanter (1983) found that civil litigation rates in the United States were approximately the same as those in England, Ontario, Australia, Denmark, and New Zealand. A study released by the National Center for State Courts (1986) examined the volume of tort litigation in 20 states; it found that tort filings increased by 9 percent from 1978 to 1984, but population increased by 8 percent at the same time. The conclusion was that there was no increase in litigation. Similar research began to slowly surface in more specialized areas. An examination of punitive damages (Daniels, 1986), for example, found that such awards are fairly rare.

Actions of Public Officials

Faced with pressure to solve the insurance crisis but with little information other than anecdotes about the nature of the crisis, several legislatures and insurance commissioners responded by creating study commissions to examine the problem. Although the study commission approach did nothing directly to solve the problem, it did allow more time to develop pertinent information and to create some temporary solutions to severe short-term problems.

Of special concern to public officials was insurance companies' cancelling insurance before the policy period expired. In a tight insurance market, cancelled policyholders had a difficult time in finding alternative insurers. States that did not have regulations prohibiting midterm cancellations began to consider them; states with such regulations began to consider longer periods of notice of cancellation. New Jersey Governor Thomas Kean placed emergency restrictions on cancellations and nonrenewals; these restrictions were lifted only after state insurance companies agreed to form Marketing Assistance Plans (MAPs), voluntary associations of insurers who agree to pool risks to underwrite insurance in a given area. One commissioner thought the actions of the insurance companies were so reprehensible that federal regulation was proposed (Herbert, 1985: 1,5A). The NAIC in June 1985 adopted a resolution that opposed midterm coverage cancellation and short notice of nonrenewals (Cain, 1985).

Other states put pressure on insurance companies to solve some of the most severe problems by joint action. California, for example, created a MAP of 26 insurance companies to offer insurance to the state's cay care centers (Cain, 1985). New Hampshire put together MAPs for day care, municipalities, and liquor liability (Ardman, 1985a). Other states followed this example (Ardman, 1985b). Insurance companies are often motivated to participate in MAPs because many insurance commissioners have the power to create joint underwriting pools, which are essentially nonvoluntary MAPs. Going one step further, the New York Superintendent of Insurance publicly proposed that the state sell insurance to meet the shortage (N.Y. Municipal, 1985).

The Legislative Battle

The battle for new state laws to limit litigation saw a great deal of action. Initially, the insurance company coalition had the field virtually to itself so that it achieved some early victories. Perhaps this coalition's greatest success was in Washington state where the legislature adopted virtually the entire list of proposed reforms (Wasilewski, 1986: 15). In California, a statewide initiative was placed on the ballot that limited joint and several liability for noneconomic damages. An estimated $12 million was spent by both sides on this election, and the measure passed with 62 percent of the vote (Hilder, 1986: 1).

The momentum of the insurance coalition slowed, however, when the legislatures of the more populous states began to address the issue. These states generally had more professional insurance regulators who could provide the legislature with a source of information not biased by the views of either coalition. New York fashioned a compromise whereby the insurance coalition received some limits on joint and several liability and structured settlements were required, but the law also allowed the Superintendent of Insurance to regulate the price of insurance by setting flexible zones of prices. Any price increases or decreases within the zone were acceptable, but any increases outside the zone were subject to state approval.

Florida went one step further. Legislation enacting some of the insurance companies' reforms was accompanied by mandatory price reductions of up to 40 percent in some insurance lines. Florida legislators reasoned that if changes in the tort system were designed to produce lower insurance costs, then rates should drop. The reaction to the Florida law was predictable. Eighteen companies announced that they would no longer write new policies in Florida in an effort to pressure the legislature to repeal the law (Kasouf, 1986: 1). This tactic had been successful earlier in pressuring West Virginia to repeal restrictive law, but Florida refused to yield. Twenty-three insurance companies and three insurance trade associations filed suit to challenge the constitutionality of the law. Heartened by Florida's example, Hawaii and North Carolina took similar actions (Hilder, 1986: 1).

Actions of Policyholders

Policyholders also took separate and joint action to lessen the impact of insurance cost and availability problems. Both large companies and municipalities can self-insure either by setting aside funds to pay for future claims or in the case of private business, establishing a captive insurance company. Such alternatives are attractive. One source revealed that of the $90 billion potential market for corporate risk, that $35 billion went to self-insurance or captives (Felter, 1985). Although the tax advantages of captive insurance companies had been restricted by the Tax Reform Act of 1984, some 2,000 captive insurance companies are currently in operation (Pine, 1985: 19). One example of captives used to solve availability problems involves bankers. Unable to get liability insurance for bank directors and officers at reasonable prices, the banking industry incorporated a captive insurance company to write such insurance and to correct high costs with a risk management program.[22]

An outside industry force also volunteered to assist in the insurance crisis. The banking industry has long wanted to get the authority to sell and underwrite insurance; efforts to get such authority in 1982 in the Garn-St Germain Act were defeated by the insurance industry's opposition. With the crisis, bankers got strong support from Robert Hunter (1985c) as one way to resolve the crisis. Banks argued that many state-chartered banks had insurance experience gained under state laws that permitted such activities. Similarly national banks in small towns have long had insurance sales authority (Bradford, 1985a).

At the federal level, several actions were taken that bolstered the banks' position. Senator Jake Garn, the Senate's leading authority on banking regulation, sponsored a bill to allow state-chartered banks to operate intrastate insurance subsidiaries. The Federal Reserve Board (Fed) issued new rules that allowed any branch of a bank located in a city of less than 5,000 people to market insurance; previously, only banks with headquarters in such cities could market insurance. In March 1986, the Supreme Court struck down an effort by the Fed to limit what are called *nonbanks*—financial institutions that do not meet the strict definition of what constitutes a bank (they either lack checking accounts or corporate loans); these nonbanks are not bound by federal restrictions on marketing insurance. Banks welcomed all these opportunities. A survey of the 100 largest U. S. banks revealed that 70 percent were planning to enter the insurance market if authority was given to do so. Insurance industry opposition to banks in insurance remained unwavering (Lease and Ruddy, 1985).

Politics at the Federal Level

While the policy battle at the state level continued, attempts were made to expand the scope of the conflict to the federal level. After an administration study, President Reagan endorsed the insurance coalition's position and recommendations.[23] The result was a proposed federal law to preempt state action in this area and impose uniform federal standards. More than 50 bills were introduced in Congress to correct all or part of the liability crisis (Greene, 1986: 77). The insurance industry endorsed the efforts of Wisconsin Senator Robert Kasten to enact a federal product liability law that was very favorable to industry.

Action at the federal level would not be easy, however, because the insurance industry and other coalition members had to compete with a wider variety of interests for access to the federal policy agenda. One group of legislators responded strongly to what was perceived as unfair tactics by the insurance companies at the state level. Particularly controversial was the threat to not write insurance in West Virginia if laws were not repealed and similar threats in Florida. Illinois Senator Paul Simon introduced a bill to modify the McCarran-Ferguson Act so that federal antitrust laws would apply to insurance companies. His bill rapidly gained support from Senators Ted Kennedy, Joseph Biden, and Howard Metzenbaum as well as banking, labor, and consumer groups. This bill would also create a Federal Insurance Commission to provide for federal regulation of insurance. Representative Peter Rodino, chair of the House Judiciary Committee, threatened to hold antitrust hearings and released his own data to argue that the insurance industry had not experienced great losses in the previous four years. With the 1986 midterm elections, tort reform was pushed to the back burner of federal legislative priorities; and no action was taken.

The Results of the Tort Reform Effort

Although generalizing about state legislative actions while efforts are still underway is difficult, some tentative conclusions can be offered. An objective analysis by the *Wall Street Journal* concluded that 32 states had adopted some type of tort reform legislation, but that few of these adoptions enacted the bulk of the civil justice reform group's wish list (Hilder, 1986: 14). States that adopted major changes in the tort system were generally smaller, less populated states. Most large states adopted only limited legislation or did not take action.

Future action on the tort reform agenda is not likely. First, the coalition found that access to the floor of the legislature was blocked by well-placed legislators who were willing to bear the wrath of the insurance coalition until more convincing data were presented.[24] With the delay, the opponents of tort reform gained ground. Individuals adjusted to higher insurance costs. Captive insurance companies were formed. Individuals who were initially unable to get insurance purchased insurance through MAPs. And preliminary information on industry profits for the last quarter of 1985 and the first quarters of 1986 revealed that the property and casualty industry was again profitable (Ross, 1987: 18). Some industries and municipalities still experienced difficulties in obtaining insurance, but most did not. In short, the crisis appeared to be over.

Cash Flow During the Liability Crisis

Before linking the liability insurance crisis to my theory of regulation, some discussion of liability insurance profits is necessary. Few financial results are understood less well than the cash-flow situation of property and casualty insurance companies. The financial condition of property and casualty companies was an issue in the liability insurance crisis. Three ratios are commonly used to assess the financial conditions of the insurance industry—the loss ratio, the combined ratio, and the overall operating ratio. These three ratios are shown in Tables 5-2, 5-3, and 5-4 for the three industry lines—medical malpractice, general liability, and commercial automobile liability—that experienced the greatest disruptions of supply during the crisis.

Each ratio requires some explanation. The *loss ratio* is the sum of insurance losses plus loss adjustment expenses divided by the total premiums earned. Each of these components merits some elaboration. Insurance accounting uses premiums earned rather than premiums written; *premiums earned* is generally a smaller number, and this use increases the size of the loss ratio. *Adjustment loss expenses* are the costs of settling claims including office costs and legal expenses. The latter is the major portion of loss adjustment expenses. *Losses* include not only losses paid out but also monies paid into reserve accounts in anticipation of future losses.

As Table 5-2 illustrates, loss ratios have deteriorated steadily in the medical malpractice insurance line over the past ten years. General liability insurance has had lower loss ratios, but they have also increased over the ten-year period. Commercial auto liability policies have the lowest loss ratios but

Table 5-2
Financial Ratios for Medical Malpractice Insurance, 1976–1985

	Loss Ratio	Combined Ratio	Operating Ratio
1976	95.4	109.8	99.4
1977	79.9	93.7	79.6
1978	88.0	104.8	87.3
1979	98.9	113.8	92.0
1980	114.1	129.2	99.8
1981	120.7	137.6	101.4
1982	133.7	150.9	109.8
1983	133.8	151.2	108.9
1984	144.9	162.2	118.3
1985	152.8	166.9	129.5

Source: *Best's Aggregate and Averages*, 1986.

Table 5–3
Financial Ratios for General Liability Insurance

	Loss Ratio	Combined Ratio	Operating Ratio
1976	79.8	107.1	96.7
1977	74.4	100.0	90.4
1978	70.5	97.3	87.5
1979	70.0	98.2	86.0
1980	77.4	107.2	92.7
1981	84.5	116.0	96.5
1982	97.0	129.4	106.4
1983	105.6	138.1	113.8
1984	120.8	151.8	125.1
1985	121.5	145.8	125.8

Source: *Best's Aggregates and Averages,* 1986.

Table 5–4
Financial Ratios for Commercial Auto Liability Insurance

	Loss Ratio	Combined Ratio	Operating Ratio
1976	77.3	103.6	97.4
1977	73.2	98.8	92.7
1978	73.5	99.9	93.7
1979	77.2	105.0	97.6
1980	80.4	109.5	101.1
1981	87.5	118.3	108.4
1982	94.0	126.4	115.3
1983	99.8	132.9	121.3
1984	111.4	143.1	130.8
1985	99.5	127.1	116.4

Source: *Best's Aggregates and Averages,* 1986.

have a similar increasing trend.

Combined ratios are the sum of losses plus loss adjustment expenses, plus underwriting expenses (commissions, etc.) divided by premiums earned minus dividends paid to policyholders. The combined ratio, because it shows all the industry's expenses but not all of its income, portrays the industry in the worst financial light. Combined ratios are often cited by the industry to argue for the depressed nature of industry profits (see Chapter 1 on the relationship of profits to combined ratios). One problem with combined ratios is that they are often so high as to stretch credibility. For this ten-year period, medical malpractice insurance operated at a combined ratio of 136.9.

Clearly, no industry can operate for ten years with an annual cash flow of minus 36.9 percent and remain in operation.

Operating ratios are nothing more than the combined ratios with the industry's investment income added to the denominator. Operating ratios show the cash flow of the industry when investment income is included in the analysis. Operating ratios, however, do not reveal the entire financial picture of the insurance industry for these three lines. First, investment income includes only interest income and capital gains that are realized. Capital gains that are not realized but continue to be held are not included. The most serious problem with this ratio, however, is that loss reserves are counted as losses when, in fact, these reserves are invested rather than spent.

Discovering the amount of money set aside by insurance industries in the form of loss reserves is difficult because the standard financial sources do not report them. Individual companies, however, do report to state insurance regulators both loss reserves and actual losses paid. As part of the documentation presented by the Insurance Information Institute to the Wisconsin Task Force on Property and Liability Insurance, the total losses actually paid in these three lines for 1980 to 1984 were listed. Using this information in addition to information from other sources will reveal a more accurate picture of the cash flow of insurance lines.

Table 5-5 shows the resulting balance sheet for the medical malpractice line. Row 1 is the total premiums earned in millions of dollars. This figure is

Table 5-5
Cash Flow in the Medical Malpractice Insurance Line (millions)

	1980	1981	1982	1983	1984	1985
1. Premiums Earned	$1,199	$1,266	$1,358	$1,508	$1,707	$2,416
2. Investment Income	353	458	558	637	749	904
3. Total Income	1,552	1,724	1,916	2,145	2,456	3,320
4. Claims Paid	500	700	800	1,100	1,200	1,700
5. Loss Adjustment Expenses	363	358	420	532	550	913
6. Underwriting Expenses	169	189	210	244	278	319
7. Total Expenses	1,032	1,247	1,430	1,876	2,038	2,932
8. Profit Estimate	520	477	486	269	418	388
9. Additions to Reserves	505	471	597	375	714	904

Total Additions to Reserves	$3,740	million
Total Profits Cumulative	$2,558	million
Estimated Capital Base 1980 =	$3.1	billion 1985 = $11.3 billion

Source: *Best's Aggregates and Averages,* 1986, and the Insurance Information Institute.

added to row 2, the total investment income, to arrive at total industry income in row 3.[25] Row 4 lists the total losses that were actually paid for claims during that year;[26] row 5 is the total loss adjustment expenses; and row 6 lists the commissions and other underwriting expenses. The sum of rows 4, 5, and 6 is the total operating expenses of the malpractice insurance industry and is listed in row 7. The difference between row 3 and row 7 is the net operating profit without considering loss reserves. These calculations reveal that medical malpractice insurance had a positive net cash flow for every year in this period.

Row 8 lists the amount of money deposited in loss reserves. Note how this amount (which is treated as an expense for tax purposes) is fairly close to the net level of operating cash flow in row 7. This pattern is consistent with behavior that would seek to protect profits from taxation by excessively contributing to the loss reserve funds. The cumulative additions to loss reserves for this six-year period is $3.74 billion or $1.2 billion more than the positive cash flow. Because a company can only shelter loss reserves for five years, something must be done with expired loss reserves. The logical place for such loss reserves is to add them to overall capital. Such action requires that the reserves be declared as income; but with ever expanding loss reserves, the net result would usually be no profits.

One way to illustrate the capital growth is to take investment income and work back to determine how much capital would be needed to generate the income that is received. By using the government bonds rate as a surrogate for the actual industry earnings rate, one can estimate the total capital available to the industry.[27] These figures for 1980 and 1985 are shown at the bottom of Table 5–5. The figures reveal a 263 percent increase in capital; this pattern is not consistent with an industry suffering major losses each year. The pattern is far more consistent with one that would be expected if an industry was able to take advantage of tax laws to accrue capital through paper losses.

Table 5–6 computes similar figures for the general liability insurance industry. The bottom line for this industry shows a cash-flow loss of $421 million over this six-year period. At the same time, the industry was able to contribute $3.75 billion to loss reserves. The capital needed to generate the reported investment income increased from $8.2 billion to $23.3 billion, an increase of 186 percent.

Table 5–7 presents the same financial figures for the commercial automobile liability line of insurance. The results for this industry show a cash-flow loss of $1.3 billion for the six-year period. This industry line was able to add $3.4 billion to loss reserves over this time period. Total capital re-

Table 5-6
Cash Flow in the General Liability Line (millions)

	1980	1981	1982	1983	1984	1985
1. Premiums Earned	$6,589	$6,103	$5,718	$5,730	$6,250	$9,317
2. Investment Income	957	1,184	1,320	1,398	1,663	1,863
3. Total Income	7,555	7,287	7,038	7,128	7,913	11,180
4. Claims Paid	2,600	3,100	3,700	4,400	5,600	6,600
5. Loss Adjustment Expenses	1,339	1,416	1,572	1,759	2,093	2,795
6. Underwriting Expenses	1,926	1,879	1,806	1,827	1,893	2,217
7. Total Expenses	5,865	6,395	7,078	7,986	9,586	11,612
8. Profit Estimate	1,690	892	-40	-858	-1,673	-432
9. Additions to Reserves	1,167	635	274	-109	-144	1,925

Total Additions to Reserves $3.75 billion
Total Cumulative Profits   -$421 million
Estimated Capital Base 1980 = $8.3 billion   1985 = $23.3 billion

Source: *Best's Aggregates and Averages*, 1986; and the Insurance Information Institute.

Table 5-7
Cash Flow for Commercial Automobile Liability Insurance (millions)

	1980	1981	1982	1983	1984	1985
1. Premiums Earned	$4,656	$4,746	$4,706	$4,710	$5,157	$6,863
2. Investment Income	396	470	533	546	639	727
3. Total Income	5,052	5,216	5,228	5,256	5,796	7,590
4. Claims Paid	2,600	3,000	3,500	3,700	4,300	5,100
5. Loss Adjustment Expenses	540	607	612	622	758	851
6. Underwriting Expenses	1,327	1,429	1,497	1,516	1,599	1,846
7. Total Expenses	4,467	5,036	5,609	5,838	6,657	7,797
8. Estimated Profits	585	180	-381	-582	-861	-207
9. Additions to Reserves	603	541	312	378	686	878

Total Additions to Reserves $3.4 billion
Cumulative Estimated Profits   -$1.3 billion
Estimated Capital Base 1980 = $3.3 billion   1985 = $9.1 billion

Source: *Best's Aggregates and Averages*, 1986, and the Insurance Information Institute.

quired to generate the listed investment income increased from $3.3 billion in 1980 to $9.1 billion in 1985, an increase of 176 percent.

The overall financial health of the three depressed lines in liability insurance does not show as dismal a picture as is often painted by individuals citing combined or even operating ratios. Although these lines may not have been generating profits according to the accounting principles used in the insurance industry, these industries have been adding greatly to reserves and have accumulated increases in capital. One line, medical malpractice insurance, has had large positive cash flows in every year examined. Claims concerning massive losses during the liability insurance crisis, therefore, should be treated with skepticism.

A Theoretical Recapitulation

The property and liability insurance crisis of 1985–1986 provides a good illustration of the recent politics of the insurance industry. The insurance industry had goals that could not be obtained within the insurance regulatory system. The proposed changes in tort liability required action by either state legislatures or the U. S. Congress. To motivate state legislatures, the insurance industry needed to raise issue salience sufficiently to place the issue on the legislative agenda.

Salience was increased with news releases and advertising campaigns to warn both the public and public officials of the crisis in the industry. An effort was made to link the rising costs of insurance with litigation and changes in legal doctrine. Unfortunately for the insurance industry, such tactics contain the seeds of its own destruction. The insurance industry does best in situations where the issues are complex but not salient. Increasing salience motivates other political actors to become involved.

The complexity of an issue increases participation costs even for salient issues. Using the perceived complexity of insurance, the industry presented a simple cause of the crisis (litigation) illustrated by a few simple statistics (combined ratios). Requests for additional information produced either a flood of unreadable documents or no response at all. Such tactics were highly successful in political communities without expertise. Small states with relatively unsophisticated insurance commissions adopted many of the proposed tort reforms. Larger states that were more likely to have some technical expertise among the regulatory bureaucrats passed only a few of the reforms.

The liability crisis illustrates that the insurance industry recognizes its own limitations in creating a policy coalition. Similar to past patterns only a part of the insurance industry was interested in the liability crisis. Throughout the crisis, the life and health insurance industry were nowhere to be seen; even among property and casualty companies, companies specializing in personal lines took almost no part in the debate. Only the companies and trade associations in the commercial liability insurance lines were active participants. This narrow base required coalition partners, and the dramatic rise in rates generated some. Small businesses, the asbestos industry, local governments, trucking companies, and others affected by the increase in rates joined the coalition. Although the insurance industry was not unified, portions of the industry were able to build a coalition with others.

The liability crisis is the best illustration so far of the active participation of consumers in insurance politics. The National Insurance Consumers Organization (NICO) provided constant opposition to the insurance industry and, at times, presented contrasting data. NICO was able to form a coalition with other consumer groups and trial attorneys as they portrayed the insurance industry as "haves" against the consumer "have-nots." Active opposition delayed the bandwagon toward reform long enough to let political officials exert control over the process.

Regulators in the larger states resisted major changes in tort laws and often demanded concessions in exchange for endorsing part of the tort reform package. Insurance law is a legislative area where professional regulators are active and continuing participants. Their levels of expertise are sufficient so that many states will not enact insurance changes over the strenuous objections of the insurance commissioner. The New York Superintendent of Insurance was able to have price regulation reinstated in exchange for some limited tort reforms advocated by the industry. Other commissioners were able to defuse the problems with blue ribbon task forces.

Political elites were also active in the crisis. Although in some states legislatures merely ratified the demands of the insurance industry (for example, Washington), in many states, political elites resisted such efforts. The Florida legislature enacted a 40 percent reduction in insurance costs in exchange for some tort reforms. Governors such as Kean of New Jersey used informal pressure to get market solutions for some of the more severe problems. More examples could be cited to demonstrate that political elites were independent actors in the process. They sought their own policy goals rather than simply accepting the insurance industry's goals.

Chapter 6

Federal Issues in Insurance Policy

Although insurance regulation is primarily a state function, nothing prevents the federal government from asserting control over part or all of the policy area. President Gerald Ford's regulatory study groups, for example, examined the antitrust exemption for insurance and recommended that it be eliminated. During the liability insurance crisis of 1985–1986, Representative Rodino threatened hearings on establishing federal regulation of insurance. Such instances are somewhat unusual, however. Because state governments are the normal place for insurance controversies to be resolved, something dramatic must occur to place an insurance issue on the federal government's agenda. As a result, insurance issues at the national level are, by definition, salient issues. The same political actors compete in the policy process with the addition of federal political elites. The salience of the issues attract political elites who see the issues as a way to build political resources.

This chapter examines five insurance issues that have been on the federal agenda—mail-order insurance, flood insurance, no-fault automobile insurance, unisex insurance rates, and taxation of insurance companies. These issues cover a wide variety of controversies in insurance politics. *Mail-order insurance* is concerned with unfair trade practices and regulatory federalism. Federal *flood insurance* seeks the regulatory goal of access and deals with the inadequacies of the private market place. *No-fault automobile insurance* addresses the efficiency of the insurance system with emphasis on the cost of litigation. *Unisex insurance* rates cover an area where insurance policy and civil rights overlap; it raises questions about the social rather than economic purposes of insurance. *Taxation of insurance companies* is a redistributive issue concerning the industry's fair share of taxes.

Mail-Order Insurance

A continuing problem for state insurance regulators has been the regulation of "foreign" insurance companies who do not have sales offices in the state. Although this problem is often referred to as the mail-order insurance problem, it is broader than that. The concern is with insurance companies that are not licensed to conduct business within a state. Unauthorized companies include not only companies that solicit customers by mail and other direct media means but excess and surplus lines companies, reinsurance companies, and companies servicing orphan policies. Excess and surplus lines companies are companies willing to write insurance on risks that domestic insurance companies are unwilling to take. Reinsurance companies are used by domestic companies to spread their risks by reinsuring a portion of their policies with another company. Orphan policies are policies owned by persons who move in from another state; policies become orphans if they are issued by companies not licensed in the destination state. Because each type of unauthorized company provides a valid insurance service, states do not want to ban all sales by unauthorized companies. Without reinsurance or excess and surplus lines insurance, many individuals in a state would be unable to get insurance. Banning orphan policies, especially in life insurance, would impose major costs on policyholders. The need is to protect policyholders from the ill effects of unauthorized insurers but allow them to attain the benefits.

An individual is entitled to purchase insurance from any company he or she desires; states cannot prohibit purchasing insurance from out-of-state companies. Because insurance was not considered commerce under the *Paul v. Virginia* decision (see Chapter 4), an insurance company could avoid regulation by incorporating in one state but doing no business in that state. Most often, the company would incorporate under the general corporation laws rather than the insurance laws. The company would sell insurance only in other states through the mail or similar methods of direct merchandizing. Any attempts by a nondomicile state to regulate such a company were frustrated. The nondomicile state had no way to enforce its laws because the foreign insurance company had no offices in the state; and, therefore, the state had no place to serve legal complaints on the company. Mail-order insurance, thus, fell outside the scope of state regulation.

Unauthorized insurance companies were an early concern of NAIC, whose first study was undertaken in 1888. A special problem was "wildcat" fire insurance companies who did not sell insurance in their domiciled state but did sell it in other states through the mail. Such companies paid no premium taxes, and policyholders had difficulty collecting payments when damages occurred (Haase, 1969: 316).

The NAIC could not reach agreement on what actions to take against unauthorized insurance companies until 1902. The futility of individual state actions logically suggested federal intervention. The NAIC had identified 86 problem companies, including 40 operating out of Chicago alone. In 1902, the NAIC executive committee requested that the Postmaster General deny the use of the mails to companies that were not authorized by their home state to sell insurance. The NAIC also requested that Congress pass appropriate legislation if the Postmaster General did not have the power to act.

If the NAIC had to rely on Congress, it might have been left in an unenviable position. Congress, shocked by the Armstrong Committee's revelations regarding excesses of the life insurance companies, was considering legislation to establish federal regulation of insurance (see Chapter 4). In order to avoid raising the salience of insurance regulation further by pointing out the inadequacies of state regulation, the NAIC soft-pedaled the issue to Congress (Haase, 1969: 318). The NAIC received cooperation from the Postmaster General; that cooperation plus the publicity generated about unauthorized insurers was successful enough for the NAIC Committee on Unauthorized Insurance to declare the problem solved in 1907 (Haase, 1969: 319).

With the resolution of the wildcat fire insurance company problem, the issue of unauthorized insurance companies dropped in salience to the NAIC. In the 1930s, the issue resurfaced with the financial success of a growing group of mail-order insurance companies. Laws prohibiting the operation of unauthorized insurance companies had no impact on these companies. Specializing in accident and health policies, the companies merely advertised the availability of insurance through either electronic or print media and relied on customers to contact them. Some of these companies were clearly fraudulent. Directed primarily at the elderly, these interstate advertisements offered benefits disproportionate to the small premiums charged. The benefits were illusory, however, because the companies often did not pay legitimate claims (Haase, 1969: 325; Hanson and Obenberger, 1966: 192).

False and deceptive interstate sale of insurance is a problem that the federal government is best suited to handle. Fearing federal legislation, the NAIC advocated uniform state laws and cooperation among insurance commissioners. Although model legislation was proposed as early as 1937, the commissioners could not agree on a solution to the problem.[1] With the renewed threat of federal legislation after the *South-Eastern* case and the McCarran-Ferguson Act (see Chapter 4), the NAIC adopted the Uniform Unauthorized Insurers Process Act in 1948 (Haase, 1969: 327). This act allowed a policyholder to sue an unauthorized insurance company in the policyholder's state of residence; the policyholder could serve process on the insurance company by filing notice with the Secretary of State. By 1954, more than 40 states had adopted this model act (Haase, 1969: 331).

The constitutionality of the Uniform Unauthorized Insurers Process Act was challenged by Travelers Health Association, a Nebraska mail-order insurance company. Travelers Health sold insurance policies through the mail in all states except Nebraska. Virginia obtained a court injunction against Travelers Health using the procedure under the uniform act. In *Travelers Health Association v. Virginia* [339 U. S. 643 (1950)] the U. S. Supreme Court held that Travelers Health had been properly subjected to Virginia's jurisdiction.

The *Travelers* case and the uniform process law did not completely solve the problem. States still had to regulate insurance companies aggressively, and most states did not have a deceptive practices law. U. S. Senate hearings on the mail-order insurance industry in 1953 and 1954 revealed that problems remained.

A constant concern of the state insurance commissioners was the FTC, the federal agency with jurisdiction over deceptive advertising. Because many mail-order insurance companies were engaged in false and misleading claims, the FTC was interested in protecting individuals from unscrupulous mail-order companies. In 1950, the FTC issued 24 voluntary mail-order insurance practice rules of conduct prohibiting a variety of deceptive practices (Hanson and Obenberger, 1966: 205); similar rules were reissued in 1956. Even though the states had been largely unsuccessful in their own efforts to prevent false claims, the insurance commissioners strongly opposed any FTC action. The FTC was perceived as the harbinger of federal regulation, the one threat that usually united all state insurance commissioners.

In response to the 1954 Senate hearings, the FTC acted against Travelers Health. The FTC issued a cease and desist order to prevent Travelers Health from publishing misleading statements in its advertising. Travelers Health countered that because it was regulated by the state of Nebraska, its actions even outside of Nebraska were exempt from federal regulation under the provisions of the McCarren-Ferguson Act. The Supreme Court in *Federal Trade Commission v. Travelers Health Association* [362 U. S. 293 (1960)] held that the conduct in question had to be regulated under the law of the state where the sale of insurance occurred. In other words, regulation had to exist in the policyholder's state of residence not just in the company's state of domicile. The FTC had the authority to regulate the interstate advertising of insurance companies.[2]

To prevent the FTC from regulating insurance advertising, the NAIC recommended an Unauthorized Insurers False Advertising Process Act in 1961. State consideration of the proposed model law was slow both as a result of opposition from the International Federation of Commercial Travelers Insurance and the Association of Insurance Advertisers (Haase, 1969:

336). In addition, state regulators expressed legitimate concerns about orphan policies, reinsurance, and excess and surplus lines insurance (Hanson and Obenberger, 1966: 211). Not until 1974 did the NAIC adopt a revised Accident and Health Model Advertising Regulation that prohibited many abuses; this regulation was adopted by 47 of the states by 1982 (Beaven and Braybrooks, 1982: 20). In 1978, the Mass Marketed Life and Health Insurance Model Act was adopted, which authorized the insurance commissioner to void insurance contracts with excessive costs.

Individual states took a stronger approach. In 1961, Wisconsin adopted its Unauthorized Insurance Law, which prohibits unauthorized insurers from operating in the state. Surplus lines insurance can be purchased only if the insurance is not available within the state and if it is purchased through a licensed agent. The harsh Wisconsin law was challenged by Ministers Life and Casualty Union, a mail-order insurance company; Ministers Life sought a declaratory judgement to void the law. The Wisconsin Supreme Court, however, upheld the law; and the U. S. Supreme Court declined to hear the case because it raised no federal question [*Ministers Life and Casualty Union v. Haase* 385 U. S. 205 (1966)]. Following the *Ministers Life* case, states approached the regulation of unauthorized insurers in a variety of different ways with more or less stringency (Huebner and Black, 1974: 570).

With the rise of state regulation, efforts by the FTC have waned. In 1964, the FTC adopted a set of Guides for the Mail Order Insurance Business, essentially administrative interpretations of the law in the area. After 1964, the FTC turned to other insurance issues such as the marketing of industrial life and price disclosure in life insurance policies.

During this time period, the mail-order insurance business, or as they prefer to be called the direct response marketing insurance industry, has grown to be a significant portion of the insurance industry. In 1985, direct response marketers had $26.1 billion of life insurance in force or approximately 5 percent of the market (ACLI, 1986: 26). The industry is highly specialized by lines, generally dealing in life and health insurance and in supplemental coverage rather than basic coverage. Direct response marketing companies argue that they fill a real need because regular companies do not want to be bothered with small supplemental health care and small life insurance policies. Lower overhead costs of direct response marketers make them profitable. Perhaps the two most popular products are group insurance which is marketed via mail to members of associations and "medigap" insurance. The former received a major boost when the NAIC model law was changed to allow professional associations to offer group insurance. Many major insurance companies such as Prudential and Teacher's Insurance and Annuity Association (TIAA) have become mail-order insurance companies with group life insurance.

The second product, medigap insurance, is designed to pay for insurance costs for elderly that are not covered by Medicare. Medigap insurance has been subject to highly critical congressional hearings. Insurance companies have adopted names that sound much like government agencies and misled potential buyers into believing that the insurance was government sponsored.[3] Problems with false and deceptive claims have not been eliminated.

The Federal Flood Insurance Program

Flood insurance is a product that private industry cannot profitably provide. Because people who live on high ground do not want flood insurance, risks due to flooding cannot be spread among enough individuals to make it economically feasible. Only by charging high rates could flood insurance companies breakeven in the long term. A viable flood insurance program requires government participation either to subsidize rates or to mandate participation and loss-control techniques.[4]

Kathy Kemp (1984), in an excellent analysis of the SEC and the FAA, illustrated the impact that crises have on regulatory policy. Flood insurance politics follows a pattern similar to the one Kemp outlined. Floods are major natural disasters; after such a disaster, the public demands that government do something to protect them from such harms. The result is an increase in political salience, and increased salience sometimes mobilizes enough policy actors to achieve some policy changes.[5] Such a pattern is not uncommon in insurance politics; the movement to prior approval rate laws in property and casualty insurance resulted from the San Francisco earthquake and fire; the medical malpractice "crisis" of the mid-1970s brought about several changes in tort laws (Meier and Copeland, 1986).

The first movement toward a national flood insurance program occurred after spring floods inundated thousands of square miles of Kansas and Missouri in 1951.[6] President Harry S Truman proposed legislation to create a $1.5 billion flood insurance program administered by private insurance companies. The federal government, through this program, was to operate as the underwriter. Truman's program failed to pass Congress in 1951, as did a similar proposal in 1952 (Weese and Ooms, 1978: 187).

In August 1954, Hurricane Carol struck the New England coast; major flooding also occurred in this area the following year. The Eastern Underwriters Association (a rate bureau) released statistical data on the extent of the damage; further mobilizing the insurance industry were a series of flood damage studies released by the American Insurance Association. In response, President Dwight D. Eisenhower sponsored the Federal Flood Indemnity Act in 1956. Eisenhower called for a five-year program, with insurance to be sold and serviced by private companies with the federal government providing reinsurance and rate subsidies (Hashmi, 1982: 20). Passing this program, Congress authorized a $2.9 billion federal commitment to flood insurance. A novel part of the program set the subsidy at 40 percent of cost, to be provided by the federal government and cooperating state governments. After July 1, 1959, the states were to pay one-half the subsidy costs (Weese and Ooms, 1978: 188).

Federal flood insurance was not to be, however. Congress failed to pass an appropriation to fund the flood control program. As a result, the federal flood control program was abolished in 1957 without ever providing any insurance.

THE NATIONAL FLOOD INSURANCE ACT

Interest in federal flood insurance continued to ebb and flow with the incidence of natural disasters. In 1960, Hurricane Donna struck the Gulf Coast, as did Hurricane Carla the following year. 1962 saw major flooding in the Northwest and along the mid-Atlantic seaboard (Weese and Ooms, 1978: 188). In response to these disasters, the insurance industry met to plot a strategy for a national flood insurance program. The resulting All-Industry Flood Insurance Committee in cooperation with the NAIC recommended a flood insurance plan based on a private risk-sharing pool and federal assistance (Weese and Ooms, 1978: 189).

In 1965, the Gulf States were hit by Hurricane Betsy. In 1964 and 1965, President Lyndon B. Johnson declared major natural disasters 34 times, the worst two-year period on record. As part of the federal government's response to these disasters, the Southeast Hurricane Disaster Relief Act, the Department of Housing and Urban Development (HUD) was instructed to prepare a report on the financial feasibility of a federal flood insurance program. Documenting flooding damages of $652 million in 1964 and $788 million in 1965, the HUD report concluded that a federal flood insurance program was both feasible and in the public interest (Weese and Ooms, 1978: 189).

After President Johnson endorsed the report, Congress held hearings on the HUD recommendations. HUD, in cooperation with individuals in private industry, proposed a National Flood Protection Act. The partnership between HUD and the industry explains the specific mechanism chosen for program implementation. HUD's initial report suggested four alternatives from a fully private system to a fully federal program. The industry-HUD proposal recommended a federal-industry partnership. Flood insurance would be sold and serviced by private industry with the federal government providing financial backup for the envisioned losses. The insurance industry enthusiastically supported the proposal. Passing both houses of Congress, President Johnson signed this program into law in 1968 (Hashmi, 1982: 20).

The National Flood Protection Act established three goals for the National Flood Insurance Program (NFIP). The first and most obvious was to provide a system of affordable flood insurance. The second goal was to control future flood losses although its importance was not as immediately apparent. Because the federal government did not envision a passive insurance program, the provision was designed to encourage communities to control flood losses through flood plain management. The effort would become the most controversial part of the program. The final goal was to save money: an effective flood insurance program coupled with a successful flood control program would save the federal government funds normally spent for disaster relief (Hashmi, 1982: 20).

The Federal Insurance Administration (FIA) was given a choice of implementation strategies; it could either run an entirely federal program or operate a program whereby private industry ran the program with support from the FIA. The FIA continued the government-industry cooperation; approximately 90 companies joined the National Flood Insurers Association, and the Association was selected by FIA to operate the program.[7]

The federal flood program became operational in 1969, but actual participation was limited. Communities could not participate in the program until they gave satisfactory assurances that they would adopt adequate flood plain management techniques. A key element in flood plain management is to prohibit development in areas likely to flood; such efforts are always controversial at the local level. By December 1969, only four communities had qualified. The inadequate progress was revealed when Hurricane Camille hit the Gulf Coast in late 1969. Congress responded to these shortcomings by authorizing an emergency flood insurance program that allowed communities to participate without completing a study to determine what actuarily sound rates would be. A community merely had to express a desire to participate and agree that future decisions would reduce flood hazards (Weese and Ooms, 1978: 192).

Growth of the program, however, continued to be slow. By the end of 1972 (the year of Hurricane Agnes), only 90,000 policies had been sold. A recent survey revealed that individuals often do not think flooding is likely and, therefore, refrain from buying flood insurance (Indiana Chapter, 1984: 210). Congress in 1973 responded with the Flood Disaster Protection Act of 1973, designed to create stronger incentives for communities to participate in the program. The Act required that individuals using any form of federal financial assistance (such as FHA loan guarantees) to purchase property in a flood plain must also purchase flood insurance. This requirement meant that communities had no choice but to join the program because without federal loan guarantees, few financial institutions would loan money for mortgages or construction.

As the program began to grow following the 1973 law, the FIA found itself involved in two major controversies. At the local level, the FIA began to oversee the flood control management techniques of local government to guarantee that they were consistent with federal goals. Land-use zoning is a power that local governments have protected vigorously from encroachment by the federal government. Federal regulations that prohibited development were strongly resented by local governments. Local governments did not have many options; however, because without compliance and the necessary federal assistance, development was not possible.[8] The National Flood Insurance Program became as much a land-use regulatory program as it was an insurance program.

The second major dispute centered on the relationship between the FIA and the insurance industry. In November 1974, J. Robert Hunter became the acting Federal Insurance Administrator. Although not known for such views at the time, Hunter eventually became the insurance industry's most severe critic, founding an organization called the National Insurance Consumers Organization (see Chapter 5). Questioning the operating efficiency of the National Fire Insurance Association program, Hunter felt program changes were needed to comply with the mandate of the National Flood Protection Act of 1973. Hunter viewed the FIA's role as setting overall policy and issuing regulations while private industry's role was to provide efficient administrative support. The insurance industry both resented and resisted what they perceived as a fundamental change in the partnership. After a bitter fight including a court challenge, the FIA exercised its option and took over complete administration of the federal flood insurance program (see Weese and Ooms, 1978: 194–201, for the details of the dispute).

With this action, the Federal Insurance Administrator became the sole flood insurance underwriter for the federal flood insurance program. A private organization was hired to run the daily operations of the program. Flood insurance policies were sold by local insurance agents who then forwarded these policies to the FIA. Claims were also handled by local agents. After several years of operating the program in this manner, the FIA recently permitted private insurers to participate again in a limited way. Private companies can now issue flood insurance, which can be reinsured with the FIA. Profits or losses are split between FIA and the insurance company (Indiana Chapter, 1984: 206).

Despite such efforts to encourage participation in the flood insurance program, program growth has been modest. In fiscal year 1986, approximately 2.12 million policies were in force generating premium income of $407 million to provide for $150 billion in insurance coverage. In 1985, the program ran at a small profit as the program does when no major natural disasters occur. The Reagan Administration, in fact, has announced a goal of making the federal flood insurance program self-sustaining (that is, operating without federal subsidies). Given the large losses that would occur with a major flood, however, such prospects are unlikely.

No-Fault Automobile Insurance

Few insurance issues have mobilized consumer forces as much as the issue of no-fault automobile insurance. Prior to 1970, the method of settling claims for automobile liability insurance was similar to the method for all liability insurance—the principle of tort liability. For one person to receive insurance compensation from another, the first person had to prove that the second party caused his or her damages (injuries, property damage). Fault was determined through the legal process. Using the legal process to determine claims was expensive, especially in terms of legal fees. The Department of Transportation (1971: 52) estimated that 23 percent of automobile insurance premiums went to pay legal fees; only 42 percent went to pay for damages to injured parties.[9] In addition, heavy reliance on the tort liability system resulted in delays, exaggerated claims, and inefficiency.

As an alternative to the tort liability system, no-fault insurance was proposed as early as 1932 and actually adopted in Saskatchewan in 1946 (Witt and Urrutia, 1984a: 12). In the United States, the issue was first placed on the policy agenda when Robert Keeton and Jeffrey O'Connell (1965) suggested the process in their book, *Basic Protection for the Accident Victim*. The operating principle of no-fault insurance is that individuals give up the right to sue others for damages; in return they are compensated for their injuries by their own insurance company regardless of fault.

No-Fault at the State Level

No-fault automobile insurance was a battle fought both at the state and federal levels. The state level was the more obvious arena because automobile insurance is regulated at the state level, not the federal level. The no-fault concept gained support from the American Insurance Association, the National Association of Independent Insurers, the American Mutual Insurance Alliance, and the National Conference of Commissioners on Uniform State Laws. Attracted by the idea that no-fault would save administrative expenses, a group of nine major insurance companies announced support for their version of no-fault in December 1972 (see Witt and Urrutia, 1984a: 12–13).

At the state level, the insurance industry was joined by consumer groups and progressive insurance commissioners. The opposition to no-fault came from the organized bar, particularly from organizations of trial attorneys. Trial attorneys, of course, make substantial legal fees from tort litigation.

Massachusetts became the first state to adopt no-fault in 1970 and implemented it the following year. The initial success of Massachusetts led to an explosion in state no-fault laws: Delaware, Florida, Oregon, South Dakota, and Virginia in 1972; Connecticut, Maryland, Michigan, and New Jersey in 1973; Arkansas, Colorado, Hawaii, Kansas, Nevada, New York, South Carolina, Utah, and Texas in 1974; Kentucky, Minnesota, Pennsylvania, and Georgia in 1975; and North Dakota in 1976 (Witt and Urrutia, 1984b: 182). According to Smith and Young (1974), the states that adopted no-fault were characterized as more innovative, urban states with more automobiles and partisan conflict in the legislature.

Although no-fault looked as if it might sweep the nation, the no-fault bandwagon stalled as quickly as it started. Trial attorneys were able to mobilize their coalitions more effectively at the state level; not a surprising fact because many state legislators are attorneys. Not a single state adopted a no-fault law after 1976. Nevada repealed its no-fault law in 1980, and several other states made modifications.

Even in states that passed no-fault laws, trial attorneys were able to gain concessions that rendered the laws ineffective. To be an effective no-fault law, the law must reduce the amount of tort litigation (See Witt and Urrutia, 1984a; 1984b; 1983; Meier, 1987a). The laws that passed varied significantly in how much litigation was restricted in return for no-fault compensation. Only three states—Michigan, New York, and Pennsylvania passed laws that greatly restricted litigation, thereby approaching a pure no-fault type of law.

Modified no-fault laws were one concession to attorneys in several states. Modified no-fault laws specify no-fault provisions up to a certain level of damages; any damages above that limit can be pursued through litigation. That is, a driver might be compensated for damages up to $10,000 on a no-fault basis; collecting greater damages would require litigation. Twelve states passed modified no-fault laws, which reserve those cases with the highest fees to the province of the trial attorneys.

Even less effective were the add-on no-fault laws; these laws—adopted in Delaware, Maryland, and Oregon—simply added no-fault coverage on top of regular automobile insurance without any restrictions on tort suits. Finally, the least effective version was optional add-on no-fault, adopted by Arkansas, South Carolina, South Dakota, Texas, and Virginia. Under this system, purchasing add-on no-fault is optional. Clearly, some forms of no-fault laws

passed were so far from a true no-fault concept with its limits on litigation
that they can be characterized as a symbolic manipulation rather than an
actual attempt to reduce litigation and the cost of automobile insurance. For
an evaluation of the effectiveness of the various types of no-fault insurance,
see Chapter 7.

No-Fault at the Federal Level

Even before the symbolic nature of many state no-fault laws was evident,
the federal government placed the issue on its agenda. No-fault was perceived
as a consumer issue, and the late 1960s and early 1970s were the height of
the consumer movement at the federal level (Nadel, 1971; Pertschuk, 1982).
The prime mover behind federal no-fault efforts was Michigan Senator Philip
Hart. In 1968, less than one year after House hearings termed the existing
automobile insurance system "unsatisfactory," Congress directed the Department of Transportation (DOT) to undertake a detailed study of the existing
insurance system (see Department of Transportation, 1971).

In 1970, while the DOT study was underway, Senator Hart held a series
of hearings and introduced several bills; no action was taken on any of them.
In 1971, Hart reintroduced his legislation. His initial proposal was broad
based. In addition to establishing a nationwide no-fault system, the bill would
guarantee insurance coverage for every licensed driver, allow group insurance policies for automobiles, require all insurance companies to publish
detailed price information, set safety standards to eliminate damage in low-
speed collisions (a bumper rule; see Meier, 1985b for a discussion of
bumper-impact regulations), and establish a nationwide set of diagnostic centers to inspect cars before consumers buy them and after they are repaired.
Such a proposal went far beyond no-fault legislation adopted by Massachusetts and supported by insurance companies. The measure was clearly a
consumer protection measure first and an insurance measure second.

At hearings, Hart's broad-based bill drew significant opposition. The
Big Three automobile manufacturers appeared to oppose bumper standards.
A large number of groups and individuals came to support the concept of no-
fault but argued that it was an area for state government action. Taking this
position was the Department of Transportation, the National Association of
Insurance Commissioners, The National Association of Insurance Agents,
the American Mutual Insurance Alliance, the National Association of Independent Insurers, and Kemper Insurance. Opposed to no-fault whether state
or federal were the American Bar Association (ABA), the American Trial
Lawyers Association (ATLA), and the National Association of Mutual Insurance Agents.[10] The only supporters of a federal law were Avis Rent-A-Car,
Royal-Globe Insurance, Consumers Union, and consumer activist Ralph

Nader. The latter two supported the entire bill although Nader contended it was too weak.

In response to the opposition generated by the broad-based bill, the proposal was slimmed down and reintroduced in 1972 as the Hart-Magnuson Bill. Warren Magnuson was chair of the Senate Commerce Committee and a sponsor of much consumer protection legislation (Nadel, 1971; Price, 1972). The Hart-Magnuson Bill focused only on no-fault; it would have required states to enact no-fault legislation containing minimum federal standards within a specified time period. If a state failed to act, a more stringent federal law would go into effect. This method of implementation, now called *partial preemption* (Reagan, 1987; Beam, 1983), was also used in environmental protection statutes and occupational safety regulation.

After hearings, the Commerce Committee reported the bill to the Senate floor. On the floor, the bill was sent to the Judiciary Committee for further study, effectively killing the legislation.[11] Similar legislation was again considered by the Commerce Committee in 1973. By 1973, the industry had become better organized although no less divisive. Eight major insurance companies that wrote more than one-third of the nation's automobile insurance met in December 1972 and agreed to press for state no-fault laws but oppose federal laws. Trial attorneys continued to oppose any no-fault bill. Support for the bill consisted of the National Committee for Effective No-Fault, which included the Consumer Federation of America (CFA), the Teamsters, the United Auto Workers (UAW), and the American Federation of Government Employees. State Farm Insurance, the nation's largest automobile insurance company, also supported the legislation. The Senate again referred the Commerce bill to the Judiciary Committee, but this time Judiciary chair James Eastland agreed to report the bill by February 15 of the following year.

1974 marked the high point of the no-fault automobile insurance effort. Not only had 20 states passed some version of no-fault automobile insurance, but the federal bill was considered on the Senate floor for the first time. After the bill was released from the Judiciary Committee, the key issue was state versus federal legislation. The pro-federal group remained similar with labor unions, consumer groups, and larger insurance companies; the opposition remained attorneys, agents, smaller insurance companies, and President Richard Nixon. After some minor amendments, the bill passed the Senate by a close vote (53-to-42) and was sent to the House for consideration. The House Subcommittee on Interstate and Foreign Commerce of the Commerce and Finance Committee completed hearings, but chair John E. Moss was unable to get a quorum of members to attend a mark-up meeting. The result was that the bill died again.

In 1975, the Senate waited for the House to take action rather than passing another bill that would be lost in a procedural morass. Because the House Commerce Committee was unable to get to the no-fault bill, no action was taken. By 1976, changes in the U. S. Senate with regard to consumer issues had begun to take place. Newly elected members of the Commerce committees were less activist on consumer issues (Pertschuk, 1982; Weingast and Moran, 1983). Although most students of consumer protection do not mark the end of the contemporary consumer movement until 1978 (see Pertschuk, 1982) with the defeat of the Agency for Consumer Advocacy, the decline in support was evident in no-fault by 1976. The Senate voted 49-to-46 on March 31, 1976, to send the no-fault bill back to committee, thereby effectively killing the legislation.

No-fault legislation was allowed one last hurrah in 1978. In 1977, no-fault was endorsed by President Jimmy Carter; both Presidents Ford and Nixon opposed the bill. By 1978, the symbolic nature of many state no-fault laws was evident; the Department of Transportation reported that only Michigan's law clearly met the standards. Coalitions supporting and opposing the bill remained essentially the same. In the House Subcommittee on Interstate and Foreign Commerce, the no-fault bill was amended to bar insurance companies from basing rates on age, sex, or geographic distinctions (see the following section on unisex insurance). The amendment was perceived as a "killer" amendment designed to alienate no-fault supporters. The House Commerce Committee rejected a motion to report the bill to the floor. This marked the last serious consideration of no-fault insurance laws by the federal government.

The Unisex Issue

Insurance companies have been likened to an automobile with four passengers: the president is steering, the sales staff has its foot on the gas, the underwriting staff has its foot on the brake, and the actuary is looking out the back window and giving directions. The actuarial basis of insurance involves establishing classes of different risks and pricing insurance for those classes based on the risk involved. Sex is one factor that has been found to be associated with differing levels of risk. As a result, women pay less for life insurance, more for annuities, less for automobile insurance, and more for health and disability insurance. The use of sex as a factor in assigning insurance risks is so ingrained in the industry that any challenge to what is perceived as a part of the scientific core of underwriting will be strongly opposed.[12]

Questions concerning the appropriateness of sex-based insurance classifications grew quite naturally out of the women's movement. Advocates of unisex rating in insurance had a multitude of forums to advocate their case. Legislation could be passed to ban sex segregated rating practices. Current practices could be challenged in courts as violations of civil rights law. Administrative action by insurance commissioners could prohibit sex-based rating practices.

LEGISLATIVE ACTION

Legislative attempts to eliminate sex-based insurance rating have met with mixed success. Proposals to eliminate sex biases in insurance developed long after equal rights had become a controversial issue so that insurance companies had a host of allies in their fight against unisex legislation. At the federal level, proponents of unisex legislation have been unable to get a favorable bill reported out of committee. At issue was what the costs of compliance would be and who would benefit from the passage of the act. While proponents (see Cicero, 1985: 211) countered that the bill would result in lower overall costs to women, a GAO (1984: 4) study was unable to establish a precise estimate of how costs would be redistributed. It did estimate that the *topping up provision* (whereby benefits would be increased to equal those of the "higher" sex) would require increased reserves of $7.7 to $15.1 billion, and administrative compliance costs would be $1.3 billion (GAO, 1984: 3, 5).

The initial Nondiscrimination in Insurance Act had major redistributive aspects, which would have applied both to group and individual insurance contracts. Health plans would have been required to provide both maternity and abortion coverage. All auto and health plans would have to comply with unisex provisions at renewal, and all pension benefits would have to be paid without regard to sex even if previous contributions were based on sex.

The insurance industry conducted a multimillion dollar campaign against this act including television advertisements warning of higher insurance premiums. Insurance companies were able to form a coalition with conservative legislators in the House of Representatives. This coalition amended the act in committee to (1) apply only to individual insurance programs not group programs, (2) require health plans with abortion benefits to be priced higher, (3) make pregnancy coverage optional in individual health plans, and (4) allow pensions to pay unequal benefits after the act passed if the contributions made were unequal. These amendments were perceived by proponents as gutting the bill, and women's groups announced that future efforts would be at the state level.[13]

124   The Political Economy of Regulation

State level efforts have produced a mixed pattern. Four states—Hawaii, Massachusetts, Michigan, and North Carolina—have passed legislation banning the use of gender-based automobile insurance rates (Bennett, 1986: 24). Of the lines of insurance involved, automobile insurance might be the least controversial in that sex is not a particularly good predictor (see Cicero, 1985: 260, note 236; but see GAO, 1984: 21), most automobile insurance for adults is already written on a unisex basis (GAO, 1984: 19), and a reasonably inexpensive substitute, mileage driven, exists. In addition, gender-based rates are normally only used for younger drivers. Montana did pass a sweeping unisex law in 1984, but eight other states rejected such laws (Fenske, 1985: 18). The Montana law prohibited gender-based rates in all lines of insurance. Although Montana is a small state, the precedent was perceived of as so dangerous that the insurance industry made its repeal a legislative priority (Fenske, 1985: 18). Bills to repeal the law in 1985 failed, and Montana's unisex law went into effect October 1, 1986. Except for equalization of auto insurance rates for those younger than age 25, little changed in Montana (Bennett, 1986: 108).

COURT CHALLENGES

The boom area of activity for gender-based insurance rates has been state and federal courts. Two separate areas have been litigated before the U. S. Supreme Court—pregnancy benefits and pensions. Pregnancy benefits in disability insurance or health insurance increase insurance costs, so some companies seek to reduce costs by excluding pregnancy from coverage. Pensions are a form of protection from old age; thus, they are similar to annuities offered by insurance companies. In fact, many pension plans are operated by insurance companies. Although the Supreme Court has been consistent within each of these areas, the two sets of precedents are conflicting.

Pregnancy Benefits. In *Geduldig v. Aiello* [417 U. S. 484 (1974)], women challenged the exlusion of pregnancy from California's disability insurance system contending that the exclusion invidiously discriminated against women in violation of the equal protection clause of the U. S. Constitution (Cicero, 1985: 220). They contended that men were compensated for all disabilities, but women were not. The Supreme Court held that the exclusion of pregnancy benefits was a legislative choice that did not violate equal protection. As long as the distinction made by the state was rationally supportable, the Supreme Court would not intervene.

In *General Electric v. Gilbert* [429 U. S. 125 (1976)] the same issue was raised, but this time plaintiffs contended that the exclusion was a violation of Title VII of the Civil Rights Act of 1964 as amended. The Court again applied a sexually neutral interpretation to the action contending that women were protected from all the risks from which men were protected.[14] The Court's position on this issue was effectively reversed by Congress in 1982 when it passed the Pregnancy Discrimination Act. This act equalized disability insurance costs related to pregnancy for all workers in organizations covered by Title VII.

Pensions. Pensions are often funded by purchasing annuity contracts from insurance companies. Because women historically live longer than men, they will collect benefits for a longer period of time. As a result, insurance companies have either paid out lower benefits to women if premiums are equal or have increased premiums if monthly benefit levels must remain equal. In *Los Angeles Department of Water and Power v. Manhart* [435 U. S. 702 (1978)], female employees were required to make larger contributions to the pension fund than were males. The Supreme Court accepted the premise that women live longer than men, but it argued that no assurance was found that any individual women working for the department would fit the generalization concerning women.[15] The Court held that predicting individual risks based on the use of group classifications was a violation of Title VII of the Civil Rights Act. The Court expressly tried to narrow its decision; it only prohibited unequal contribution schedules and stated that they did not intend "to revolutionize the insurance and pension industries" (435 U. S. at 717). The Court also suggested that nothing would prevent an employer from setting aside equal pension amounts and letting employers purchase whatever annuity protection they could on the open market.[16]

In *Arizona v. Norris* [103 S. Ct. 3492 (1983)], the Supreme Court was presented with a challenge to a pension plan that required equal contributions but paid lower monthly benefits to women than men. Although this was analogous to the hypothetical example cited in *Manhart,* the Supreme Court held that unequal benefits also violate Title VII and the Equal Pay Act (Genthner, 1985: 302). The actuarial benefits of gender-based rating had to yield to the social goals embodied within the statutes.[17] The decision affected only pension benefits earned after the Court's decision.

The extent to which the dicta in *Arizona v. Norris* can be applied to other areas of insurance is unclear. In both *Norris* and *Manhart,* insurance was linked to the workplace so that laws requiring equal pay could be brought to play. Attacks on other gender-based insurance ratings such as private life insurance contracts, automobile insurance, and private health insurance will be more difficult. Such litigation is underway. The National Organization of Women (NOW) filed a class-action suit against Mutual of Omaha in Washington D.C. for discrimination against women in individual health and disability insurance policies (Fenske, 1985: 18). The suit was dismissed by the court in October 1985; a second suit filed against Metropolitan Life in New York was dismissed in mid 1987. Several similar suits are still pending.

ADMINISTRATIVE ACTION

An interesting twist on gender-based classifications has occurred by administrative action in Pennsylvania. In 1980, a young, unmarried male brought a class-action suit challenging automobile insurance rates of Harleysville Mutual Insurance Company as sexually discriminatory. The claim was brought under the equal protection clause of the Fourteenth Amendment to the U. S. Constitution and the Pennsylvania Equal Rights Amendment. In *Murphy v. Harleysville Mutual Insurance* [282 Pa Super 144, 422 A2d 1097 (1980)] the Pennsylvania Supreme Court held that "state action" was required to apply either of these constitutional provisions, and that purely private actions were not affected (Milbourne, 1985: 269).[18] Murphy's claim was rejected.

The Pennsylvania Insurance Commissioner then noted that he was entitled to consider all relevant factors in setting insurance rates. Noting the Pennsylvania Equal Rights Amendment was an expression of public policy, the Commissioner announced that he would approve no gender-based rates because they would be contrary to public policy. The Commissioner's action was immediately challenged in court by an insurance company. In *Hartford Accident and Indemnity v. Insurance Commissioner* [482 A2d 542 (Pa 1984)], the Pennsylvania Supreme Court upheld this action. The ratemaking power of the Commissioner to set rates that were "not excessive, inadequate or unfairly discriminatory" gave the Commissioner power to consider factors other than actuarial soundness (Milbourne, 1985: 273n). After failing in court, the insurance industry lobbied the Pennsylvania legislature to prohibit unisex rating. In late 1986, the Pennsylvania legislature passed such a ban over the Governor's veto. This ban was then challenged in court by women's groups as unconstitutional.

The Pennsylvania case raises an interesting scenario. In virtually every state that regulates insurance rates, the statute requires that the rates shall be "not excessive, inadequate, or unfairly discriminatory." If the logic of the Pennsylvania Supreme Court is correct, then approximately two-thirds of the insurance commissioners have the power to mandate unisex insurance rates under their price regulation statute. Such a scenario is unlikely, however, because most insurance commissioners are fairly conservative when making policy that affects the actuarial base of insurance companies.

Federal Taxes

Perhaps the insurance industry's most salient federal concern is taxes. The concern is twofold. First, insurance companies are corporations and are subject to federal corporate income taxes. Second, employees can receive insurance as part of their total compensation packages and, in the process, avoid paying taxes on these fringe benefits. Both issues have been considered by Congress in recent years as efforts to reduce the size of the federal deficit have become paramount. Both merit further discussion.

CORPORATE INCOME TAX

In one sense, insurance companies are similar to other corporations: they pay the same federal corporate income taxes that other corporations do. In another sense, insurance companies have clear tax advantages. Insurance companies operate under a system of accounting rules adopted by NAIC and accepted by the federal government in 1921. Unlike other accounting systems, the NAIC insurance accounting system allows certain costs to be deducted immediately such as reserves to satisfy future claims and expenses related to the sale of insurance. The normal business practice is to spread such costs over a period of time. At the same time, income is prorated over the length of the policy. The net result of such accounting practices understates taxable income (GAO, 1985b: 11).

In 1921, the federal government adopted the industry's distinction between life insurance companies and property and casualty insurance companies. Life insurance companies were to be taxed on income from investments only (Garfin, 1982: 1). Profits for life insurance companies are difficult to determine on a yearly basis because losses will not be paid until many years in the future. Property and casualty companies were taxed on their profits and losses from underwriting. Because many property and casualty policies also have payoffs several years into the future (especially if occurrence policies are written), property and casualty companies are allowed to set aside reserves and deduct them from their taxable incomes. The liberal deduction policies mean that for most years property and casualty companies report net losses or small profits.

Life Insurance. Life insurance company taxation changed in 1959 when members of Congress perceived that life insurance companies were not paying their fair share of taxes and that the returns from this tax were highly variable because payments fluctuated with investment income. A compromise among Congress, the Treasury Department, and the life insurance industry resulted in the Life Insurance Company Income Tax Act of 1959. This act attempted to raise about $500 million in revenue for fiscal year 1960, tax life insurance companies on total net income at corporate rates, and maintain a proper tax balance between stock and mutual companies (Garfin, 1982: 1).

The stock versus mutual distinction is important from the government's perspective because mutuals have far more options to avoid federal taxes.

Because mutuals are technically owned by the policyholders, a dividend paid to a policyholder is not the same as a dividend paid to a stockholder. The mutual dividend is a mixture of (1) a reduction in the premium, (2) interest income to the policyholder, (3) dividend income to the policyholder as a result of his or her ownership in the company, (4) repayment of part of the principal invested in the company, and (5) a capital gain on the amount invested in the ownership share (Aaron, 1983: 24). Unfortunately, no precise way to allocate a dividend among these five categories exists. To avoid a distinct preference for mutual companies, therefore, the 1959 law has different rules for deducting dividends for stock and mutual companies.

Calculation of a life insurance company's taxable income under this law was extremely complex. First, *phase 1 income* is calculated, which is essentially investment income. Next, *phase 2 income* is calculated, which is the gain from operations before dividends and special deductions. Income tax is paid on the smaller of the two amounts (Garfin, 1982: 2).

Under the 1959 law, life insurance companies paid the bulk of the taxes paid by insurance companies. In any given year, life insurance companies pay approximately 70 percent of the taxes paid by all insurance companies (see Table 6–1). In 1982, for example, life insurance companies paid $1,189 million in taxes compared to $441 million for nonlife companies. The tax difference results even though the premium income of life and property and casualty companies was relatively equal (in 1985 life premiums were $156 billion and property and casualty premiums were $144 billion).

Because life insurance companies are heavy investors in government and corporate bonds, their investment incomes greatly increased as interest rates rose in the late 1970s. Taxable income also increased (Aaron, 1983: 19). The result was that life insurance companies felt that they were paying more than their fair share of taxes. In 1960, under the new law, life insurance companies paid $529 million in federal taxes or 2.4 percent of all corporate income taxes. By 1978, they paid $2,772 million or 4.3 percent of all corporate taxes (see Table 6–2).

Because insurance is an industry where technical nuances are examined continually, any loophole that exists in an insurance tax law will be found sooner or later. A loophole was found in section 820 of the Internal Revenue Code that made a special provision for coinsurance. This section was adopted to avoid tax problems with reinsurance. Reinsurance is a process whereby one insurance company reinsures part of its risk with another insurance company. To avoid taxing reinsurance proceeds twice, once as investment income to one company and once as operating income to the other company, Section

Table 6-1
Insurance Taxes for Selected Years

Year	Tax (millions)	Percent Paid by Life Companies
1982	$1,630	72.9
1981	1,859	65.4
1980	2,879	72.9
1979	3,956	75.2
1978	4,091	67.7
1977	3,238	59.6
1975	1,861	69.9
1961	746	77.2
1960	702	75.3
1958	583	78.0

Source: IRS, *Statistics of Income: Corporate Income Tax Returns,* annual.

Table 6-2
Life Insurance Taxes as a Percentage of All Corporate Taxes

Year	Taxes (millions)	Life Percent of All	Industry Percent of All
1982	$1,189	2.5	3.4
1981	1,217	2.0	3.1
1980	2,101	3.3	4.5
1979	2,978	4.5	6.0
1978	2,772	4.3	6.3
1977	2,263	4.0	5.7
1975	1,783	4.4	4.6
1961	576	2.6	3.3
1960	529	2.4	3.2
1958	455	2.4	3.1

Source: IRS, *Statistics of Income: Corporate Income Tax Returns,* annual.

820 exempted the investment income from reinsurance from taxation. In 1978, an insurance company discovered that if it had a large phase 1 income it could reinsure some policies with a company with negative phase 2 income, the result would be a reduction in taxes for the first firm and no increase in taxes for the second firm (Garfin, 1982: 7). This loophole, known as Modco 820 for modified coinsurance 820, was remarkably successful in reducing the tax liability of life insurance companies. Income taxes paid by life insurance companies dropped from $2,978 million in 1979 to $1,189 million in 1982. Given an increase in premiums and investment returns, Aaron (1983: 1) estimates that this loophole saved the life insurance industry $2 billion per year in taxes.

With federal government budget deficits exceeding $200 billion per year in the 1980s, a $2 billion loophole was a prime target when Congress raised taxes in 1982. The Tax Equity and Fiscal Responsibility Act of 1982 (TEFRA) closed the loophole but set 1984 as the effective date for closing (GAO, 1985c: 1; Aaron, 1983: 1). This temporary closure with a delayed effective date permitted the life insurance industry to negotiate the details of the tax increase with Congress. Some evidence exists that Congress desired such negotiation because the tax code for insurance companies is so complex that often experts cannot tell how a change in the law will affect revenues. The Deficit Reduction Act of 1984 reflected the negotiated compromise. Life insurance companies would be taxed at the normal corporate rate (Section 820 was closed), but they would be allowed to deduct 20 percent of their income from insurance operations; small insurance companies with taxable incomes of less than $3 million were allowed to deduct 60 percent of their incomes (Harman, 1985: 63). The different perceptions of this law are illustrated in that the GAO (1985c) felt the law reduced taxes by $1.4 billion annually (compared to pre-loophole rates) while the insurance industry claimed it was a $3.1 billion increase (Fenske, 1985: 16). In 1985, life insurance companies paid $4.1 billion in federal income taxes (ACLI, 1986: 7).

Property and Casualty Insurance. After resolving the tax issue with regard to life insurance companies, Congress turned to the property and casualty industry. Again, the motivation was to increase taxes in response to the growing federal deficit. The agenda was set with a report from the GAO (1985b) that examined the tax laws governing the property and casualty insurance industry. The GAO had three specific suggestions. First, the deduction of loss reserves was questioned. The GAO noted that loss reserves serve a valid insurance function by providing funds for future payment of losses but that loss reserves earned income while they were held in reserve. This income, the GAO felt, was in excess of needed reserves and should be taxed. The specific mechanism was to require insurance companies to discount reserves by the gain in investment income. The GAO estimated that a 5 percent discount rate would have produced $485 million in tax revenues (GAO, 1985b: 19).

Second, GAO again challenged the NAIC accounting procedures that allowed deducting the costs of selling a policy immediately rather than prorating these costs over the term of the policy. Premium income was counted on a prorated basis so that income and expenses did not match. GAO (1985b: 24) estimated that these accounting rules reduced tax revenues by $164 million in 1982.

Third, GAO raised questions about the protection against loss (PAL) accounts of mutual insurance companies. Because mutuals do not have access to the capital markets as stock companies do, they cannot raise crucially needed capital when faced with a serious underwriting loss. Mutuals, therefore, are allowed to maintain additional reserves in a PAL account; such reserves are not taxed; no estimate was made of the revenue loss from PAL accounts (GAO, 1985b: 26–7). The GAO estimated that the property and casualty insurance companies had profits of approximately $75 billion from 1975 to 1984 but paid a negative $125 million in federal taxes.

The property and casualty industry's reaction was vehement. The industry submitted 92 pages of responses to the GAO report, challenging GAO's accounting and presenting the argument that the property and casualty industry, at large, lost money; therefore, it could not afford to pay additional taxes (van Aartrijk, 1985: 24).

To keep the pressure on the insurance industry, Congressman Fortney "Pete" Stark requested a second GAO report to cost out various methods of increasing the tax on property and casualty companies. GAO costed out five tax proposals, including minimum taxes on net income and premium taxes; when the tax figures for the 20 largest property and casualty companies were presented, only four of those companies had paid any federal income tax in 1984 (GAO, 1985a: chart 21). To put further pressure on property and casualty companies, Stark inserted a 20 percent tax on net income for property and casualty companies starting in 1988 in the 1985 House version of the tax reform bill. Such a tax was estimated to raise $4.8 billion. Stark, a subcommittee chair in the House Ways and Means Committee, was perceived as taking this action to force the property and casualty companies to negotiate a tax increase compromise. The question was not *if* property and casualty companies would pay additional taxes but *how much* they would pay.

INDIVIDUAL INCOME TAXES

The relationship of insurance benefits to individual income taxes was raised by President Reagan in his tax simplification effort in 1985. The President proposed that the U. S. tax system be simplified by eliminating deductions and credits and having only three tax categories. To simplify taxes in this manner requires a major reduction in tax deductions. The Office of Management and Budget (OMB) responded with a list of the loopholes and how much each loophole cost the federal government. Four major loopholes were related to the insurance industry: employer deductions for medical insurance, employer deductions for life insurance, employer deductions for accident and disability insurance, and the inside cash build-up of life insurance policies. The first three are fringe benefits and can be discussed as a single item.

Insurance is a popular fringe benefit for both employers and employees.

In 1920, the IRS ruled that less than $50,000 of group term life insurance provided by an employer was not income subject to taxation (Johnson, 1968: 383; MacAvoy, 1977: 73; Hira and Sivertsen, 1986: 66). Similar rules apply to health and accident insurance (Dickerson, 1968: 674). Insurance is preferable to wages from an employee's standpoint because wages will be taxed but the insurance will not. From an employer's standpoint, both wages and insurance are business deductions but with wages the employer must also make social security contributions. OMB (1985: G-43-47) has estimated that the deduction for health insurance cost the federal government $23.7 billion in lost revenues in 1986. Group life insurance deductions cost $2.22 billion, and accident and disability insurance deductions cost $130 million.

The second individual income tax issue related to insurance is taxing the inside build-up of life insurance. Life insurance can be divided into two parts—insurance and savings. The amount of money necessary to pay death benefits and cover the insurance company's operating expenses is called the *pure premium*. The pure premium is close to the price charged for term life insurance. Whole life insurance, in contrast, charges a premium in excess of the pure premium; and this difference is invested or "saved" for the policyholder. The price of whole life insurance is higher in the earlier years of a policy than the corresponding price of term insurance but lower in later years when some portion of the savings go to pay the pure premium. This savings portion of an insurance policy is also called the inside build-up.

The tax consequences of the inside build-up of an insurance policy were minor when whole life was the main product of the life insurance industry. The savings rate was always conservative so that the savings would equal the paid-up value of the insurance at the end of the payment period. Often, life insurance savings' interest rates were as low as two or three percent when more attractive rates could have been attained in passbook savings accounts. As inflation and interest rates approached and exceeded double digits, the attractiveness of whole life insurance declined because it was perceived as a bad investment.[19]

This situation changed in 1979 when E. F. Hutton Life, a subsidiary of the brokerage firm, invented the universal life policy, which pays market interest rates on the savings portion of life insurance. The policyholder can increase his or her contributions to the life insurance policy and either increase the value of the insurance or simply add to the savings. Increases in the savings portion of the life insurance are tax free unless the policyholder withdraws them. Universal life, therefore, combines term insurance with a money market fund that is not taxed. If the policyholder needs funds, he or she can borrow against the cash value of the universal life policy. Any interest paid in this borrowing is tax deductible. By saving via life insurance, the policyholder avoids the taxes ordinarily paid when saving with a bank or a brokerage firm.

Universal life became a major insurance marketing innovation. By 1985, 6.8 million universal life policies were in force with a total face value of $563.6 billion. This figure represents 9.1 percent of the total life insurance in force in the United States (ACLI, 1986: 29). OMB (1985: G–43) estimated that the failure to tax the inside cash build-up of life insurance resulted in a $3.655 billion loss in federal tax revenue.

The initial proposal for tax reform came from the Treasury Department under the direction of President Ronald Reagan who made tax reform the priority of his second term. The initial proposal (called Treasury I) advocated taxing the inside build-up of life insurance and taxing all employer-paid insurance as income. The battle over tax reform involves literally hundreds of interests; it pits Congress against the President; state governments against the federal government; labor against business; and industry against industry. The insurance industry is only one actor among many (Clark, 1986a: 928), but it lost no time in mobilizing to fight the proposed taxes. In each case, the industry had allies. The life insurance companies could count on the advocates of reducing taxes on savings in their battle over the inside cash build-up. The life and health companies could join with organized labor who strongly favored not taxing fringe benefits.

On the deductibility of employer-paid insurance, the industry was able to strike a blow before the proposals were even considered by Congress. Senator Robert Packwood, chair of the Senate Finance Committee, was persuaded to lobby the Treasury Department to delete this proposal. Packwood was successful; the second administration proposal (called Treasury II) proposed taxing just the first $10 per month in health care benefits for individuals and the first $25 for families (Cohen, 1985a: 2361).

With the introduction of Treasury II, the focus of tax reform shifted to the House. The Senate was reluctant to consider a controversial issue like tax reform;[20] Representative Daniel Rostenkowski, the chair of the House Ways and Means Committee, was willing to take on the issue, allegedly to demonstrate his leadership in hopes of a possible bid to be Speaker (Cohen, 1985a: 2357). Rostenkowski also wanted to place political pressure on the Republican Senate for the 1986 midterm election.

In the Ways and Means Committee, the insurance industry won almost everything that it sought. The inside build-up provisions were deleted in response to industry pressure. Organized labor strongly opposed taxing fringe benefits so those provisions were also deleted from the Ways and Means bill (Cohen, 1985b: 2727). To make up for the revenue lost by deleting these and other items, the Democratic-controlled committee increased the taxes on corporations (including Pete Stark's minimum tax on property and casualty companies). The special 20 percent deduction for life insurance companies passed in 1984 was repealed. The Ways and Means proposal passed the House December 17, 1985.

By mid-1986, issues concerning taxation of insurance were no longer part of the discussion. The Republican alternative discussed in the Senate Finance Committee proposed an increase in excise taxes in place of the increased corporate income tax advocated by the House. The conflict now was between Democrats and Republicans with businesses lined up on both sides of the issue (Clark, 1986b: 1059–1060). The individual income tax side of insurance had effectively avoided any changes.

The final version of the tax bill approved by the House-Senate Conference Committee and signed by President Reagan in October 1986 contained some minor changes that increased the previously negotiated tax liability for property and casualty companies. Property and casualty companies were unable to get favorable transition rules similar to other industries (for example, the steel industry), and actually lost some ground in the final version. Twenty percent of any increase in unearned premium reserves was included as taxable income, loss reserves had to be discounted, PAL accounts were restricted, and a 15 percent tax was placed on all tax exempt income earned after August 7, 1986. The five-year tax increase for property and casualty companies was estimated between $7.4 and $7.5 billion. The bottom line was that insurance fringe benefits would not be taxed, but insurance company income would.

A Theoretical Recapitulation

The five federal issues of insurance regulation illustrate the political economy of insurance when issues are salient. In each case, the industry was generally divided, or only part of the industry was interested in the policy. As a result, federal issues are issues where political elites have greater influence.

Mail-order insurance is an issue that falls through the cracks in state regulation because mail-order companies operate in interstate commerce. Mail-order insurance is an issue that divides the industry; mail-order companies prefer as little regulation as possible, while traditional companies oppose these low-cost competitors. Bureaucratic values and their role in regulation is well illustrated by this issue. The FTC's interest in the area is a reflection of how the FTC defines its sphere of influence; the FTC considers interstate sales and deceptive advertising as part of its policy domain regardless of the industry involved. The FTC's past activism served as a catalyst to state action because insurance regulators feared the federal government's entry into insurance regulation. Even though state regulators do not have the tools to combat interstate mail-order insurance, they prefer to avoid federal assistance. Political elites at the federal level have played both a stimulus role and a resolution role. Congressional hearings stimulated the FTC to take action against Travelers in the 1950s, and most mail-order disputes are usually resolved by the courts.

Federal flood insurance is an issue area with high salience as a result of natural disasters. Again, it is an issue where political elites dominate. Flood insurance programs received presidential endorsements from Truman, Eisenhower, and Johnson before Congress eventually passed a law. Congressional elites took the initiative in amending the federal flood law in 1969 and again in 1973 to fix problems in the initial program. Bureaucratic values are also involved. Desires for program expansion were instrumental in HUD initially recommending a flood insurance program; Robert Hunter played a key role in pushing private insurance companies out of the program in the 1970s. Federal flood insurance is an area where the insurance industry clearly does not dominate the policy process. Although the industry was active in lobbying for a program and wants to participate in the program, it was booted out of the program by Hunter and is now only a minor participant.

No-fault automobile insurance is an issue area of consumer activism. In this case, consumers united with a faction of the insurance industry, the large automobile direct writers, to support a federal no-fault law. Industry was again split with mutual companies and agents opposing federal action. Such a division allowed political elites to play a key but unsuccessful role. Senators Philip Hart and Warren Magnuson placed the issue on the policy agenda; after both men left the Senate, the issue died, as did many other consumer issues of the time.

Unisex insurance rating is an issue area dominated by the courts. Groups outside the insurance area (for example, women's groups) were seeking to expand the impact of anti-sex discrimination laws, in effect to draw insurance into a different policy arena. Such action was possible, in part, because Congress had passed legislation making employment discrimination illegal. In addition, Congress effectively overruled the Supreme Court's Decision regarding pregnancy benefits with the Pregnancy Discrimination Act. Even regulatory bureaucrats played an active role; the Pennsylvania Insurance Commissioner announced a policy of not approving gender-based insurance rates, which was subsequently overturned by the state legislature. In unisex insurance issues, the insurance industry is seeing the scope of the conflict expanded to areas that are not the industry's forte. This unfamiliarity might explain its inappropriate techniques. Given that salient issues are less likely to be resolved in favor of insurance companies' interests, using an ad campaign to warn the public of the dangers of unisex insurance rates does not appear to be an effective technique unless the industry feels it has greater influence among federal political elites.

Federal taxation of insurance companies and insurance benefits reveals a policy arena where insurance companies are only one of hundreds of interests. Huge federal deficits raised tax reform to a redistributive policy battle between Democrats and Republicans. In such a situation, the insurance industry can win only with strong allies. Fringe benefits were spared greater taxation in part because the industry had allies among labor unions and businesses. In the area of increased taxes on insurance companies, the industry lost. The interesting aspect of the tax issue is the way political elites finessed the complexity problem. Rather than trying to understand the complexities of insurance tax accounting, Congress twice enacted simple and direct taxes and challenged the industry to negotiate a different policy. Such a tactic forces insurance companies to provide expertise to policymakers or suffer under what they perceive is an unfair tax.

Chapter 7

An Empirical Examination of State Insurance Regulation

Chapter 2 presented a regulatory theory that was used as the general framework to examine federal issues in insurance regulation and the historical development of state insurance regulation. This chapter tests additional portions of that regulatory theory with a 50-state analysis of current insurance regulatory policies. Policy will be viewed as a function of the resources of four actors—insurance industry groups, consumer groups, regulatory bureaucrats, and political elites. Each set of actors is assumed to have policy goals. Industry groups will favor regulation that benefits the industry and oppose regulation that imposes costs on it. Consumer groups will favor lower prices and stringent regulation of the insurance industry. Regulatory bureaucrats will favor increases in regulatory authority and regulation that restricts industry discretion. Political elites will favor regulatory policies consistent with the policy values that they hold; that is, they may favor or oppose regulation depending on their policy values. The ability of each group to attain their policy ends is a function of the resources that they can convert into political influence.

This chapter first operationalizes a set of variables that measure the resources that the four actors possess. These operationally defined variables are then used to test the theory of regulation in several state-level insurance policy areas. Included are analyses of regulatory stringency, insurance company premium taxes, insurance prices, the results of the no-fault automobile insurance experiment, and other state policy restrictions on insurance companies. The tests proceed in two steps. First, the policy is examined as a product of industry forces only, a pure Stigler (1971) view of regulation. Second, the policy is reexamined with a multi-interest model using indicators of all four regulatory policy participants.

Industry

Previous efforts to examine the relationship of industry pressures to regulatory policy outputs have been marred by treating industry as a monolithic group. Both the historical examination of state regulatory policy (Chapters 4 and 5) and the analysis of federal insurance issues (Chapter 6) revealed that the insurance industry often had divided policy goals. This chapter does not assume that the insurance industry has monolithic goals but rather will operationalize insurance industry resources in a way to permit some analytic conclusions about the various interests within the industry.

According to George Stigler (1971), a key industry resource in regulatory battles is size (see also Rourke, 1984). A large industry has access to important potential political resources, such as campaign contributions and potential votes. In addition, a large industry is more likely to be important to the state's economic base; this economic dependence permits an insurance company to threaten to leave the state if certain policies are not enacted.[1] Policymakers in such a state may see an industry as a resource to be protected rather than as an industry to be regulated. Two measures of size are used— financial and employment. The financial size of the insurance industry will be measured by the industry's per capita premium income.[2] This figure omits investment income because insurance companies do not allocate investment income across states; that is, insurance companies account for investment income only in the aggregate not on a state-by-state basis. The employment measure of insurance will be the number of people employed in the insurance industry per 100,000 state population.[3]

Within the insurance industry, small companies must be distinguished from larger companies. In other areas of regulation, regulatory policy has had a differential impact on different size firms (see Pashigian, 1983; Meier, 1987b). Large insurance companies have the necessary resources to act independently from the rest of the industry. They need not rely on rate bureaus to determine the rates they will charge. They also have sufficient resources to take political action independent from the industry trade associations. One measure of large firm dominance is the three-firm concentration ratio—the percentage of the insurance market that is controlled by the largest three firms.[4] A second indicator of large firm interests is the proportion of the insurance market held by direct writers. Because direct writers have lower overhead costs (see Joskow, 1973; Ippolito, 1979) and are less inclined to participate in industry cartels, they are often a force for greater competition in the industry.[5]

The third major segment of the industry is the agents. Conflict between agents and insurance companies dates back at least 130 years. In general, insurance agents oppose policies aimed at encouraging greater competition.

Their major asset in this effort, other than substantial political resources, is the legal recognition that clients are the property of the agents not the insurance companies. Two measures of agents' resources are used—the number of members in the Independent Insurance Agents of America (IIAA) per 100,000 state population and the number of chartered underwriters per 100,000 people. The IIAA is the major professional association for independent insurance agents. The underwriters' measure is the sum of the members of the Chartered Property and Casualty Underwriters (CPCU) and the Chartered Life Underwriters (CLU).[6]

With slight adjustments, these six variables are used in the initial industry analysis of insurance regulation. Whenever a single line of the insurance industry is examined, adjustments are made to convert the measure to that line. For example, when the automobile insurance industry is assessed, the financial resources measures, the three-firm concentration ratio, and the direct writers measure are for the automobile insurance portion of the industry. In this case, only the CPCU measure of chartered underwriters is used.

Potential Consumer Groups

Measuring the resources of consumer groups is more difficult than it is for industry groups. Consumer groups tend to be *ad hoc* forming for one issue and disbanding afterward. For groups interested in insurance, many are organized in one state but not in others (Miles and Bhambri, 1983). The one national organization, NICO, can best be described as the effort of a single individual rather than the concerted effort of thousands of individual members. In combination, these facts mean that a single good measure of consumer group activities does not exist.

Two surrogate measures of consumer resources in insurance politics are used. These are not direct measures of consumer activities but rather measures of the consumer orientation of the state. This variable is termed *potential consumer groups*. The first is a multistate measure of consumer group members that combines the membership totals for Consumers Union and Common Cause. Consumers Union membership rolls include individuals interested in consumer issues, but Consumers Union is not an active lobby organization.[7] Common Cause is not technically a consumer group, but it supports some consumer issues and recruits the same type of people that most consumer groups do—middle-class, urban, and well-educated people (Nadel, 1971; Sigelman and Smith, 1980). As an illustration of common membership patterns, the per capita state membership for these two groups is strongly correlated ($r = .78$). The indicator used in this study is the combined per capita membership of both groups.[8] Using this indicator does not imply that these particular groups are active in insurance policy; merely that large memberships in these groups are likely to exist in states that either produce more consumer activists who participate in salient insurance issues or have political elites more receptive to consumer issues.[9] The measure has been used successfully to predict state policies in other areas of consumer protection (Meier, 1987b).[10]

The membership variables tap common attitudes that relate to consumerism. Interest groups are more than common attitudes; however, there must be some contact (Truman, 1951). The best measure of contact is probably urbanism; Stigler (1971) used urbanism as a contact measure for producer groups; Miles and Bhambri (1983) found that consumer activism by insurance commissioners was highly correlated with urbanism.[11] The percentage of persons living in urban areas, therefore, is used as a measure of consumer contact.[12]

Bureaucratic Resources

Bureaucracies should have greater influence on public policy when public policies are complex. Complex policies permit the bureaucracy to use its specialized skills to resolve policy problems. The actual position taken by the bureaucracy on any issue, however, will depend on the values held by the career bureaucrats.

The key to bureaucratic knowledge is the ability to specialize, an ability that increases as the organization becomes larger (Berry, 1984). To measure the size of the regulatory bureaucracy, a composite measure was constructed from the insurance department's budget, the total number of employees, the total number of examiners, and the salary paid to the insurance commissioner. The specific indicator was a factor score combining these four variables.[13]

Bureaucratic values should also affect public policy (Berry, 1984; Meier and Nigro, 1976). The best way to assess the values of insurance regulators is to survey all 50 insurance departments, not a particularly feasible option. Assuming that an insurance department's policy decisions reflect the values held by its bureaucrats, a surrogate measure was constructed. The National Association of Insurance Commissioners has recommended a series of model laws and regulations; many deal with consumer protection issues in insurance. Sixteen such model laws and regulations were identified, and a measure of department consumer orientation was created by giving the department credit if it adopted these models either by law or administrative regulation.[14] This measure recognizes that most insurance laws passed by legislatures are passed at the recommendation of the state insurance department.

Political Elites

Public policy should reflect the policy values held by political elites who participate in the process (Mazmanian and Sabatier, 1980; Hofferbert, 1969). In regulatory theory, the key distinction is between policies that benefit the industry and those that benefit others such as consumers (Sabatier, 1977). If the consumer protection values of state legislatures could be measured, then these values should be positively correlated with state insurance policies that benefit consumers.[15] To construct such a measure, an assumption was made that a political party within a state holds reasonably consistent policy values over time (Downs, 1957). Such an assumption is not unrealistic because political parties develop positions over several elections and need to maintain some consistency to retain loyal supporters.

Using this assumption, the Consumer Federation of America (CFA) ratings of federal legislators were averaged for both the Republican and Democratic delegations for each state (both the House and the Senate for 1982 and 1983). Next, the party composition of each house of the state legislature as well as the governor's office was determined for the period from 1970 to 1983. Weighting the lower house, the upper house, and the governor's office equally, a Democratic and Republican percentage of control was calculated. This party percentage was used to adjust the party consumer scores calculated by the CFA measures. The result was a consumer protection score that reflected both party strength and the party's orientation toward consumer policies. This score had a theoretical range from 1 to 100 with higher numbers indicating proconsumer orientations. The actual range was from 10.0 in Alaska to 76.4 in Rhode Island; this elite measure of consumerism is correlated with state consumer protection policies in noninsurance areas (Meier, 1987b).[16]

A second political elite measure is the traditional party competition measure. V. O. Key (1951) argued that competitive parties were necessary to produce policies favoring the disadvantaged in society. Although Key's hypothesis has had only weak empirical support in literature, a theoretical reason exists why competitive party systems might foster more consumer protection policies. In a noncompetitive system, insurance interests need only to ally themselves with the dominant political party; noninsurance interests are unlikely to have the political resources to overcome such an alliance. In a competitive system, insurance interests need to appeal to both parties;

the result should be a relative balance between the parties on insurance issues. Such an equilibrium means that groups with fewer resources can tip the balance of power in their favor or at least be able to modify the pro-producer orientation of the political elites. Competitive party states, therefore, should be more responsive to consumer interests. The measure used is the competitiveness of the party system from 1970 to 1983.[17] The mean, standard deviation, and range of this variable and the other independent variables are found in Table 7-1.

Table 7-1
Independent Variables Used

	Mean	Std. Dev.	Low	High
Insurance Industry				
Income per capita	$805	150	$577	$1,450
Employment per 100K	793	270	375	1,976
Concentration percent	25.0	4.4	17.8	37.4
Direct Writers percent	53.1	10.0	28.5	72.7
Agents per 100K	16.7	6.2	6.1	36.2
Underwriters per 100K	26.3	9.6	9.4	58.5
Consumer Groups				
Members per 100K	1,427	433	580	2,450
Contact (percent urban)	61.4	22.8	15.3	94.9
Bureaucracy				
Budget (millions)	3.57	5.25	.33	25.99
Employees	117	155	18	766
Examiners	20	29	0	180
Commissioners salary	44,167	10,708	24,351	70,000
Political Elites				
Consumer Orientation	44.6	13.5	10.0	76.4
Party Competition	.80	.13	.51	.96

COMPARING THE THEORIES

Comparing Stigler's theory of economic regulation to the multi-interest model of regulation is relatively straight forward. First, only industry variables are used to predict public policy variables. Stigler's theory of regulation is supported if the explained variation (after adjustment for degrees of freedom) is higher than that of the multi-interest model *and* if the coefficients all have signs in the same direction as predicted by industry interests.

Second, the multi-interest model is operationalized to predict policy. The multi-interest model is evaluated on the basis of comparing the regression coefficients with the hypotheses listed above. This model is judged in comparison with the Stigler model in terms of both adjusted explained variation and in consistency with the hypotheses generated in Chapter 2.

Regulatory Stringency

Solvency is a goal accepted by almost all commentators on insurance regulation. If insurance companies are not solvent, then insurance contracts have little value. Such solvency regulations as financial requirements and entry restrictions vary substantially among states. To assess the impact of industry resources and other political forces on the stringency of insurance regulation, five indicators of regulatory stringency are used: minimum policy standards, minimum capital requirements, domiciled companies, licensed companies, and guaranty fund assessments.

The NAIC recommends minimum standards for almost every type of insurance policy. One indicator of how strictly a state regulates insurance companies is the number of model policy standards adopted by the state. A model policy standard specifies the policy's form and content required by the state. The average state adopted 10.7 of the NAIC's 17 minimum policy standards (see Table 7-2).

Table 7-2
Dependent Variables: Stringent Regulation

Minimum Standards	Mean	Std. Dev.	Low	High
NAIC Models	10.7	2.3	5.0	15.0
Guaranty Fund Payments				
per capita	$1.35	1.65	.02	8.65
Minimum Capital Life				
Insurance in 1,000s	687	575	70	3,000
Domestic Insurance Companies				
per 100K	3.52	4.76	.80	27.70
Licensed Insurance Companies				
per 100K	59.5	53.7	5.1	204.0

States also regulate the creation of insurance companies by establishing the minimum amount of capital required to write insurance in the state. The greater the minimum capital required by a state, the more difficult marginal companies find incorporating in the state and selling insurance. A second indicator of stringent regulation, therefore, is the minimum capital required by each state to sell life insurance.[18]

Related to minimum capital are several other requirements for incorporating an insurance company. In insurance regulation a form of Gresham's Law (see Kimball, 1969b: 423) exists whereby insurance companies choose to domicile in states that are less strict about regulatory requirements. For example, 616 life insurance companies are domiciled in Arizona, a state with a reputation for few requirements, while only 80 are domiciled in New York, a much larger state with more restrictive requirements. The third indicator of regulatory stringency is the number of insurance companies domiciled in the state per 100,000 population (see Table 7-2). Similar to the domiciled companies' measure as an indicator of stringency is the number of insurance companies licensed to do business in each state. By setting high licensing requirements, a state can limit the insurance business to only the most solvent companies. The measure is the number of insurance companies licensed per 100,000 population.[19]

The final measure of regulatory stringency concerns the action of the state regulatory system after insolvencies. In response to the threat of federal regulation, all states adopted guaranty fund legislation in the 1970s (Lilly, 1976: 112; Lewis, 1981: 121). Guaranty laws cover policyholder losses under specified conditions and up to certain limits (Wenck, 1983: 225). In 49 states, legal provisions were established to assess all licensed insurance companies for policyholders' losses that result from an insolvency.[20] Assessments reflect, in part, laws governing guaranty assessments and the aggressiveness of the insurance commissioner in administering the law (Lewis, 1981: 10). The maximum assessment in most states is 2 percent of premiums (Wenck, 1983: 225). The measure of stringency is the per capita guaranty fund assessment for property and casualty companies since 1969.[21]

A state with stringent requirements for selling insurance would have adopted many of the minimum standards, have a high minimum capital requirement, have fewer companies domiciled in the state, have fewer companies licensed to sell insurance, and have larger guaranty fund assessments. These indicators had intercorrelations that reflected this pattern. All 20 intercorrelations between these variables were in the correct direction.

The first step in determining the correlates of stringent insurance regulation is Stigler's hypothesis that regulation reflects industry interests. Table 7-3 shows the relationships between the six indicators of industry resources and the measures of stringent regulation. The first two rows, those for industry income and industry employment, show that industry resources are strongly related to regulation. In all five cases industry employment is correlated with *stronger* regulation; three of these five relationships are statistically significant. In three of five cases (minimum standards, guaranty fund assessments, and minimum capital) industry income is also associated with stronger regulation. These findings do not necessarily refute Stigler because existing firms could be supporting regulatory restrictions to limit competition.

What does differ markedly from Stigler's theory is that various segments of the industry react differently to regulation. All ten relationships for agents and chartered underwriters show support for less stringent regulation. Five of

Table 7–3
Stringent Regulation: Insurance Industry Model

Independent Variables	Dependent Variables				
	Minimum Standards	Guaranty Fund	Minimum Capital	Domestic Companies	Licensed Companies
Income	.05	.58*	.02	.12	.40*
Employment	.37	.05	.96*	−.84*	−.67*
Agents	−.39*	−.19	−.44*	.15	.32*
Underwriters	−.23	−.07	−.73*	.90*	.06
Concentration	−.57*	−.11	−.01	.03	.13
Direct Writers	.53*	.06	−.39*	.13	−.09
R²	.45	.36	.36	.20	.41
F	5.9	3.9	3.8	1.8	4.9

*p < .05.
All coefficients are standardized regression coefficients.

these relationships are statistically significant. As this pattern reveals, agents have regulatory interests different from those of the insurance companies. Further in support of a multiple interest industry are the relationships for large companies. More concentrated markets are associated with less vigorous regulation. Similarly direct writers are correlated with higher minimum standards (significantly), greater guaranty fund assessments, and fewer licensed companies.[22] Direct writers stand in opposition to agents on all three issues, not surprising because direct writers sell without agents.

The level of explanation for the six industry variables is moderate to weak. Industry resources explain 45 percent of the variance in minimum standards and 41 percent for licensed companies. For guaranty fund assessments and minimum capital requirements, the level of explanation is 36 percent. For domestic insurance companies, the level of explanation is a mere 20 percent.

Operationalizing the multi-interest model of regulation generally increases the levels of explanation.[23] Table 7–4 shows dramatically different results from those in Table 7–3. The strongest determinant of stringent regulation is not the industry but rather the regulatory bureaucracy. In every case, larger regulatory bureaucracies (and thus more likely to be specialized and professionalized) support more stringent regulation of the insurance industry, a finding consistent with those of Gormley (1983) and Berry (1984) for utility regulation. In three cases, the size of the bureaucracy has the strongest single relationship with the dependent variable; in four of five cases, the relationship is statistically significant. The size relationships are usually sup-

Table 7-4
Stringent Regulation: The Multi-Interest Model

Independent Variables	Dependent Variables				
	Minimum Standards	Guaranty Fund	Minimum Capital	Domestic Companies	Licensed Companies
Industry					
Income	-.12	.56*	-.25	.18	.29*
Employment	-.10	-.29**	.08	-.12	-.33*
Bureaucracy					
Size	.42*	.37*	.59*	-.25	-.30*
Values	.24	.17	-.21	.10	-.10
Political Elites					
Consumerism	-.31**	.09	.22**	-.03	-.14
Competition	.03	.14	.25*	.06	.15**
Potential Consumer Groups					
Contact	.18	.06	-.01	-.03	-.45*
Members	.17	-.04	.16	.09	.33*
R^2	.41	.51	.53	.11	.75
F	3.5	5.2	5.6	.6	15.0

*$p < .05$.
**$p < .1$.
All coefficients are standardized regression coefficients.

ported by the bureaucratic values measure but not consistently. Industry is the other major force. Although the relationships are in opposite directions, industry resources are strongly related to the guaranty fund and licensed companies indicators.

Although the complex, but unsalient, characteristics of insurance regulation suggest that the industry and the bureaucracy are the only active participants in insurance regulation, the results in Table 7-4 indicate otherwise. Party competition is associated with higher minimum capital requirements as is the political elites' consumer orientation. These relationships suggest that political elites can be forces for consumer-oriented regulatory policies. Unfortunately, the negative relationship between consumer orientation and minimum standards and the positive relationship between competition and licensed companies suggest otherwise. The pattern of relationships for these indicators is not consistent enough to generalize.

Finally, with the exception of licensing, political consumer groups appear to have little impact on regulatory stringency. Potential consumer contact is significantly related to more licensed firms, but membership in consumer organizations is negatively related to more licensed companies. No logical explanation for this pattern exists. Although the relationships are not statistically significant, both potential consumer measures are associated with more laws requiring minimum policy standards.

Taxing Insurance Companies

The tradition in taxing "self-regulated" industries is to tax them just enough to pay for the regulatory agency. That pattern does not hold for the insurance industry. Less than $200 million is spent by regulatory agencies whereas state taxes on insurance companies total approximately $4 billion. The largest insurance specific tax is the premium tax, essentially a sales tax on insurance sold. Determining the level of premium taxes is not easy because states provide for numerous exceptions and exclusions. This analysis uses the net premium tax rate; it is the total dollar value of premium taxes paid divided by the total dollar value of premiums. The average net premium tax was 2.28 percent in 1983 with a range from 1.08 percent to 4.65 percent (see Table 7–5).

Two other tax measures relate insurance taxes to population—the per capita premium tax and the per capita insurance tax. By including licensing fees and other special assessments paid by insurance companies, the insurance tax is larger than the premium tax. In 1983, the average state collected $18.06 per person in premium taxes and $18.84 in all insurance taxes. Without a doubt, premium taxes constitute the bulk of state taxes paid by insurance companies (see Table 7–5).

The final measure of tax policy concerns tax discrimination against foreign insurance companies. Before the U. S. Supreme Court declared such practices unconstitutional in 1985, many states charged foreign insurance companies a higher tax rate than domestic insurance companies paid. The average state charged out-of-state companies .65 percent more in premium

Table 7–5
Insurance Industry Taxation: Dependent Variables

	Mean	Std. Dev.	Low	High
Premium Tax Rate	2.28%	1.72	1.08%	4.65%
Insurance Taxes per capita	$18.84	5.66	$10.37	$34.20
Premium Taxes per capita	$18.06	5.57	$9.63	$32.50
Tax Discrimination	.65%	.96	0.0 %	4.0 %

taxes than they charged domestic companies. The level of discrimination ranged from 0 percent to 4 percent. Although this system of taxation is being altered to met the constitutional requirements, it illustrates a policy designed to protect local insurance companies.[24]

Taxation is a public policy that subjects Stigler's (1971) regulatory theory to a clear-cut test. Insurance companies have little interest in paying higher taxes; and if Stigler is correct, greater insurance company resources should be associated with lower levels of taxation. The results of the industry model of insurance taxation are shown in Table 7-6.

Industry factors explain only a modest portion of the variation in taxation policy. Only one predicted relationship between the industry forces and premium tax rates is significant; states with more chartered underwriters have lower premium tax rates. This negative relationship with underwriters also holds for per capita premium taxes and per capita insurance taxes. In fact, underwriters are the only significant, negative force in any area of taxation (direct writers are a negative force, but the relationships are not significant). Industry resources, on the other hand, are generally associated with higher taxation. The significant relationship between industry income and per capita taxes, however, is probably not the result of industry demanding higher taxes. Rather, the relationship most likely results from a legislative effort to link taxes with income. Accordingly, it represents political rather than industry forces.

Most industry variables appear unrelated to tax policy. No relationships

Table 7-6
Taxation of Insurance Companies: Insurance Industry Model

Independent Variables	Dependent Variables			
	Premium Tax Rate	Taxes (per capita)	Premium Tax (per capita)	Tax Discrimination
Insurance Income	−.16	.50*	.48*	.11
Insurance Employment	.12	.10	.06	−.23
Independent Agents	.05	.04	.04	.04
Underwriters	−.53**	−.48**	−.44	.17
Concentration	.07	.06	.07	.31**
Direct Writers	−.14	−.17	−.16	−.10
R^2	.23	.27	.25	.09
F	2.2	2.6	2.4	.7

*$p < .05$.
**$p < .1$.
All coefficients are standardized regression coefficients.

for employment, agents, direct writers, or concentration are significant, a fact reflected in the low levels of explained variation. As expected, the tax discrimination pattern is different from the others. Tax discrimination is explained only poorly by industry factors; the sole significant relationship is a positive coefficient for industry concentration. The direction of causality for this relationship might go either way. Although more concentrated industries may support greater interstate tax discrimination, tax discrimination may also result in greater industry concentration.

The multi-interest explanation of tax policy is a slight improvement over the insurance industry model.[25] No additional significant relationships are found, but the first three columns of Table 7-7 show some consistent patterns. The industry continues to exhibit a mixed pattern with income related to higher taxes and chartered underwriters associated with lower taxes. Perhaps the most interesting finding in Table 7-7 is that all six relationships for the bureaucratic variables are negative. This pattern can be explained. Because premium taxes do not go into the agency's budget, the bureaucracy has no reason to support higher taxes on its industry, especially if the regulator is concerned with solvency. Second, the bureaucracy relationships may also reflect the regulator's acceptance of the industry view that higher taxes raise

Table 7-7
Taxation of Insurance Companies: Multi-Interest Model

Independent Variables	Dependent Variables			
	Premium Tax Rate	Taxes (per capita)	Premium Tax (per capita)	Tax Discrimination
Industry				
Income	-.11	.52*	.53*	.12
Underwriters	-.16	-.15	-.15	-.04
Bureaucracy				
Size	-.14	-.20	-.18	-.06
Values	-.19	-.17	-.15	-.12
Political Elites				
Consumerism	.06	.06	.06	-.02
Party Competition	-.16	-.19	-.17	.02
Potential Consumer Groups				
Contact	-.21	-.19	-.19	.25
Members	.00	.04	.04	-.22
R^2	.35	.37	.37	.07
F	2.7	3.0	3.0	.4

*p < .05.
**p < .1.
All coefficients are standardized regression coefficients.

the price of insurance to consumers. Third, taxation is primarily a legislative policy arena not a bureaucratic one.

The absence of a clear consumer position on taxes perhaps explains the mixed findings for both political elites and potential consumer groups. The political elite's consumer orientation is unrelated to taxes. Competition is related consistently to lower taxes. The pattern for potential consumer groups defies explanation. Contact is consistently associated with lower taxes, and membership is unrelated to taxes.

The multi-interest model fares no better in predicting tax discrimination than the insurance industry model did. None of the eight relationships is significant, and the level of explanation is so low that it is essentially zero. Tax discrimination is obviously a function of variables not considered here.

Regulating Insurance Prices

Approximately two-thirds of the states directly regulate the price of some property and casualty insurance lines; most of these states also regulate the price of individual policies issued by Blue Cross and Blue Shield. Comparing prices directly is difficult without some consideration of the risk involved for each policy (Harrington, 1984; Witt and Miller, 1981). Fortunately, industry-wide figures are kept that adjust prices for risk. The adjusted loss ratio (ALR) divides the claims paid to policyholders by the premiums paid in, adjusted for any dividend payments to policyholders. The adjusted loss ratio is widely accepted in the industry as a measure of price (Harrington, 1984; Witt and Miller, 1981; Witt and Urrutia, 1983; and see Chapter 5). The higher the ALR, the greater the proportion of premiums paid out in claims; and, therefore, the lower the price of the insurance is relative to risk. The mean loss ratios for eight different insurance lines are listed in Table 7-8.[26]

As an illustration, the adjusted loss ratio for automobile insurance is 65.7. This figure can be interpreted as follows: insurance companies pay 65.7¢ in claims for every $1 of premium income they collect. Although the accepted industry rule of thumb is that ALRs of less than 65 are profitable, the breakeven point varies by line of insurance. Analysis presented in Table 1–18 revealed that the ALR breakeven point for all property and casualty lines in combination was approximately 81. A second pattern worthy of note in Table 7–8 is the standard deviations. These deviations show the variation in ALRs across states; consequently, they are a rough indicator of the predict-

Table 7-8
Insurance Prices: Adjusted Loss Ratios

	Mean	Std. Dev.	Low	High
Life Insurance	34.7	3.3	25.8	46.5
Health Insurance—Private	79.9	6.7	69.0	104.6
Health Insurance—Blues	98.7	11.4	92.8	175.0
All Property and Casualty	64.6	4.0	58.5	77.6
Automobile	65.7	4.4	58.5	77.6
Homeowners	62.2	9.3	49.6	93.3
Commercial Multiple Peril	54.2	8.4	41.7	95.0
Medical Malpractice	71.6	28.9	30.8	209.0
General Liability	54.3	9.6	39.6	78.0

ability of losses in a line of insurance. Of particular interest is the large standard deviation for medical malpractice insurance.

PRICES IN LIFE INSURANCE

As noted above, the price of life insurance and private health insurance is not directly regulated. Regulators indirectly affect prices via regulations affecting reserves and investments. Investment regulation, as a technical area away from the public's view, should be affected little by public pressure. Prices, therefore, should reflect industry interests.

The insurance industry model for prices in the life and health insurance areas is shown in Table 7-9. Although a modest level of explanation is

Table 7-9
Prices of Life and Health Insurance:
Insurance Industry Model

Independent Variables	Dependent Variables		
	Life Insurance	Health—Private	Health—Blues
Insurance Income	.08	.38*	.10
Insurance Employment	.56*	.15	.17
Independent Agents	−.45*	−.18	.54*
CLU Members	−.73*	−.06	−.02
Company Assets	.02	−.16	−.08
Number of Companies	−.19	−.18	.06
R^2	.41	.13	.31
F	4.9	1.1	3.2

*$p < .05$.
All coefficients are standardized regression coefficients.

achieved for life insurance and the Blues, private health insurance prices can
not be explained. The most striking relationships are those between agents
and life insurance prices. Both the number of independent agents and the
number of CLUs are associated with higher life insurance prices. The same
relationship, although not significant, holds for private health insurance. The
agency system has been condemned as inefficient and expensive because
agents have an incentive to select the insurance policy with the highest commissions (see Joskow, 1973). These relationships support that view by showing a strong linkage between agents and higher prices in insurance lines
dominated by the agency system.

As the positive relationships between industry income and employment
indicate, size is associated with lower prices. What these relationships probably reflect are some economies of scale in terms of national advertising and
the in-roads made into the market by group life sales. Even if such relationships reflect economic considerations, they have political implications because small life insurance companies cannot adapt as well to lower prices as
larger firms can.

The relationships between the price charged by the Blues and the industry variables are shown for comparison purposes only. Because the Blues
are dominated by the medical profession and have a slightly different role
in the health payment system, little reason exists why insurance industry
variables should affect the price of this type of health insurance. The single
significant relationship, therefore, is probably spurious.

The multi-interest model of life insurance prices is somewhat surprising
(see Table 7-10). Because prices in life and health insurance are not directly
regulated, the lack of relationships between bureaucratic variables and prices
is not unexpected. Neither is the lack of relationship between the political
elite variables and price because legislation affecting reserves and investments, and thus price, is highly technical. What is surprising is the relationships for potential consumer groups. Consumer contact is significantly
associated with lower prices for life and private health insurance. The relationships for consumer groups members is also in the same direction but not
significant.

The mechanism by which consumer groups achieve lower prices for
health and life insurance is probably the market. Although data are lacking,
one would suspect that consumer activism is high in the same locations
where alternative means of purchasing insurance are available. Consumer
organizations may be able to persuade their members that group life insurance is a better buy than individual life insurance policies or that term insur-

Table 7-10
Prices of Life and Health Insurance:
Multi-Interest Model

Independent Variables	Dependent Variables		
	Life Insurance	Health—Private	Health—Blues
Industry			
CLU Members	−.64*	−.16	−.11
Agents	−.13	−.01	.51*
Bureaucracy			
Size	.11	.03	−.02
Values	.13	−.07	.16
Political Elites			
Consumerism	.05	−.12	−.10
Party Competition	.07	.04	.09
Potential Consumer Groups			
Contact	.47*	.49*	−.08
Members	.20	.04	−.05
R^2	.55	.21	.32
F	6.4	1.4	2.4

*$p < .05$.
All coefficients are standardized regression coefficients.

ance is preferable to whole life. In the health insurance area, alternatives such as HMOs can be used to reduce costs. Although the appropriate linkage mechanism is pure speculation, the consumer education activities of consumer groups make such a linkage plausible.[27]

The multi-interest model of Blue Cross and Blue Shield prices performs no better than the insurance industry model.[28] The process of determining prices in this area is essentially unexplained. Given the high ALR for the Blues (98.7), the probable determinant of price is cost with insurance regulators responsive to arguments based on cost (similar to Berry's, 1984 findings for utility prices).[29]

PROPERTY AND CASUALTY INSURANCE PRICES

The insurance industry correlates for property and casualty insurance prices are shown in Table 7-11. If Stigler's assessment of regulation is correct, then relationships between industry variables and ALRs should be negative; that is, the industry should favor higher prices. A quick glance at the coefficients of determination suggests that, except for automobile and general liability insurance, insurance prices are independent of industry resources.

Table 7-11
Property and Casualty Insurance Prices:
The Insurance Industry Model

Independent Variables	Dependent Variables					
	All P/C	Auto	Home	Com.[a]	Med.[b]	Lia.[c]
Industry Income	.26**	.54*	−.26	.03	.22	.64*
Industry Employment	.05	.19	−.10	.11	.29**	−.17
Independent Agents	−.00	−.13	.04	−.26**	−.06	.02
CPCU Members	.08	.01	.09	−.11	−.06	.13
Concentration	.15	.35	.21	.04	−.27**	.15
Direct Writers	.10	−.08	.04	−.06	−.04	−.10
Number of Companies	−.16	.01	−.17	−.10	−.12	−.27*
R^2	.14	.39	.16	.09	.15	.55
F	1.0	3.9	1.1	.6	1.0	7.4

*p < .05.
**p < .1.
[a]Commercial multiple peril insurance.
[b]Medical malpractice insurance.
[c]General liability insurance.
All coefficients are standardized regression coefficients.

Showing even less support for Stigler's theory is the direction of the relationships; more than one-half the coefficients in the table are positive. The strongest evidence supporting Stigler is the relationship for the number of companies; the more companies licensed to sell insurance, the higher the price. In addition to supporting Stigler's view of regulation, this finding also has implications for structural economists who feel that competition is a function of the number of firms in a market place (see Armentano, 1982).

Among the more interesting relationships are those for income and concentration. Both high income and concentration are associated with lower prices. In the case of income, three of these relationships are significant. Because the larger firms in the property and casualty field are direct writers who have lower costs, this finding is not surprising. Direct writers have no interest in high prices because high prices protect other firms and deprive direct writers of their competitive advantages. That these relationships appear for income and concentration but not percentage of direct writers is a function of collinearity (see Table 7-12).

Also worthy of note is the lack of relationships for agents. Because agents have less control over the property and casualty market, their impact on prices is less. Lack of influence by agents is one reason why direct writers have steadily gained market percentage at the expense of the agency system.

In the case of property and casualty insurance prices, the multi-industry model predicts far better than the insurance industry model.[30] As the coefficients in Table 7-12 indicate, industry is not without a role in the regulation of insurance prices. Industry income is significantly related to prices in four cases (general property and casualty, auto, commercial multiple peril, and liability), and the proportion of direct writers is similarly related in one case (auto). All five of these relationships are positive indicating industry supports lower prices. Because both variables tap the strength of direct writers, the support for lower prices is consistent with one market segment's economic self-interest.

Equally clear is the role that political elites play in setting insurance prices. The consumer orientation of political elites is significantly related to lower prices for property and casualty insurance in general and automobile insurance in particular. Because automobile insurance is the most visible area of property and casualty insurance where the policyholder is a normal citizen (as opposed to a physician, business owner, etc.), this relationship suggests

Table 7-12
Property and Casualty Insurance Prices:
The Multi-Interest Model

Independent Variables	Dependent Variables					
	All P/C	Auto	Home	Com.[a]	Med.[b]	Lia.[c]
Industry						
Income	.45*	.60*	−.12	.33**	−.16	.54*
Direct Writers	.24	.27*	.25	−.21	−.12	.01
Bureaucracy						
Size	.02	−.04	.01	.00	.20	.05
Values	−.21	−.19	−.24	−.09	−.38*	−.11
Political Elites						
Consumerism	.53*	.45*	.21	−.13	.04	−.09
Party Competition	−.11	−.05	.00	−.15	.28	−.04
Potential Consumer Groups						
Contact	.32**	.22	−.14	.52*	−.08	.27**
Members	−.37**	−.28	−.25	−.55*	.45*	.04
R^2	.45	.56	.29	.38	.33	.51
F	4.2	6.6	2.1	3.1	2.6	5.4

*p < .05.
**p < .1.
[a]Commercial multiple peril insurance.
[b]Medical malpractice insurance.
[c]General liability insurance.
All coefficients are standardized regression coefficients.

that political elites create pressures in the regulatory system for lower prices in personal lines of insurance.

The consistent negative relationships between bureaucratic values and ALRs also merit some discussion. Consumer protection values in the bureaucracy are associated with higher prices. Although this pattern of relationships (significant in the malpractice case) might appear inconsistent, it is not. The primary concern of most regulators is solvency; the literature contains many statements by regulators that prices must be set high enough to generate sufficient return on investment to guarantee solvency (similar to utility regulation, see Gormley, 1983: 19). Solvency and higher prices can, therefore, be viewed in some ways as proconsumer action.

The potential consumer group variables reveal an inconsistent pattern. Although the contact variable is generally associated with lower prices— significantly so in general property and casualty, commercial multiple peril, and general liability insurance, the membership variable is usually associated with higher prices—significantly in the case of commercial insurance and general property and casualty insurance. The obvious explanation for membership's negative relationships might be the direction of causality is reversed. Rather than consumers pressing for higher prices, the more logical interpretation is that higher prices stimulate greater consumer mobilization.

In combination, Tables 7–11 and 7–12 show a great deal of support for modifying Stigler's theory of regulation. Industry resources are generally unable to predict regulated prices; and when they do, the industry favors lower prices. Industry pressures, in addition, are only one force in the regulatory area. The regulatory bureaucracy, political elites, and possibly even consumer groups play a role in regulating prices. The roles may not be as direct as the role played by the industry; but, at a minimum, these other actors create an environment that prevents industry groups from dominating the regulatory process.

The Impact of Regulation on Price

Although one purpose of regulation is to affect the price of the regulated product, economic critics have long charged that regulation distorts the market-clearing price mechanism (MacAvoy, 1979). Regulation can distort market prices in two ways. Those who view regulation as a reflection of industry pressures (Stigler, 1971; Posner, 1976; Peltzman, 1974; Kolko, 1965) expect prices in a regulatory system to be higher. If monopoly or near monopoly conditions exist, however, price regulation could have the opposite effect. It could lower artificially high monopoly prices (Harrington, 1984). Because the insurance industry does not have the structural characteristics of a monopoly, the more logical hypothesis is that regulation increases the price of insurance.

To test this notion, each of the ALRs for property and casualty lines was analyzed in terms of the type of regulatory law. Although numerous ratemaking laws exist, they can be divided into two types: competitive ratemaking laws and noncompetitive ratemaking laws (Witt and Miller, 1981). Under a competitive ratemaking law, an insurance company does not need the regulator's prior approval to change rates. Approximately one-third of all states use competitive rate laws, but the actual number varies by line of insurance.[31] By comparing states with competitive laws to states with noncompetitive laws, the impact of regulation can be assessed (but see Harrington, 1984).

The impact of regulation is determined by using the ALRs as the dependent variables with a dummy independent variable coded *1* if the state used a competitive ratemaking law.[32] The slope in this regression shows the difference in ALR between competitive and noncompetitive states. A positive slope means that competitive states have higher ALRs and, thus, lower prices. The slopes for all six property and casualty lines are shown in Table 7–13.

In two insurance lines—commercial multiple peril and general liability—prices are lower in competitive ratemaking states. In the other four product lines, prices are higher in competitive rating states. The important finding in Table 7–13, however, is the last column on statistical significance. In no case are the rates in regulated states significantly different from the rates in less regulated states, a finding consistent with the other empirical literature (see Harrington, 1984). The clear conclusion is that regulation, in general, has no impact on the price of insurance.[33] The reason should be obvious. Regulation involves discretion; whether regulation results in higher prices is a function of the values and abilities of the regulators, not the process of setting prices.

Table 7–13
The Impact of Competitive Rating Laws
on Property and Casualty Insurance Prices

Dependent Variables	Slope	R^2	p
All Property and Casualty	−.84	.009	.50
Automobile Insurance	−.89	.009	.51
Homeowners' Insurance	−2.20	.012	.45
Commercial Multiple Peril	1.93	.011	.46
Medical Malpractice	−5.36	.007	.55
General Liability	1.84	.008	.53

Independent Variable = Competitive Rate Law.

Litigation and the Price of Insurance

In recent years, the insurance industry has blamed many of its problems on the legal profession. Particularly in the medical malpractice area, but also in the other areas of property and casualty insurance, legal fees claim a large portion of expenses. In automobile insurance, legal fees are an estimated 23 percent of premiums (Witt and Urrutia, 1984b: 11). Massive damage awards are perceived as destabilizing the insurance industry (Insurance Information Institute, 1985; see also Chapter 5).

The insurance industry's contention raises the question of whether or not litigation is affecting the stability of the insurance industry or if legal awards are simply a reflection of decisions that insurance companies would make anyway. Because accurate information on court cases filed that involve insurance company payouts is not available, secondary measures of litigation need to be developed.[34] The cynic would argue that a simple measure of the number of lawyers would suffice because lawyers need to find things to do and, thus, they generate their own business. The number of lawyers per 100,000 population will tap the volume of legal talent. A second measure of litigation is the number of law suits filed in state courts. Unfortunately, data from state courts vary greatly among states in terms of definitions, coverage, and quality. The only partially reliable measure is the number of civil suits filed per 100,000 persons, and this measure is of questionable validity. Perhaps the best measure available is the number of federal tort cases filed. Tort cases are more likely to involve insurance companies, and federal court data are far more reliable than state court data. Unfortunately, federal court data reveal only the tip of the legal iceberg because most torts are filed in state courts.[35]

The relationships between litigation and the cost of insurance is revealed in Table 7-14. To prevent conclusions based on spurious results, the regression equations in Table 7-14 control for both industry income and the proportion of insurance written by direct writers. The only litigation variable that is significantly related to the adjusted loss ratio for the property and casualty lines is the number of federal tort cases filed. Statistically significant relationships exist between the tort cases measure and the ALR for liability insurance, commercial multiple peril insurance, auto insurance, and overall property and casualty insurance. These relationships are positive (as they are also for homeowners' insurance and medical malpractice insurance) suggesting that more litigation results in insurance companies paying a larger portion of premiums in claims.

The table implies that lawyers are popular in dealing with insurance companies because they are able to get larger claims for their clients. What is not clear from the table is whether policyholders actually receive more

Table 7-14
Litigation and the Price of Insurance

Independent Variables	Dependent Variables					
	All P/C	Auto	Home	Com.[a]	Med.[b]	Lia.[c]
Industry						
Income	.18	.60*	−.21	−.12	.05	.55*
Direct Writers	.12	.17	.22	−.06	.00	.12
Litigation Variables						
Lawyers	.06	−.15	−.09	.18	.15	.17
Tort Suits Filed	.44*	.21**	.10	.40*	.23	.30*
Civil Suits Filed	−.12	−.00	−.21	−.28	.04	−.09
R^2	.30	.44	.19	.22	.08	.53
F	3.6	6.6	2.0	2.4	.9	9.7

*$p < .05$.
**$p < .1$.
[a]Commercial multiple peril insurance.
[b]Medical malpractice insurance.
[c]General liability insurance.
All coefficients are standardized regression coefficients.

money because attorney's fees must be paid out of the award. Whether policyholders benefit more, however, the table does show why insurance companies do not look favorably on the legal profession.

No-Fault Automobile Insurance

The results in Table 7-14 raise the question, why do not insurance companies aggressively pursue legislation that resolves disputes by means other than litigation? Litigation costs the insurance companies not only higher payouts but also the increased overhead costs to defend lawsuits. To be sure, some direct writers, such as State Farm, and many organizations of insurance professionals have been strong advocates of no-fault automobile insurance (Witt and Urrutia, 1984b: 12–13), but in general such pressures have not resulted in any recent legislation (see Chapter 4).

The no-fault automobile insurance experience, however, provides a good opportunity to examine what happens to insurance costs when alternative dispute resolution procedures are used. Most auto insurance operates under the principle of tort liability compensation; to collect damages from another person, one person must prove that the second person was somehow at fault. Under the principle of no-fault insurance, claims are paid without any assessment of liability.

In 1971, Massachusetts was the first state to adopt a form of no-fault automobile insurance. In the next five years, 23 other states adopted various versions of no-fault auto insurance, and federal legislation was considered that would have required no-fault automobile insurance (see Chapter 6). As the result of opposition by the legal community, the movement to no-fault automobile insurance systems was effectively stalled. Not a single state adopted a no-fault law after North Dakota did in 1976, and Nevada repealed its no-fault law in 1980.

All no-fault insurance is not identical; it comes in four basic varieties: A pure no-fault system provides payments for all personal injuries regardless of fault; in exchange for such protection, the individual relinquishes his or her right to sue for damages. Only three states have no-fault systems that approach a pure no-fault system by limiting court action—Michigan, New York, and Pennsylvania (Witt and Urrutia, 1984a: 182). The majority of states adopting no-fault laws have modified plans that cover losses up to a certain limit. Above that limit, tort claims can be filed for additional damages.

A third form of no-fault is referred to as add-on no-fault because no-fault insurance is simply added on to regular insurance and no limitations are placed on tort suits. The final form of no-fault is add-on no-fault insurance where the purchase of the no-fault add-on is optional, at best a pseudo form of no-fault (Witt and Urrutia, 1984a: 182; Witt and Urrutia, 1983).

The touted benefit of no-fault automobile insurance is that, by eliminating the costly determination of fault, costs will decline as will the price of insurance. To assess the impact of various no-fault plans on the cost of insurance (the ALR), a series of dummy variables was coded *1* if the state had a specific type of no-fault and coded *0* otherwise. Dummy variables were created for "optional add-on no-fault," "add-on no-fault," "modified no-fault," and "no-fault." These codes were consistent with the four types of no-fault described above.

When this series of dummy variables is used as independent variables in a regression with the automobile insurance ALR[36] the predicted pattern results (see Table 7–15). Under optional add-on plans, consumers are no better off than under tort liability systems. Add-on no-fault results in a saving of 3.05 percent. Neither the optional add-on nor the add-on coefficients are statistically significant. States that adopt pseudo forms of no-fault are engaging in symbolic politics by making superficial changes that have little impact on the distribution of benefits (Edelman, 1964).

The real benefits to consumers come from those plans that more closely recognize the causal linkage between determining fault and price. Modified no-fault plans reduce the ALR by 3.13 percentiles, and no-fault plans make a

Table 7–15
The Impact of No-Fault Insurance on Price
Four Types of No-Fault

Type of No-Fault	Slope	t
Optional Add-On	.52	.31
Add-On No-Fault	3.05	1.44
Modified No-Fault	3.13	2.58
No-Fault	7.05	3.33

Intercept = 66.6
$R^2 = .27$ F = 4.03

7.05 percentile reduction.[37] Both savings are statistically significant. Although a 7 percentile improvement in an ALR might not appear large, when contrasted with the ALR of 66.6 (see the intercept in Table 7–15) in tort liability states, no-fault systems increase the benefits paid to policyholders by 10.6 percent.

To determine if the results in Table 7–15 might be a function of other variables rather than just no-fault, a multivariate model of automobile insurance prices was constructed. Based on the previous analysis of insurance prices (Table 7–11), four additional variables were included in the model— the size of the industry (per capita premiums), direct writers (percent of the auto insurance market controlled by), federal tort litigation (number of suits per 100,000 population), and the consumer orientation variable for political elites.

Because only no-fault systems and modified no-fault systems had a significant impact in the univariate regression, dummy variables for these two systems were the only no-fault variables included. The results of this six variable regression are shown in Table 7–16. Positive slopes indicate higher ALRs and, thus, lower insurance prices. All six variables are positively related to the ALR, and together they explain 57 percent of the variation.[38]

Table 7–16
Impact of No-Fault Controlling for Other Factors Affecting Price

Independent Variable	Slope	Beta	t
No-Fault	5.18	.32	3.08
Modified No-Fault	2.06	.23	2.12
Insurance Income	.02	.29	2.63
Direct Writers	.12	.30	2.65
Federal Torts Filed	.18	.31	3.01
Political Elites Consumerism	.11	.39	3.33

Intercept = 48.57
$R^2 = .57$ F = 9.37

Although no-fault laws are not the strongest influences on the price of automobile insurance, they are a significant factor after controlling for industry resources, litigation, and political elites. The impact of no-fault laws on insurance prices is clearly not spurious. Even with controls, no-fault systems reduce the risk-adjusted cost of insurance by 5.18 percentiles, and modified no-fault systems have an impact of 2.06 percentiles. Although this might not appear to be a substantial gain, it is when contrasted with the size of the automobile insurance market. If similar gains could be achieved from a nationwide no-fault system, consumers would gain $3.7 billion in either lower prices or higher benefits.

Other State Restrictions on Automobile Insurance

No-fault laws are only one of many ways that state legislators or other policymakers can affect the price of automobile insurance. Five types of automobile insurance laws or policies are examined to determine their impact on price. *Mandatory insurance laws* require that everyone have insurance to operate a motor vehicle; by eliminating most problems of uninsured motorists, mandatory insurance should reduce the price of insurance. The *involuntary* or *shared insurance market* is used by many states to force companies to insure risks they prefer not to insure; the use of shared markets varies dramatically by state ranging from 30 percent of the market in Massachusetts to .03 percent in Utah. By forcing companies to insure higher risks, large shared-risk plans should be associated with higher ALRs. *Financial responsibility laws* require individuals to provide proof of financial responsibility after an accident. The higher the financial responsibility requirement, the lower the ALRs because uninsured high-risk drivers are eliminated from the market. The *family purpose doctrine* imposes liability on a parent for the driving accidents of a dependent; family purpose laws should result in higher ALRs for auto insurance. Finally, some states are even more strict about minors, using *permissive use statutes,* whereby owners are liable for accidents by any individual who uses the vehicle with permission; such laws should be associated with higher ALRs.

The impact of these five laws on the adjusted loss ratio of automobile insurance is shown in Table 7–17. In each case the law or policy was used an an independent variable in a regression on the ALR. Two of the laws, the family purpose doctrine and the permissive use statute, have no impact on the price of automobile insurance. The size of the shared market has a barely significant impact on price. For every one percent of the auto market insured through the shared market, the ALR increases by .14. All things being equal,

Table 7-17
The Impact of State Restrictions on Auto Insurance Prices

Restriction	Slope	t	p	r²
Mandatory Insurance	2.31	1.91	.06	.07
Size of Shared Market	.14	1.67	.10	.06
Financial Responsibility	−.08	2.78	.01	.14
Family Purpose Doctrine	.96	.74	ns	.01
Permissive Use Statute	.47	.38	ns	.00

Dependent variable is automobile insurance ALR.
ns = Not significant.

this means that prices would increase by 4.2 percent in a state such as Massachusetts with a 30 percent shared market.

Mandatory insurance laws also have a significant impact on the price of insurance; a mandatory law is associated with a 2.3 percentile increase in the ALR; that is, it lowers the price of insurance. Stricter financial responsibility laws have the opposite impact. For each $1,000 in financial responsibility required, the ALR for auto insurance increases by .08 percentiles. A requirement of $100,000, all things being equal, would translate into an 8 percentile increase in price.[39]

The Impact of Price on Availability

Economists often claim that regulation will set prices too low and, as a result, shortages will develop. The data here provide a good opportunity to examine the empirical relationship between price and supply. In classical economic theory, the lower the price of a good, the more of the good that will be demanded. If the price is too low, however, individuals will refuse to supply it (MacAvoy, 1979).

In the area of automobile insurance, good indicators of price (the ALR) and availability exist. Data are available on the percent of insured automobiles and the percentage of automobiles insured in the voluntary market (as opposed to the involuntary or shared market). Using price as an independent variable in a regression to predict the proportion of vehicles insured, therefore, can tell us if lower prices lead to shortages.

The results of this regression are shown in Table 7-18. A negative slope indicates that higher ALRs (lower prices) are associated with fewer insured automobiles. The slope for the voluntary market regression is -1.00, indicating that for every one percentile drop in price (as expressed by the ALR), an additional one percent of the drivers will be unable to get automobile insurance in the voluntary market. The relationship is significant but explains only a small portion of the variance.

Table 7–18
Impact of Price on Availability
Automobile Insurance

Availability	Intercept	Slope	t	r²
Percent Automobiles Insured	129.9	–.60	1.93	.07
Percent Automobiles Insured in Voluntary Market	151.0	–1.00	2.35	.10

Dependent variable is the automobile insurance ALR.

The regression for the voluntary market does not tell the entire story, however. Some individuals who cannot obtain insurance in the voluntary market will purchase insurance in the shared market. The regression for total automobiles insured (both voluntary and involuntary) shows a slope of -.60, which suggests that for every one percentile decrease in price, six-tenths of one percent of individuals will not obtain insurance. In combination, both regressions imply that a one percentile decline in price will result in a one percent decline in vehicles insured in the voluntary market, but that 40 percent of those eliminated from the voluntary market will obtain insurance through the shared market.

The regression equations in Table 7–18 can be used to speculate about the nature of the insurance market. If one assumes that all things will remain equal, the equations can be solved to determine what ALR would result in a price high enough to insure 100 percent of all vehicles. For universal voluntary insurance, the ALR would need to be 51 percent or less or about 14 percentiles below the current rate. Including the involuntary market, an ALR of 49 percent would be needed. Because the voluntary market would satisfy all demand before the combination market would, the figure for the voluntary market appears to be more realistic.

Access to Insurance

A goal of many federal insurance programs and some state insurance regulators is universal access to insurance at "reasonable" prices. Without some type of government subsidy, however, universal access is not a popular goal with the insurance industry. Without subsidies and with price restrictions, universal access means that some policyholders are cross-subsidizing other policyholders. The high risks exploit the low risks as it were.

Two types of access program are fairly popular, the shared automobile insurance market discussed above and fair access to insurance requirements (FAIR) plans. FAIR plans provide insurance to individuals who reside in areas where insurance companies cannot provide low-cost insurance. Combining these two measures of access to insurance, a single indicator of policy on access to insurance was created.[40]

Because access to insurance is a policy decision that rests with the regulatory system, this portion of the analysis will omit the industry only model and proceed directly to the multi-interest model. The results of this model (see Table 7–19) reveal an interesting pattern. The single most important predictor of access to insurance is membership in consumer organizations. The larger the potential consumer organizations' membership is, the greater the access to insurance. The relationship is consistent with the view that consumer groups would push for greater access.

Two other significant relationships are less interpretable. Greater access to insurance is associated with more employment in the insurance industry and less competitive party systems. The first relationship can be explained in terms of causation. Greater access to insurance means that more individuals with higher claims percentages will be insured. Such individuals will not only cost the insurance companies more in money, but they will also require

Table 7–19
Access to Insurance: Multi-Interest Model

Industry	Slope
Income	−.15
Employment	.27**
Bureaucracy	
Size	.18
Values	−.15
Political Elites	
Consumerism	.19
Party Competition	−.25**
Potential Consumer Groups	
Contact	.16
Members	.33**
$R^2 = .46$ $F = 4.32$	

**$p < .1$.
All coefficients are standardized regression coefficients.

that more employees be hired to service the demand. The competition relationship is directly contrary to theoretical expectations.

Conclusion

This chapter presents an empirical examination of state insurance regulatory policy using all 50 states as units of analysis. The research uses both
industry models of regulation and multi-interest models of regulation to explain regulatory policy in a wide variety of insurance areas. Insurance regulation is an area generally characterized by complexity and a lack of salience.
Accordingly, if George Stigler's view that regulation is designed for and
benefits the regulated holds anywhere, it should hold for state insurance
regulation. The overall impression from the analysis, however, is that the
insurance industry does not dominate the regulatory process. First, the insurance industry lacks the unity necessary to resolve all regulatory issues within
a consistent subsystem. Agents have interests different from those of insurance companies. Direct writers seek goals different from either agents or
national insurance companies. Property and casualty companies face demands different from those faced by life and health insurers. Industry, therefore, is seldom in unanimous agreement about regulatory policy.
    Second, interests other than the industry have an impact on regulatory
policy. Bureaucratic actors, political elites, and possibly even consumer
groups were able to influence the policy outputs of the insurance regulatory
system. Each set of actors has goals that differ from those of the industry.
Any good explanation of regulatory policy, therefore, must be based on more
complex models than George Stigler's simple supply and demand model.
The Stigler version of capture theory provides no better empirical support for
what is happening in regulation than the market failures' explanation. Regulatory policy, similar to most other policies, is a function of myriad political, economic, and organizational forces that are constrained by the policy
environment.

Chapter 8

The Political Economy of Insurance Regulation

Insurance is virtually an unknown industry to social scientists despite the industry's massive size. Insurance companies control more than $1 trillion in assets and have sales of $300 billion per year. Insurance is the largest state-regulated industry in the United States.

Empirical Findings

The political economy of insurance regulation results from a complex interaction of industry groups, consumer interests, regulatory bureaucrats, and political elites. Insurance is often incorrectly perceived as a regulatory system where the insurance industry dominates policymaking. In this view, insurance regulators are captured by the industry they were established to regulate. Such a situation is most likely to occur when the policy environment contains issues that are complex but not salient as the insurance policy environment is.

Despite conditions favorable to industry domination of the policy process, one cannot conclude that insurance regulation is captured by the insurance industry. First, capture does not occur because the industry is too divided to agree on policy goals. Insurance is not one industry; it is several industries, each with different goals and policy objectives. These differences are rooted in the historical development of insurance as a monoline industry whereby companies specialized in a single line of insurance. As a result, life insurance companies are simply not concerned with questions of price regulation and liability that occupy much time of property and casualty companies. Within lines of insurance, large companies are more likely to be interested in competition and less likely to seek collusive regulation than are small companies. Direct writers are direct competitors to the agency system;

167

agents often seek protected markets and higher prices while direct writers seek to undercut prices and expand markets. The result of these and many other conflicting interests in the insurance industries means that the industries are rarely ever united in favor of a policy goal. Without unity, policymakers can play one portion of the industry against other portions.

Second, insurance policy takes place in too many forums for the industry to dominate.[1] All 50 states regulate insurance but do so in a variety of different ways. The federal government also affects the insurance industry by structuring its environment and creating some direct regulation or threatening to regulate directly. For the insurance industry to capture insurance regulation, it would have to dominate at least 51 separate policy systems each with a different political environment and different political actors. Such domination is not unachievable, but with the divisions in the industry, it is not likely.

A variety of actors other than the insurance industry play a role in the insurance regulatory process including regulatory bureaucrats, political elites, and consumers. Of these, the most important are the regulatory bureaucrats. Bureaucracy is an institution designed to handle complexity. Bureaucracies can specialize, deal with complex problems over time, and, in a series of steps, approximate a solution. In larger states with reasonably sized insurance commissions, the regulatory bureaucracy can compete with the insurance industry as an equal. The smaller states with few examiners and no actuaries must rely on NAIC for data or place themselves totally at the mercy of the insurance industry.

The history of insurance regulation contains numerous important policy decisions whereby the regulatory bureaucracy imposed a policy solution different from that sought by the industry. The McCarran-Ferguson Act was a much different exemption of insurance from federal antitrust laws than the insurance industry requested. The All-Industry laws that were passed to trigger the antitrust exemption were much stricter than the industry's proposals. Where the industry wanted a simple ratification of their right to collude and set prices, the insurance regulators established a prior approval system.

The movement to greater competition in ratemaking during the 1950s, 1960s, and 1970s was often over the objections of the major segments of the insurance industry. Regulatory commissioners granted deviations, allowed multiline insurance pricing, and eventually advocated competitive ratemaking statutes in numerous states. In the process, the insurance industry was placed in a more uncertain economic environment; and the consumer benefitted from increased competition.

Political elites, key members of the executive, legislative, and the judicial branches, also play a role in insurance policy. Perhaps their most important role is indirect. Political elites create an environment of expectations that regulatory bureaucrats must meet. Insurance commissioners know that certain actions will be unacceptable to key legislators; therefore, these actions will not be considered. In a state with a professional and progressive legislature, the zone of discretion available to the insurance commissioner widens in terms of consumer protection policies. In a state with conservative, part-time legislators, the insurance commissioner must be careful not to offend the insurance industry.

Political elites do more than create a climate of expectations. They also pass legislation that sets insurance policy. Insurance policy has detailed laws, and the industry has a reputation for incorporating such precision in its actions. Legislation is often used to specify exact policy forms or to delegate this authority to the commissioner. The NAIC's sponsorship of model legislation has greatly assisted the smaller states in this regard.

A good illustration of the role political elites play in the insurance regulatory process is the property and casualty insurance crisis of 1985–1986. New Jersey Governor Thomas Kean directly intervened to pressure insurance companies to create a Marketing Assistance Plan to provide insurance for small businesses that could not get it. The Florida legislature enacted several proposed tort reforms and in exchange unilaterally cut specified insurance rates by up to 40 percent. In many states, political elites did nothing more than slow down the process of considering tort reforms. This delay allowed additional information to enter the debate and permitted policymakers to assess the impact of the large 1985 rate increases. Those states that were able to resist the initial stampede to tort reform eventually found little reason to adopt insurance industry proposals.

Although consumers are the least active group in insurance policy, they influence the policy environment. States with strong consumer movements or potentially strong consumer movements have a policy environment less receptive to insurance industry demands. Potential consumer group membership was highly correlated with policies designed to increase access to insurance at the state level. Consumer groups were part of the anti-tort-reform coalition in the liability insurance crisis of 1985–1986. Although NICO hardly packs the clout of the Insurance Services Office, its presence during policy debates often illuminates consumer issues in insurance.

The political economy of insurance regulation is an interesting study in federalism. Unlike other areas dealing with interstate commerce, the federal government has not preempted state regulation of insurance. By passing the McCarran-Ferguson Act with an antitrust exemption for the insurance industry, the federal government has delegated most insurance regulatory policy to the states. This delegation is voluntary; however, and the federal government at any time could decide that federal regulation of insurance is in the public interest. Such legislation is currently pending in Congress. Although passage is unlikely without some major stimulus event, the threat of such legislation often motivates state regulators to act.

Despite federal delegation of insurance regulation, many insurance issues are placed on the federal policy agenda. Federal issues differ from state issues in that federal issues are always more salient (they need to be simply to get on the federal agenda) than state issues and usually less complex. As such, they occur in a policy environment that is more conducive to political elites and federal bureaucrats participating in the process.

The mail-order insurance problem, for example, illustrates the ability of the Federal Trade Commission to play a catalytic role. The FTC's willingness to act against deceptive advertising among mail-order insurance companies was a prime stimulant for the states to take action. The no-fault automobile insurance controversy at the federal level reveals a policy arena where industry was split. Agents were eventually able to triumph over large insurance companies in defeating a federal no-fault law. The result has been an increase in costs to the consuming public.

The federal proposals concerning unisex insurance rating plunged the insurance industry into a debate over social goals. The industry does not feel comfortable with social goals; it prefers issues where the actuarial base of the industry is not threatened. The fact that unisex rating of insurance is even raised illustrates that insurance companies are unable to control the policy agenda. Federalism has allowed women's groups to pursue this issue in a variety of forums; partial victories have been won in court, in Congress, in some state legislatures, and with a regulator or two.

Federal flood insurance was a policy innovation advocated by insurance companies, but they were unable to control the program once it was established. Private firms were, in fact, eliminated from the program in a policy dispute with the Federal Insurance Administrator. Perhaps the best illustration of the insurance industry's political limitations was the increase of insurance company taxes by the federal government in the 1980s. Despite the awesome complexity of insurance accounting, Congress was able to increase taxes on insurance companies. The complexity problem was finessed by passing temporary legislation and forcing the industry to negotiate its own tax increase.

This study of regulation was undertaken for theoretical reasons. The results of the analysis suggest that the time has long passed to abandon George Stigler's simplistic supply and demand regulatory theory. Stigler's theory was incorrect when he proposed it in 1971, and it has not improved with age. Regulatory policy is more than just competition between interest groups; if it were, Stigler's arguments about capture might well be correct.

Political officials cannot be realistically viewed as neutral monitors of the interest group process who are willing to grant the demands of the most powerful groups. Regulatory bureaucrats are an independent force in insurance policy and in many cases are a force for pro-consumer policy. Not all insurance regulators fit this role; a regulator needs a professionalized, supportive agency to be a consumer advocate. An insurance commissioner who administers an agency of 20 to 30 employees rarely has the expertise to oppose industry recommendations. In larger states, however, insurance commissioners have instituted progressive policies and through the NAIC exported them to other states.

Political elites are the other group that must be considered an independent actor. Political elites, such as legislators, must first be considered a separate actor from regulatory bureaucrats; treating them as one entity as Stigler does simply ignores the different interests the two groups have. Political elites can and do intervene in the insurance regulatory process. When they do intervene, they seek policies consistent with their own policy goals. Pro-consumer elites seek pro-consumer policies; pro-industry elites seek pro-industry policies. In many cases, political elites do not have to intervene; simply the threat that they might keeps an insurance regulator somewhat responsive to the general policy goals of political elites.

Finally, Stigler's view of regulatory policy ignores the important role that the political environment plays in regulatory policy. Complex and unsalient issues are ideal for creating a situation where only the industry and the regulatory bureaucracy can effectively participate. When issues become salient or less complex, political elites and even consumer groups can play a more effective role. Although insurance issues are generally complex and unsalient, they vary. No-fault automobile insurance is a salient and simple policy issue as is unisex insurance rating. If such salient issues are placed on the agenda, the insurance industry is at a disadvantage. It becomes just another group advocating its own self-interest. The industry can no longer simply argue that the policy issue is one that is best decided as a matter of expertise.

In sum, the political economy of insurance regulation is richly varied. Not all insurance regulation is established for the industry at the industry's request. Policies vary from state to state and from issue to issue. Policy outcomes follow a reasonably predictable pattern; they are an interaction between the interests of industry, consumers, regulators, and political elites within an environment that structures the opportunities available for each group.

Policy Recommendations

Although the primary purpose of this analysis was to test theories of regulatory policy, many of the findings have policy implications. The following recommendations reflect the author's bias that the purpose of insurance regulation is to protect the consumers' interests. The insurance consumer may benefit from regulation in a variety of ways. First, if regulation improves the financial solidity of insurance companies, a policyholder's claims are more likely to be paid. Second, regulatory policies can enhance efficiency so that the consumer is able to purchase insurance at a reasonable cost. Third, regulatory policies can increase access to insurance so that individuals who might not otherwise be able to purchase insurance can now do so. Fourth, regulatory decisions can increase the choices available to consumers and provide information to make rational choices. Although these four benefits often conflict with each other and some benefit certain classes of consumers at the expense of others, they provide the supporting justifications for the following recommendations.

REGULATORY RESOURCES

This study finds that states with ample resources committed to insurance regulation are more likely to have policies that benefit the consumer. A large regulatory bureaucracy acts as a counter weight to insurance industry claims. A large agency does not necessarily overrule industry claims but, rather, subjects them to probing analysis. In such a situation, individuals advocating consumer interests (such as regulators or legislators) can draw on the bureaucracy's resources to support their policy claims. Accordingly, states should augment the resources available to insurance commissioners. An insurance regulatory agency with fewer than 30 employees (and some exist) and no insurance examiners is in no position to vigorously regulate the industry.

Funding to increase insurance regulatory resources is available. Only about 5 percent of insurance premium taxes are spent on insurance regulation; the remainder go into the state general revenue fund. If budget constraints are too severe, then a small increase in the premium tax (as little as a 5 percent increase) earmarked for the insurance regulatory commission could double commission budgets.

These additional resources could be spent in a variety of ways. First, insurance commissioners should be paid realistic salaries. Some insurance commissioners earn less than $30,000 per year. How a state can attract a competent commissioner to regulate multibillion dollar corporations with such salaries is impossible to tell. Restrictions on the qualifications of the commissioners should also be abolished. Some states require that their commissioner have worked in the insurance industry for a given number of years. Recruitment from the industry plus low pay will virtually guarantee a weak regulatory commissioner.[2]

Second, additional resources could add badly needed professionals to insurance commissions. Unlike many other regulatory agencies, insurance commissions have not attracted many economists in recent years. The impact of economists in federal regulatory reforms in airline transportation, surface transportation, banking deregulation, and consumer protection suggests that their expertise might also be valuable in insurance regulation (Derthick and Quirk, 1985). At a minimum, economists see insurance somewhat differently stressing the incentives that high insurance costs create for changing behavior (see Schwartz and Komisar, 1978). This viewpoint is valuable. Many innovations in fire protection were implemented because insurance companies threatened to raise rates unless changes were adopted. Economists could provide this viewpoint in other areas of insurance.

Third, insurance commissions employ very few actuaries, the individuals that the industry relies on to calculate rates and make other statistical determinations. Although commissions might not need more actuaries per se, they do need staff with similar skills. Information from insurance companies cannot be rationally analyzed without both statistical and computer skills. Every commission should employ both statisticians and management information systems personnel. These individuals could work closely with the industry to make reporting forms consistent with regulatory needs for information.[3]

Fourth, smaller states need to employ more consumer specialists. Large states often publish valuable consumer information comparing prices or complaints lodged against insurance companies. This valuable service is unavailable in many smaller states. In addition, these individuals could mediate complaints filed against companies.

PRICE REGULATION

This study and several others (Harrington, 1984) find that price regulation by insurance commissions has no impact on the price of insurance, probably because insurance regulatory commissions, with a few exceptions, lack the expertise to set rates rationally. Surprisingly, many commissions that have the expertise to regulate rates (for example, New York and California), rely heavily on the market to set insurance prices. Given this finding, justifying the expenditure of resources on prior approval price regulation systems is difficult.

This conclusion is especially pertinent to the individual lines of insurance (automobile insurance, homeowners' insurance, etc.). Such markets are competitive or potentially competitive. The number of sellers is reasonably large, and some sellers (the direct writers) are aggressive competitors. Consumers in these markets need information (see below) rather than rigid price regulation. At most, states should require rates to be filed so that general price trends can be monitored.

In business lines of insurance (general liability, malpractice, commercial multiple peril, etc.) the market clearly has fewer sellers. This market also has fewer buyers, thereby resembling oligopsony. Businesses that purchase insurance are not at an information disadvantage with regard to insurance companies; in fact, large businesses actually can use their market position to either demand attractive rates or to self-insure. Small businesses have the option of creating captives or joint risk-sharing pools with other similar businesses or hiring an agent to reduce the information asymmetry. A market with few buyers and few sellers is bound to create some temporary inequities. What is unclear is how government price regulation could improve such a situation. If prices are set too low, insurance companies will simply abandon the market. If they are set too high, businesses will be unable to buy insurance. Prices in this situation are a zero sum game, and price regulation offers no panacea that will benefit both insurance companies and the insured. Market-set prices appear to be a more flexible way to create incentives either to arrive at equilibrium prices or to find alternative methods of reducing risk.

CONSUMER INFORMATION

Without the burdens of price regulation, insurance commissions will have additional resources available to provide information to consumers. Certain forms of insurance are reasonably uniform so that rational choices could be made with the correct information. Some state insurance commissions already provide price comparisons for automobile and homeowners' insurance policies. Such practices should be universal and published frequently. The claims side of the insurance transaction is also important. Some insurance companies provide better claims service than others. Those insurance commissions that do not compile insurance companies' complaint ratings should do so and publish them. A consumer could then the necessary trade-offs between price and service.[4]

The life insurance market also needs better consumer information. Although insurance companies have been highly critical of the FTC's attempts to compare life insurance policies, such comparisons provide valuable information. Because the insurance regulator knows the costs of the pure life insurance premium, the expenses of the company, and the company's investment income, the insurance commission has all the information to publish good cost comparisons for life insurance products. Although many insurance companies would oppose such action, those companies with high benefits-to-premiums ratios should support such government action.

The final consumer information program regards policy readability. NAIC's model laws on readable policies are a step in the right direction. Those laws or improved versions of them should be adopted in all 50 states. Insurance is one of the few areas of commerce where a consumer purchases a product and has almost no idea what has been purchased. The general common law doctrine that contracts should be interpreted to favor the party who did not draft the contract is not an adequate protection for unreadable policies. Such an interpretation benefits policyholders with lawyers—not policyholders in general.

BANKS AND INSURANCE

Consistent with the goal of providing consumers more choices, current federal and state laws that restrict the entry of bank holding companies and banks into the insurance business should be repealed. The past 15 years have seen the barriers between the various financial services industries eroded by technology and economics. Insurance companies have not been shy about entering into traditional banking businesses. Insurance companies now offer universal life insurance policies as a direct competitor to both bank-held IRAs and traditional savings accounts. Ordinary life insurance has always been a means of saving funds for retirement or for an estate. Insurance companies perform services similar to banks; they take deposits (premiums) that individuals can vary under certain policies; they make loans to both policyholders and to corporations via purchases of commercial paper. If banking is a business that is not inconsistent with operating an insurance company, then insurance is surely not a business inconsistent with operating a bank.

The entry of banks into insurance raises a wide variety of other regulatory issues with regard to banks and federal regulation. Such issues as deposit insurance, financial solvency, and so forth can be handled within the bank regulatory system. Consumers would benefit from more competitors in the "insurance" side of financial services. Banks, in turn, would be able to compete with insurance companies and securities firms in the same markets that insurance companies and securities firms currently provide "bank-like" services.

TAXING LIFE INSURANCE

Consumer choice in financial services and in insurance specifically is enhanced if all competitors are operating under similar rules. If regulatory and tax policies are neutral with respect to various financial institutions, then consumers will select financial services on the basis of highest returns rather than on the basis of tax breaks. The current tax distinction between life insurance and other forms of savings is irrational. No societal or consumer purpose is served by taxing most forms of savings and exempting savings via life insurance. Universal life in particular is so close to a money market mutual fund that it should be treated as such.[5]

NO-FAULT AUTOMOBILE INSURANCE

The evidence presented herein and by other research convincingly demonstrates that policyholders benefit from real forms of no-fault automobile insurance. Under no-fault systems that limit litigation, consumers receive a larger benefits to premiums ratio. The portion of premiums that pay for company expenses is similarly reduced. The experiment conducted by the states has served its purpose. Although the prospects of federal legislation are unlikely, the consuming public would be well served by a federal no-fault automobile insurance law. Failing federal legislation, well-drafted state legislation would have an equally positive impact in those states where a no-fault law could be passed.

ALTERNATIVE DISPUTE RESOLUTION MECHANISMS

A true no-fault automobile insurance system essentially eliminates the use of the tort system to determine fault. No-fault processes are only one of several alternative methods of resolving disputes. The current system of dispute resolution in liability insurance relies almost completely on the legal process through litigation. The present tort system has a variety of problems. First, it is inefficient; a large portion of premiums goes to pay the costs of resolving claims rather than compensating injured parties. Second, the tort system is inequitable. Medical malpractice liability insurance provides an excellent illustration of inequitable treatment. A few injured individuals are compensated for their injuries and often overcompensated through punitive damages and other mechanisms. The overwhelming majority of parties injured by medical treatment are not compensated or are compensated less than the extent of their injuries (Danzon, 1985). Third, the tort system is slow. Cases often drag on for years under a bewildering procedural morass of discovery and pretrial maneuvering. Parties are often not compensated for years after the injury. Fourth, the legal system often lacks the expertise to decide claims intelligently. Jurors are not trained in the techniques of assessing injury costs; judges are also generalists. Occasional reports of bizarre decisions should not come as a surprise. One is never sure if the tort system rewards meritorious claims or possession of legal talent.

The optimal dispute resolution process for insurance claims is not obvious. What is obvious is that the current system has substantial limitations.

Efficiency, equity, timeliness, and rationality should be the goals used to evaluate alternative dispute resolution mechanisms. Several possibilities exist. Arbitration might be used to settle disputes. A government agency might be staffed with liability and injury experts who would make a ruling after an investigation of the claim. Specialized courts similar to those for workers' compensation might provide more equitable results.

Alternative dispute resolution processes are the key to real tort reform. Major policy disputes about such issues as contingency fee limits, caps on pain and suffering, limitations on rules of procedure that were discussed in the 1985–1986 liability insurance crisis are a waste of time. Good empirical studies (Sloan, 1986; Copeland and Meier, 1986) have shown that these proposals have virtually no impact on the cost of medical malpractice insurance. State legislatures should experiment with real alternatives to tort litigation if the objective is to provide a liability system that is more efficient, equitable, timely, and rational.

RISK AND SOCIETY

Citizens of the United States now purchase more than one-half of the insurance sold in the entire world. Americans seek to protect themselves from the ill effects of death coming too early (life insurance), death coming too late (annuities), workplace injuries, automobile accidents, bad weather, household accidents, and countless other events. Americans' concern with risk has spawned innovative lawsuits, which, in turn, have generated innovative judicial rulings. Many of these rulings have had a positive effect; others are difficult to justify. Why a homeowners' insurance policy should be liable for the transmission of a social disease is difficult to understand. Why a liability insurance policy written to cover pollution damages from sudden and accidental spills should be interpreted to cover gradual leakage is also mystifying.

Creating a risk-free society through the insurance mechanism is neither possible nor desirable. Governments need to take a role in defining insurance risks. Certain risks are clearly societal risks and should be borne by society at large. Hauling hazardous waste and disposing of it property at the present time is a societal problem. Private insurance companies can no more offer reasonably priced insurance for this risk than they can for the risk of a nuclear accident. Because the problem needs to be solved, the risks involved should be defined as government risks with a compensation system established. An especially valuable contribution might be a government risk policy that defines the types of risks considered societal problems and provides for compensation systems for injuries.

An equally valuable policy would be one that recognized that a risk-free society is not possible. Individuals and companies are not compensated for a wide variety of economic and personal risks. Federal deposit insurance should not be used, for example, to protect the owners of financial institutions from the consequences of their own actions; badly managed institutions should be allowed to fail. Risk in investments are compensated by higher rates of return; individuals seeking risk-free investments should buy savings bonds. Similarly, no government policy whether or not supplemented by private insurance policies can protect individuals from the daily risks of life. Insurance companies should lead the way in educating consumers about the purpose of insurance. Life quite clearly contains risks; they should be recognized as such. Protecting individuals from every potential risk in life is both inefficient and undesirable.

Conclusion

The chapter has two purposes. First, the empirical findings of the analysis were recapitulated. The implications of the analysis for regulatory theory is the focus, and the author argues that Stigler's theory of economic regulation is inferior to a multi-interest view of regulatory policy. Second, several policy recommendations that grew out of the analysis are discussed, including augmenting bureaucratic resources, creating more consumer choices in insurance, eliminating price regulation, providing alternative dispute resolution processes, and establishing government policy in regard to risk.

Notes

1. Even economists do not devote much attention to the political economy of insurance. Only two major articles have appeared: Joskow (1973) and Ippolito (1979).

2. Private health insurance companies are so designated to distinguish them from the Blue Cross and Blue Shield organizations. The Blues, as they are known, are physician-dominated and are designed more to provide payment for physician and hospital services; insurance is the means to do this. Despite the similar services, the private health insurance companies and the Blues are not considered part of the same industry.

3. The recent spurt in annuities can be attributed to the popular nature of universal life insurance. Universal life essentially combines a form of term insurance with the equivalent of a money market fund that will eventually pay off as an annuity. Because of the tax consequences related to insurance, investments made this way are not taxed until the funds are actually returned to the policyholder. The tax avoidance nature of universal life has made it the most popular product in the industry.

4. Many insurance policies can be divided into two parts—insurance and savings. The insurance portion is that portion of premiums that go to pay for death benefits based on actuarial tables. Premiums are usually larger than the amount needed to pay for the pure insurance portion of the policy. These funds are invested; they eventually accumulate so that when the policy is fully paid the total savings will equal the face value of the policy. These savings are the cash value of the insurance policy.

5. The private passenger automobile insurance buyer does have options in purchasing insurance, but these are selected from the options that the insurance company makes available. The large commercial automobile insurance buyer can have policies designed specifically for them.

6. The Insurance Information Institute has begun to report profit comparisons, but it uses insurance industry accounting and compares these figures to profit figures taken from *Forbes*. As expected, this comparison shows that the insurance industry's profits lag far behind those of other industries.

179

7. The life insurance industry profit figure is probably an underestimate because mutual insurance companies technically do not make profits. Their cash flows would not be represented in these figures. Because mutual firms tend to be the largest and most successful in the industry, the estimate is probably somewhat low.

8. The prices for insurance stocks are taken from the life and health edition of *Best's Review*. This monthly stock index was used for the final figures for December of each year. The New York Stock Exchange index was taken from its annual report. Property and casualty insurance stocks alone grew by 28.3 percent in 1985, the year of the property and casualty insurance "crisis." This figure compares favorably to the 26.1 percent increase in the New York Stock Exchange index for 1985.

Chapter 2

1. In at least some of these examples, Stigler's view of the world is open to question. Brown (1985) presents evidence that CAB policies did not benefit the largest members of the airline industry and that benefits were restricted to the scheduled trunk airlines only in times of economic stress. FDIC restrictions on entry should be interpreted in the light of recent economic arguments that federal regulation sponsored more banks than economic conditions warranted (see Carron, 1983).

2. This first statement that smaller firms somehow exploit the larger firms has generated a great deal of discussion in the literature. The point was first made by Bauer, Pool, and Dexter (1963) and popularized by Mancur Olson (1965). Numerous others have focused on what has become known as the "free rider problem." Small firms are viewed as free riders because they can benefit from the actions of larger firms without political investments of their own.

3. High-quality roads might indicate that state legislatures are rational in making policy. Such legislatures probably have higher weight limits when they have roads that can bear those limits.

4. If Stigler had shown positive relationships between the number of truckers, the income of truckers, and these weight limits, then the claim of capture might have been plausible. For a contemporary argument about the lack of influence of truckers on federal policy circa 1970 see Kohlmeier (1969).

5. Stigler does not distinguish between legislative actors and administrative regulators despite the common situation where administrative rules diverge from legislative policy. Weingast and Moran (1983) have recently attempted to justify this position by arguing that legislators dominate administrative actors so that one need not be concerned with the actions of administrators. Given the findings of many studies of regulation (see Wilson, 1980a; Meier, 1985b), this assertion is absurd. See Moe (1985) for a comprehensive critique of the Weingast and Moran argument.

6. Actually, Stigler confuses an interest group's resources with the factors that make it difficult for an interest to organize. Given two similar potential interest

groups, the smaller group has fewer organizational costs and, therefore, is more likely to organize. Given two interest groups that are already organized, the larger group has greater potential resources. Economists in general and Stigler in particular have extremely simplistic views of interest groups; they often ignore myriad incentives that interest groups can offer members (see Wilson, 1973) and rarely ever consider the internal dynamics of these groups and how they affect the actions that they take (Browne, 1977; Moe, 1980; Berry, 1984).

7. The enthusiasm of economists for George Stigler's work is best illustrated by his winning the 1982 Nobel Prize for economics, which specifically referred to his theory of economic regulation.

8. Efficiency is probably not a goal of regulation (see Litan and Nordhaus, 1983; Meier, 1985b: 275). Regulation is a political process, and, as such, it is concerned with the distribution of political and economic power. Individuals seek to be regulated or to have others regulated because they are dissatisfied with the current distribution of economic or political power.

9. The best explication of public interest theory, even though the context is not regulation, is Stokey and Zeckhauser (1978). This view still flourishes in the economics profession (see MacAvoy, 1979; Noll and Owen, 1983) and has picked up some adherents among political scientists (Stone, 1982).

10. One might argue as Gormley (1982: 298) does that *pluralism* and *capture* are distinct theories, but based on who benefits from regulation, the process of both is similar—interest groups determining public policy.

11. Some economists might argue that the EPA is captured by environmentalists, but this view so perverts the theory as to render it useless.

12. Exactly what Posner means by *atheoretical* is not clear. The difference between Bernstein and Stigler is that Bernstein has a more elaborate explanation for why agencies serve the interests of the regulated. Stigler merely asserts that regulation should follow a supply-and-demand relationship while Bernstein spins out an elaborate life-cycle analogy. Posner's criticisms of Bernstein are also criticisms of Stigler because both have the same empirical failings even though Posner seeks to save Stigler and bury Bernstein.

Posner, in fact, criticizes all political scientists as being atheoretical in that their theories do not explain why some interest groups are effective and others are not. In doing so, Posner demonstrates his lack of knowledge of the literature. Both Zeigler (1964), whom he cites, and Rourke (1969), whom he does not, have elaborate specifications as to what factors increase the probability that an interest group will affect public policy.

13. The reader should note that fire insurance companies were able to obtain protective legislation for a period of time despite the fact that they had the ability to establish a private cartel and that they were not concentrated in any geographic area. See Chapter 5.

14. This is the basic tenet of pluralism. Posner's reformulation of Stigler is nothing more than warmed-over political science pluralism placed in supply-and-demand terminology.

15. Peltzman is making the same point in a more limited way that Wilson (1980b) does. Wilson argues that when benefits are concentrated but costs are dispersed, the industry (usually a producer group) will control the regulatory process.

16. I do not mean to argue that the current model is simpler than the economic theory of regulation; it is much more complex. I only mean to argue that the need to operationalize each of the variables in both a historical and a cross-sectional approach will prevent me from using some concepts that can be used only with in-depth case study methods. See Meier (1985b) for a more elaborate political theory of regulation applied to a series of case studies.

17. A more elaborate theory would include additional actors such as journalists, professional experts, judges, proxy advocates, etc. (see Sabatier, 1983; Heclo, 1978; Gormley, 1982; 313). To keep the theory parsimonious, only four are used. In the historical sections of this book, the designations of actors become more specific and at times other actors are included.

18. Exceptions to this rule exist. The CAB appeared to cheerfully preside over the demise of the CAB, and the FCC of the 1980s has shown little interest in regulation.

19. *Political elites* include the elected chief executive, legislators, and judges. It does not include agency (career) bureaucrats or the insurance commissioners.

Chapter 3

1. Japan, the number two nation, has its percentage of the market distorted because the Japanese are major purchasers of life insurance. To illustrate, the property and casualty insurance market in Japan is only one-seventh the size of the U. S. market, but the life insurance market is five-eighths the size of the U. S. market. The Japanese market for life insurance can be explained by the poor-quality pension systems in Japan. The total worldwide market for insurance in 1984 was estimated to be $498 billion (Insurance Information Institute, 1986: 15).

2. To be fair to the SEC, two cases of reasonably vigorous regulation have occurred. When Stanley Sporkin was director of enforcement, many firms were prosecuted for failing to disclose information to stockholders. This was the mechanism used to prosecute corporations that illegally contributed money to President Nixon's reelection campaign in 1972. Beginning in 1986, the SEC began a major effort to combat insider trading. Although this effort is too recent to evaluate, it does appear to be a departure from the SEC's normal emphasis on self-regulation.

3. This act also separated banking from investment banking, thereby prohibiting banks from underwriting stock issues.

4. State banks in some states are authorized by state law to sell insurance. This has resulted in a loophole whereby bank holding companies have attempted to purchase banks in certain states (primarily South Dakota). These state banks could be turned into what were called "nonbanks" by eliminating either checking accounts or commercial loans. The nonbank loophole has been litigated unsuccessfully by the Federal Reserve; it is currently on the national legislative agenda. Although many observers expect this loophole to be closed, no one can predict what Congress will ultimately do.

5. The reader should be aware that federal health care insurance programs have major regulatory implications. Because the federal government is such a large purchaser of health care through Medicare and Medicaid and because the federal government has been interested in controlling costs, the federal government has instituted a form of price regulation in health care. Using diagnostic review groups (DRGs) the federal government pays only a specified amount for each diagnosed illness. This program has established a cap on fees that health care providers can charge the federal government. Private insurance companies have been exerting similar pressures on health care providers.

6. The line between an insurance program and a welfare program is a fine one. To be considered an insurance program, the individual must make some direct payments that can be considered equivalent to premiums. If benefits similar to insurance are offered, such as the supplemental income program for the blind, disabled, and aged or the Aid to Families with Dependent Children (AFDC) program, and the benefits are paid for by general tax revenues, the program is considered a welfare program.

7. Several other areas of federal insurance activity have private sector competition. Some private deposit insurance companies still exist, but with the recent defaults of savings associations in Ohio and Maryland, demand for private deposit insurance has dropped. Private insurance companies could easily provide life insurance directly to veterans and in many cases companies exist that market specifically to veterans. Private mortgage insurance exists, and some secondary mortgage market institutions insist that mortgages be insured. Credit life is a form of loan guarantee insurance that is offered by private insurance companies.

8. Companies with their legal origins in another country are called *alien companies*.

9. In actuality, a bewildering array of processes exist for filing rates. A file-and-use law requires the company to file a rate and wait for a given period before using the rate. If closely monitored by the state, this type of law is fairly similar to a prior approval law. A use-and-file law requires that rates be filed, but companies can use the rates immediately. Subsequent action by the regulator is required to reject the rate.

In many cases, it is not the type of law on the books but the way the law is implemented that affects whether prices are set by the market or by regulatory agencies.

10. The 5 percent figure has no economic basis. Premium income is only one source of income to insurance companies; the other major source of income is from investments. Initially investment income was not to be considered in establishing rates. A recent survey of insurance commissioners, however, revealed that most states at least look at investment income when setting some rates (Hurtz, 1984: 18). The NAIC has modified its stand also; it now holds that investment income should be considered to some degree. The estimates of return on equity for insurance companies presented in Chapter 1 reveal that returns in insurance are roughly equal to the returns for all other industries although returns in insurance are more volatile.

11. Even the most rabid free market economist would accept the principle that government must enforce contracts. Without government enforcement of contracts, economic relations are simply impossible. Contracts could, of course, be enforced by courts rather than regulators, but the sheer volume of insurance contracts make this impossible. Currently courts interpret a limited number of insurance forms as provided by state regulators.

12. See also Chapter 5 on the property and casualty insurance crisis of 1985–1986. Many individuals, including some insurance companies and consumer advocate Robert Hunter, blamed the crisis on excessive competition. An alternative view of competition and solvency in a cross-national perspective is presented by Finsinger and Pauly (1986).

13. Access as a regulatory goal is very similar to the goal of equity, which is often expressed in regulatory policy (Meier, 1985b). Access goals are almost always raised by individuals who seek to provide greater equity in the benefits of insurance coverage.

Chapter 4

1. Patterson (1927: 515) argues that the first regulation of insurance took place in Florence, Italy. A special administrative agency to regulate insurance was found in a 1523 Florentine statute.

2. The Presbyterian Ministers' Fund was actually an annuity company rather than a life insurance company; its product was aimed at retirement incomes not death benefits (Miller, 1982: 79).

3. Patterson (1927: 521) also argues that the corporate form makes insurance regulation feasible by limiting the number of individuals that need regulation.

4. An *alien insurance company* is one that is domiciled in another country. A *foreign company* is one domiciled in another state. The *place of domicile* is the place where the company is incorporated.

5. Local boards to restrict competition were created as early as 1819 (Hanson, Dineen, and Johnson, 1974: 10).

6. This is a pattern that will be repeated many times during the political history of insurance regulation. The most recent time it occurred was during the liability insurance crisis of 1985–1986.

7. In 1866, a bill was introduced to establish federal regulation of insurance companies. Many life insurance companies favored this bill (Buley, 1953: 83). During President Theodore Roosevelt's Administration, another unsuccessful effort was made to establish insurance regulation within the Department of Commerce.

8. In 1918, New York adopted a new standard fire policy and this gradually replaced the 1886 policy. The 1918 policy remained the norm until the adoption of the 1943 New York policy form (Lilly, 1976: 106).

9. Term insurance provides only for death benefits for a limited term. It has no cash value. Whole life insurance, which is more expensive than term insurance, builds a cash value. The greater use of whole life insurance means that insurance companies have greater reserves to invest.

10. Under Wright, the life insurance companies did rather well. The number of policies in force quintupled from 1858 to 1867 (Buley, 1953: 63). Wright was forced out under the guise of administrative restructuring. Massachusetts reduced the number of insurance commissioners from two to one, and Wright was the one eliminated.

11. Hughes, of course, goes on to become Governor of New York, a candidate for President, and Chief Justice of the U. S. Supreme Court.

12. Early state legislation often limited the size of dividend that a stock insurance company could pay. The option was to organize as a mutual company so that the dividend could include part of the organization's "profits," thereby circumventing the law. To avoid the problem of policyholders controlling the company, a number of companies were able to persuade legislatures to eliminate policyholder voting in mutual companies (Post, 1976: 99).

13. The salience of insurance at this time is illustrated by President Theodore Roosevelt's holding a conference on insurance regulation. He also made several comments with regard to insurance in his first address to Congress later that year (Buley, 1953: 237).

14. The Appleton rule actually preceded the Armstrong Committee investigation; but without the legislation that followed the Armstrong Committee investigation, the Appleton rule would have had little impact. The Supreme Court upheld the extraterritorial aspects of the Appleton rule in *Fireman's Insurance v. Beha* 278 U. S. 580 (1929).

15. The Appleton rule also limited the growth of companies doing business in New York. The result was that the companies not operating in New York often grew at much faster rates (Krooss and Blyn, 1970: 144).

16. The response of life insurance companies to the Appleton rule is to avoid New York. In 1972, only 103 of the 1,790 life insurance companies operating in the United States were licensed to sell insurance in New York. In 1900, 37.5 percent of all life insurance companies were licensed in New York (Weisbart, 1975: 39). A survey of companies not licensed in New York revealed that 85 percent stated they did not seek admission to New York to avoid the Appleton rule (Weisbart, 1975: 43). Most companies wanted to avoid the expense limitation law, although some companies also cited the lack of investment flexibility and the group life minimum premium law.

17. The committee accepted the industry's argument that competition was the problem. They did not consider other causes of insolvency including mismanagement of funds, inadequate reserves, and absence of good loss statistics (Hanson, Dineen, and Johnson, 1974: 18 note 31).

18. The conclusion that anticompact laws have failed was interesting because New York did not have an anticompact law.

19. Wisconsin did regulate the price of life insurance in 1907. The objective was to hold the price of life insurance down by limiting company expenses. The premium was determined by the pure premium, the assumed interest rate, and an additional one-third added for expenses. No other state followed this policy innovation.

20. The federal government also has a major impact on the investment decisions of life insurance companies (see O'Leary, 1953). This impact, primarily through monetary and fiscal policy, is discussed in the chapter on federal regulation of insurance.

21. INA was originally given authority to insure lives but issued very few life insurance policies. Those policies it did issue were for short periods of time, such as the time necessary to travel from location A to location B.

22. In part because of mandatory investment statutes, life insurance companies were advocates of federal regulation of insurance. Although the *Paul* case was brought by fire insurance companies, life insurance companies continued to favor federal regulation for the next several decades (Orren, 1974: 26).

23. The variation in investment laws explains some of the bizarre pattern of where insurance companies are domiciled. In 1985, only 80 life insurance companies were domiciled in New York, while a record 616 were domiciled in Arizona.

24. States also regulate investments via their ability to evaluate the value of life insurance investments. This practice has become fairly uniform due to the NAIC's efforts. The only clear-cut manipulation of this valuation process occurred during the Great Depression when certain valuation rules were adopted to avoid declaring insurance companies with nonproducing assets bankrupt.

25. Armentano (1982) and a variety of other economists argue that conspiracies are inherently unstable. Conspiracies must have some type of enforcement mechanism that allows them to control potential cheaters. For insurance bureaus, both the information and the access to reinsurance were controls.

26. At this time, the nation was divided into four parts by the insurance companies with separate rate bureaus for each of the regions. The South-Eastern Underwriters Association essentially controlled insurance functions in the southeastern United States. Other regional bureaus were the Eastern Underwriters Association, the Western Underwriters Association, and the Board of Fire Underwriters of the Pacific.

27. These returns on premiums were not unusual at the time. Between 1936 and 1941, Wisconsin fire insurance companies collected $128 million in premiums and paid only $52 million in claims (Kimball, 1960: 105).

28. According to Rose (1969: 690), these fears were exaggerated because these state regulatory laws would be exempt from antitrust laws under the state action criterion of *Parker v. Brown* (see below).

29. Two additional criticisms of the decision were heard. Justice Jackson raised the issue that this was an attempt to establish federal regulation. Although insurance companies once preferred federal regulation to state regulation when state regulation appeared to be more vigorous than federal regulation would be, by 1944 and the domination of the New Deal and federal activism, the industry preferred state regulation. One insurance executive remarked that the industry would rather be regulated by 50 monkeys than by one gorilla. The second issue regarded the Supreme Court's deviation from its customary procedures of not deciding constitutional questions unless an absolute majority of the court agreed. This was essentially a criticism of the 4-to-3 majority (see Rose, 1967: 686).

30. Tactics of the insurance industry are fairly predictable. A similar grassroots lobby effort was undertaken during the liability crisis of 1985–1986 with some effort to get Congress to pass a federal tort reform law.

31. McCarran and Ferguson were strong supporters of the insurance industry. Their defection and that of other Senators from the insurance industry coalition left the coalition with too little support to impose its own solution. The support of McCarran, Ferguson, and other key legislators was the result of adroit lobbying by the NAIC.

32. The McCarran-Ferguson Act was introduced on January 18, 1945, and was signed into law fewer than two months later setting records for consideration of legislation. Although Attorney General Biddle had removed any pressure from prosecution, the states had another deadline. March 1 was the date set for payment of most premium taxes; without legislation, such taxes were in doubt. In addition, the NAIC was successful in mobilizing the industry and legislators to support what they presented as a compromise bill (see Weller, 1978: 597).

33. The court accepted a similar interpretation of federalism when it accept the Appleton rule (see above). Perhaps the distinction is that the Appleton rule extended real regulation, whereas the Nebraska did not.

34. For slightly different numbers, see Crane (1972: 512), who presents figures for 1925 and 1942.

35. Kimball and Boyce (1958: 552) argue that rate regulation was more prevalent than Mosher and Marryott do. They argue that 33 states had mechanisms to regulate insurance rates but admit that in some states the mechanisms were "purely paper machinery". They conclude that "though ostensibly there was control in two-thirds of the states, insurance ratemaking was as yet largely uncontrolled in the United States."

36. New York, of course, was a leader in establishing protective legislation for insurance. As a result of the Merritt Commission investigations, New York adopted rate regulation that permitted insurance companies to set rates in concert. New York was recognized as a leader in this area of regulation even though the first rate regulation law was passed by Kansas in 1909.

37. Before the McCarran-Ferguson Act was passed and the governing concept was the *Parker v. Brown* decision that exempted regulation under state action, the stock insurance companies had advocated prior approval laws. This previous support for prior approval was instrumental in pressuring the stock companies to support prior approval in the NAIC model legislation.

38. The subscriber aspect was added to gain the support of the mutual companies who were not members and often lacked sufficient information to calculate rates. Membership allowed the mutuals to charge the same rates as the bureau members; this portion of the act also prohibited the bureau from discriminating against any company for paying dividends (Long, 1978: 248).

39. Actually, Armentano feels that government-supported cartels are not unstable. He feels that insurance regulation, much like professions regulation, is an area where stable cartels are likely. Even with the coercive power of the state supporting the insurance cartels, however, by the mid-1980s, they were no longer dominant force in insurance politics.

40. The United States is the only country to have required monoline insurance (Bickelhaupt, 1961: 13).

41. An interesting political note is that some of the large existing companies, such as INA and Aetna, were covered by grandfather clauses thereby enabling them to retain their multiline operations.

42. Bickelhaupt (1961: 28) argues that the fleet movement was not particularly successful because many fleets were composed of companies operating in the same line of insurance.

Chapter 5

1. Much of the information presented here was gathered while the author served as a member of the Wisconsin Task Force on Property and Casualty Insurance

during 1986. The conclusions and analysis presented are the author's and do not reflect the thinking of the task force.

2. All figures for the industry and the various lines are taken from *Best's Aggregates and Averages,* 1985, the accepted source in the industry for overall financial statistics.

3. The ISO figure released in January 1985 proved to be inaccurate. Approximately $3 billion in new capital came into the property and casualty industry in the last quarter of 1984. Inflation dropped and the stock market boomed, both of which eased the burden somewhat. In addition, the industry received a $1.7 income tax refund (Bradford, 1985c: 40).

4. Investment income as a percentage of premiums varies greatly by lines. For the years between 1980 and 1984, the investment income by lines is as follows: private passenger auto liability (8.7 percent), private passenger auto physical damage (2.4 percent), homeowners' (4.2 percent), group accident and health (17.5 percent), commercial auto liability (10.7 percent), commercial auto physical damage (2.4 percent), general liability (21.5 percent), medical malpractice (39.2 percent), reinsurance, (13.7 percent). Figures are from *Best's Aggregates and Averages,* 1985: 78–79.

5. Lloyds withdrawal came with some criticisms of the American judicial system. Essentially, Lloyds felt that the tort system in the United States was not predictable; therefore, no systematic way to price risks was found. As a result, Lloyds could not afford to offer reinsurance in such a market.

6. The New Jersey Supreme Court subsequently modified this rule by exempting pharmaceutical companies, see *Feldman v. Lederle* 460 A. 2d 203 (1983).

7. The case that permitted civil rights suits against local governments is *Monroe v. Page* 365 U. S. 167 (1961).

8. Legal costs are not directly broken out in insurance company aggregate reports. Legal costs are included in the category of loss adjustment expenses, which also includes the costs of settling claims. According to industry claims, approximately 90 percent of loss adjustment expenses are legal fees. The 1980–1984 loss adjustment expenses as a percentage of premium income for the major lines of insurance are as follows: private passenger auto liability (11.9 percent), private passenger auto physical damage (8.3 percent), homeowners' (6.9 percent), group accident and health (3.2 percent), commercial auto liability (13.1 percent), commercial auto physical damage (7.5 percent), general liability (19.3 percent), medical malpractice (25.1 percent), reinsurance (4.7 percent), all property and casualty lines (10.4 percent). A good comparison of the 10.4 percent figure for all property and casualty lines is the ALR of 70.2 percent. Approximately $1 in legal fees is spent for every $7 paid in claims (or set aside in reserve funds to pay future claims). All data are from *Best's Aggregates and Averages,* 1985: 78–79.

9. This statement was made to the author by the president of a large insurance company. He contended that any concern with the level of prices was a concern for

190   The Political Economy of Regulation

policyholders, but that the insurance industry was quite willing to insure greater risks at higher premiums.

10. A curious problem was created in pollution liability insurance because federal environmental regulation required financial responsibility for individuals involved in pollution control and hazardous waste industries. Insurance is the easiest way to establish financial responsibility.

11. New York was self-insured. In 1983, it settled 5,671 claims for a total of $78 million (King, 1985: 72).

12. This coalition formed in a variety of states. Although the author has no idea how many states had active coalitions for "reform of civil justice," a brief perusal of the popular literature suggests that as many as three-fourths of the states had reasonably well-organized efforts. Reports frequently appeared both in the local press and the national media about such coalition efforts.

13. Negligence standards have been changing rapidly. Under the doctrine of contributory negligence, a plaintiff shown to be negligent in any way could recover nothing. Under comparative negligence, each party is liable based on the party's contribution to the negligent situation. Under modified comparative negligence, a plaintiff could collect only from individuals who were more negligent than the plaintiff was.

14. Joint and several liability means that each defendant found liable is responsible for paying the entire amount of the award even if only a small amount negligent. Municipalities are most concerned with joint and several liability since they might be found 5 to 10 percent liable in an auto accident for failure to maintain a street or stop sign. If the primary defendant is unable to pay, the municipality would be liable for the entire judgment.

15. The extent to which the reforms would have reduced costs is open to question. For two analyses of the legal reforms enacted during the 1970s medical malpractice crisis see Sloan (1985) and Copeland and Meier (1986). Both studies conclude that the tort reforms of that era had little impact on the cost of medical malpractice insurance.

16. A *captive insurance company* is one that is owned by the individuals who are insured.

17. These groups were, however, on opposite sides in the no-fault automobile insurance debates.

18. Advocating prior approval rate laws is a strange position for a consumer group to take. These laws were used in the past to allow insurance companies to set prices collusively. The result of such practices in the past was higher prices for consumers. Given the low opinion that NICO held of most state insurance commissioners, one can only wonder why Hunter would be willing to trust this group with greater rate regulatory powers.

19. *Actuaries* are the individuals who perform the statistical work for the insurance industry. The profession requires a series of demanding exams. Actuaries are crucial in determining the rates necessary to underwrite insurance at a profit.

20. One way to illustrate the distorting effects of a few large cases is to examine some specific figures. In 1978, the average award was determined by Jury Verdict Research to be $1.7 million. This large figure was distorted by the award of $127 million to an individual involved in a tort suit concerning Ford Motor Company's Pinto. This award was later reduced to $6.7 million. If the actual award, rather than the jury award, is used, the mean for 1978 drops to $538,000.

21. For example, insurance companies do not keep statistics on the punitive damages that they pay or the claims that arise under joint and several liability. Such information is costly to code. Because neither accounting practices nor regulations required such numbers, insurance data forms were not designed to collect such information.

22. Insurance business that leaves the traditional insurance industry and goes to captives or other insurance mechanisms rarely ever returns to the industry. Gaps in coverage have often created the opening for specialty companies to develop and grow into giants. Wausau Insurance, for example, was created because other insurance companies refused to sell insurance to the lumber industry in Wisconsin. After World War II and the boom in auto transportation, many companies reduced automobile insurance. This created the opportunity for State Farm and other direct writers to dominate the automobile insurance market.

23. Tort reform is the type of issue that is attractive to President Reagan. It is an issue area with a wealth of horrifying anecdotes, and the President has a fondness for anecdotes in making policy decisions.

24. An example of this occurred in Wisconsin. State Representative Tom Hauke, who chaired the House committee with jurisdiction over insurance, bottled up reform proposals.

25. Investment income is calculated by taking the total premiums earned in the line of insurance and multiplying that number by the ratio of investment income to premiums earned, which is supplied by *Best's Aggregates and Averages,* 1986: 83.

26. The actual paid claims figure for 1985 is estimated by the author because industry figures did not include this year. I have made an exceedingly generous estimate of 1985 losses paid given the past losses experienced by the industry. If anything, paid losses for 1985 are overestimated.

27. This is a defensive strategy because property and casualty companies invest heavily in government bonds. In 1985, the last year with available data, 62 percent of the property and casualty companies' assets were invested in government bonds. Because many of these bonds were tax-free municipal bonds, the interest rates may well have been lower than those used in the analysis. This bias will result in underestimating the needed capital because lower interest rates require greater capital to

produce the same amount of income. The interest rate used for each of the years was 11.55 (1980), 14.44 (1981), 12.92 (1982), 10.45 (1983), 9.50 (1984) and 8.00 (1985). This was the annual average interest rate for three year government Treasury Bills. Using the AAA corporate bond rate produced similar results.

Chapter 6

1. One state's deceptive company might be another state's legitimate business. In addition, an insurance commissioner had no motivation to protect citizens of other states.

2. This power was limited to only those states that did not regulate. If the state to which the material was sent did regulate unfair trade practices, the FTC was not permitted to regulate [see *FTC v. National Casualty* 357 U. S. 560 (1958)].

3. The name Medicare Supplements has been used, as has Medicare 65 (Hanson and Obenberger, 1966: 194). A company that specializes in selling to veterans of the armed forces, for example, might be called U. S. Veterans Life. The FTC has required many such companies to expressly state in the advertisements that the company is not affiliated with the U. S. government or the VA. Well-known individuals who appear in the advertisements are often identified as stockholders or compensated spokespersons.

4. Unlike loss control techniques in fire insurance, an area where insurance companies have been remarkably successful, loss control in flood insurance requires changes to people's property other than the property that is insured. Flood prevention requires substantial use of land-use restrictions. Only governments have the power to coerce such changes in behavior.

5. One major source of flooding is from hurricanes. In a seminal work by Abney and Hill (1969), hurricanes were shown to have an impact on mass political behavior. My analysis will illustrate that hurricanes also have a significant impact on elite behavior, thus contributing to the growing literature on hurricanes and politics.

6. A federal flood insurance program is not as much as a break with precedent as it first appears. The federal government had long been involved in flood control programs through the U. S. Army Corps of Engineers. The step from flood control programs to flood insurance programs is a logical extension of the federal government's earlier role.

7. The industry effort to provide cooperation with the federal government was not insignificant. The companies associated with the National Flood Insurers Association contributed $42 million in capital to underwrite the effort. The initial effort began much more cooperative than it ended (Weese and Ooms, 1978: 191).

8. Resistance to the regulations involved in the flood insurance program was especially strong in cities such as Houston with its strong antifederal government

orientation. Houston, the only major city without zoning laws, was accustomed to allowing the market decide what development would be undertaken. The result of this *laissez-faire* policy was extensive construction in flood plains and flood control techniques that simply transferred water somewhere else quickly.

9. The 23 percent figure for automobile liability insurance compares similarly to other forms of liability insurance. Legal defense fees are included in what the industry calls loss adjustment expenses. The bulk of the expenses in this area are for legal fees. For medical malpractice insurance, 25.1 percent of premiums went to pay for legal defense costs; plaintiff costs are not reported to state insurance commissioners. In general liability insurance, 19.3 percent of premiums went to pay for legal defense costs in between 1980 and 1984. In other lines, the percentages for 1984 are as follows: automobile liability private (11.4 percent), commercial automobile liability (14.9 percent), general liability insurance (38.5 percent), and medical malpractice insurance (32.8 percent). All figures are from *Best's Aggregates & Averages,* 1985. Other lines of insurance that do not rely on tort liability such as fire insurance have much smaller legal defense costs.

10. Agents who represent mutual insurance companies and agents in general oppose no-fault because no-fault is pushed by the large direct writers. These companies do not use agents and are able to operate with lower costs. If no-fault places a cost squeeze on the insurance industry, direct writers can absorb additional costs easier than mutuals and agents can.

11. The Judiciary Committee could claim jurisdiction on two grounds. First, by eliminating the tort liability system, no-fault was a bill that clearly concerned the judiciary. Second, the issue of federal versus state regulation of insurance was considered under the McCarran-Ferguson Act, an antitrust statute. Antitrust was under the jurisdiction of Judiciary. Senator Phillip Hart was also a member of the Judiciary Committee when he initially held his hearings.

12. The literature on sex segregated insurance classification has become massive. See Benston (1982: 491, note 10), Austin (1983), Genthner (1985), Cicero (1985), and Milbourne (1985). The hearings conducted concerning the Fair Insurance Practices Act in 1983 illustrate the range of the political debate. Proponents of unisex insurance even challenge the actuarial base of gender contending that past patterns of results may not hold in a world where sex roles are changing rapidly (see Brilmayer, Hekeler, Laycock, and Sullivan, 1980).

13. The decision to focus on the state level reflects political realism. Given the ability of the insurance companies to link sex to their actuarial base and the current ideological distribution of members of Congress, major redistributive legislation concerning sex is unlikely to pass the U. S. Congress. If such a bill passed, the probability of veto would be great.

14. Justice William Rehnquist obviously meant that while women were not protected from disability due to pregnancy neither were men.

15. Even on a unisex basis, the Supreme Court's criticism still applies to any pension plan because no individual, regardless how rated, will automatically receive the benefits intended for the group.

16. While this implies that equal pension benefits might not be required, the court effectively rejected this position in the *Norris* case.

17. Clearly the court's decisions with regard to pregnancy and pensions are not consistent. How one can distinguish between disability benefits for pregnancy, which is clearly based on sex, from differences in pensions, which are related to sex differences in lifespan, is difficult to see. Congressional action with the Pregnancy Discrimination Act has made policies in these two areas consistent by reversing the court on the pregnancy rulings.

18. One could argue that the court erred on the concept of state action. Rates charged by Harleysville were approved by the state insurance commissioner, and this could be interpreted as state action.

19. The logical alternative to whole life was to purchase term insurance with a death benefit equal to the whole life policy and then to place the difference in some other savings or investment mechanism.

20. As Senator Charles E. Grassley said, "The benefit of tax reform is not significant enough to take the risk of irritating the minority of people who are concerned about issues such as [insurance] inside build-up and repeal of the investment tax credit." Quoted in Cohen, 1985a: 2356.

Chapter 7

1. A large firm, however, has a credibility problem in threatening to leave since the firm has large fixed costs in the state.

2. Data for premium income by state are taken from the Insurance Information Institute (1984) for property and casualty insurance companies and from ACLI (1984) for life and health insurance companies. Population figures are from the 1980 census.

3. Employment figures are from the U. S. Bureau of Census *Industry of Employment* statistics. The insurance industry argues that these figures significantly underestimate the total employment in insurance (see Chapter 1). Because no reason exists why these underestimates would vary by state, the census figures were used rather than attempting to apportion industry figures by state.

4. The three firm concentration ratio is used because *Best's Review* publishes the sales figures for the top three firms in each state. More traditional measures such as the four firm or eight firm concentration ratio are not available by state. These figures are only available for property and casualty insurance lines.

5. The direct writer figures are also from *Best's Review* for 1983. Direct writers are generally a property and casualty insurance phenomenon; the measure is the portion of property and casualty insurance sales in the state that are written by direct writers.

6. Agent strength was measured in these two ways rather than the total number of agents because the total number of agents includes many agents who work for direct writers as captive agents. Independent agents are more likely to resist the political advances of the insurance companies. They are likely to be independent small business persons with political ties in the local community. Data on members for 1984 were gathered directly from IIAA, CPCU, and CLU by the author.

7. Ralph Nader, in fact, resigned from the board of the Consumers Union in the late 1960s because they were not active in lobbying for consumer-oriented legislation (Nadel, 1971).

8. Because the Consumers Union is much larger than Common Cause, membership figures were standardized before they were added. The membership figures were taken from totals provided by the national office of each organization. An interesting empirical phenomenon is that membership in Common Cause is also correlated with membership in the Sierra Club ($r = .57$) and the Audubon Society ($r = .50$). For Consumers Union these correlations are .56 for the Sierra Club and .66 for the Audubon Society.

9. Consumer influence may well manifest itself in insurance issues through the actions of political elites. Political elites with consumer-oriented values see electoral benefits from advocating consumer issues. Bureaucrats might also infer from potential consumer groups that they can gain allies among either the public or among political elites if they take pro-consumer actions.

10. Actually, this indicator might not measure group strength at all but, rather, mass political attitudes. If this is the case, then mass political attitudes probably affect insurance policy through the type of political elites that represent such individuals in the legislature.

11. Exactly what *urbanism* is is difficult to determine. Urbanism might be a surrogate for a style of politics that focus on redistributive issues and thus provides benefits for consumers. My interpretation of urbanism as a surrogate for consumer contact is not the only plausible interpretation.

12. One other possible measure of consumer group activity would be a total of all the registered lobbyists in this area. Lists of registered lobbyists proved to be unusable because the volume of registration was related to how strict the registration law was in the state rather than the level of group organization. In addition, identifying consumer groups from myriad lobbyists was difficult.

13. The first factor accounted for 78 percent of the variation in the individual indicators. The interrelationships between these variables did not change when they

were changed to per capita measures. The insurance commissioner's salary was taken from a survey conducted by the Ohio Insurance Institute. Their most recent survey covered the year 1981. To fill some gaps in the data, I contacted several insurance departments.

14. Sixteen specific model laws and regulations were identified by the author from those proposed by the NAIC. These models cover topics such as the simplification of insurance policies, disclosure of prices, unfair claims settlement procedures, and prohibitions against discrimination in insurance. Information on which states adopted the models either by regulation or by law was provided by the NAIC. The final measure is simply the total number of models adopted by each state.

15. This portion of the analysis removes judges from the category of political elites. No discernable way exists to measure the influence of judges on insurance issues for all 50 states.

16. Similar measures of political elite attitudes have been used by Nice (1985) with some degree of success in predicting policy actions.

17. Specifically, the percentage of seats in the legislature and the distribution of vote for the governor were used to calculate an average Democratic percentage. This figure was then folded at 50 percent to measure how close the "average" election was. The figure was then subtracted from 100 so that larger numbers indicated more competitive states.

18. The minimum capital requirement for life insurance is used because that requirement is easiest to compare across states. Requirements for property and casualty companies vary by line of business and are difficult to compare across states. Data are from ACLI's library in Washington, D. C.

19. The number of domiciled property and casualty companies was determined by examining Best's ratings of all property and casualty insurance companies in the United States. The number of domiciled life insurance companies was taken from ACLI (1984). The general measure for this variable is the sum of these two values. The licensed companies data are from the Ohio Insurance Institute supplemented by the author's own survey.

20. New York has a preassessment system whereby insurance companies are assessed for insolvencies before the fact. In practice, this means that the New York law is more strict than any of the other state laws because it requires payments for insolvencies before they occur.

21. The guaranty fund assessment data appear in Insurance Information Institute (1984). Guaranty funds are controlled by a board of directors from the insurance companies and, therefore, may resist assessments (Lewis, 1981: 120). Assessments also reflect stringency because the insurance commissioner must examine the company to discover the insolvency and then seek a court order for liquidation, rehabilitation, or commissioner supervision (Prybutok, 1982: 91).

22. The anomaly for direct writers, the significant correlation between direct writers' percent of the market and lower minimum capital requirements, can be explained. Direct writers are heavily involved in property and casualty insurance rather than life insurance. The minimum capital measure is for life insurance. Because direct writers generally have little interest in minimum life insurance capital requirements, this relationship is probably spurious.

23. The only fair way to compare the explanatory ability of the multi-interest model with the industry model is to compare the adjusted coefficients of determination. These coefficients are adjusted for degrees of freedom so that the natural advantage of the eight variable model is cancelled out. The adjusted coefficients for the industry model and the multi-interest model are as follows (multi-interest model in parentheses): minimum standards, .38 (.28); guaranty fund assessments, .26 (.41); minimum capital, .26 (.43); domestic companies, .08 (-.06); licensed companies, .32 (.62). By this standard, the multi-interest model performed better in three of the five cases.

24. The data on premium taxes were taken from the Insurance Information Institute (1984). Data on taxes other than premium taxes were taken from a survey done by the Ohio Insurance Institute. Information on tax discrimination was gathered from documents in NAIC's library in Kansas City, MO.

25. In terms of adjusted multiple coefficients of determination, the multi-interest model is again superior to the industry model. The coefficients for the industry model (multi-interest model in parentheses) are .13 (.23) for premium tax rates, .16 (.25) for insurance taxes per capita, .14 (.26) for premium taxes per capita, and -.03 (-.10) for discrimination. Only in the case of tax discrimination does the industry model predict better, and in that case the effective level of prediction is zero.

26. The figures in Table 7–8 are the mean adjusted loss ratios for the 50 states. They are not the same as the industrywide loss ratios in Table 1–10 because they are not weighted by premium volume before averaging. As a result, the figures in Table 7–8 are not comparable to those noted in earlier parts of this book. The ALRs for life and health insurance are for 1983 and were calculated from data presented in ACLI (1984). The ALRs for all the property and casualty lines are taken from *Best's Review* and are the averages for the years 1976 to 1983. Because the property and casualty ALRs are based on longer time periods which should smooth out any irregularities that result from idiosyncratic events, the property and casualty ALRs are more reliable than the life and health ALRs. In fact, the life and health industry does not use the ALR in reporting information.

27. An alternative explanation is that the market in urban areas might well be more competitive, thereby driving the price down.

28. The multi-industry model does work better for life insurance and private health insurance. The adjusted coefficients of determination for the insurance industry model (and the multi-interest model) are .32 (.45) for life, .21 (.19) for the Blues, and .00 (.06) for private health companies.

29. Regulators are more likely to be persuaded by cost arguments from the Blue Cross and Blue Shield companies than from other companies because the Blues operate with such a low overhead. The ALR for the Blues is more than 30 points higher than the average ALR for other property and casualty insurance companies.

30. The adjusted coefficients of determination for the industry model (and the multi-interest model) are .00 (.34) for property and casualty, .29 (.47) for auto, .02 (.15) for home, -.06 (.26) for commercial multiple peril, .00 (.16) for medical malpractice, and .48 (.42) for general liability. Only for general liability does the industry model predict better. For an extended case of modelling the price of medical malpractice insurance see Meier and Copeland (1986).

31. Information on the type of rate law was taken from records in NAIC's library.

32. A more sophisticated model could be used that controls for a variety of factors that might affect the price of insurance (see Harrington, 1984). This option shows little more than the simple relationships in Table 7–13 reveal. Only two research studies have ever shown that insurance regulation affects price. Pauly, Kunreuther, and Kleindorfer (1986: 100) found that insurance regulation affected automobile insurance prices from 1975 to 1977 but that this impact had disappeared by 1978 to 1980. These findings may well be a function of anomalies in the underwriting cycle. The GAO (1986b: 99) recently released a report claiming that regulation affected the price of insurance, but this report had several serious flaws. First, the study used a pooled time series, which artificially increased the number of cases from 44 to 352. Second, any states that changed types of regulation between 1975 and 1982 were omitted from the analysis even though a pooled time series could accommodate changes. Third, the classification of states with competitive rate systems includes some states that operate file and use systems that resemble prior approval systems. Fourth, the impact of the regulation variable by itself in the risk-adjusted equation is not significant (it is significant in the average dollar-cost equation but this measure of cost has serious flaws). Fifth, only for an interaction between urbanism and regulation is there a significant impact, but urbanism has been reduced to a dummy variable coded above or below the median level of urbanism. In short, so many flaws affect the validity of the GAO study that it can be disregarded.

33. This findings does not mean that specific regulatory policies do not affect the price of insurance. They do. The results only show that the overall impact of regulation in two-thirds of the states does not result in appreciably different prices from the competitive pricing states. Substantial variation still exists in prices among states (see Table 7–8). These variations can be affected by specific regulatory policies in operation in one state but not in another.

34. The author was often amazed at the data that insurance companies did not collect. Even simple information such as the amounts paid out in punitive damages are not collected.

35. The attorneys' data are taken from the U. S. Bureau of Census figures on occupations for 1980. The state civil suits data are from the National Center for State Courts, *State Court Caseload Statistics: Annual Report 1980* (Williamsburg, VA, 1984). The federal data on torts are from the *Annual Report of the Director of the Administrative Office of the United States Courts* (Washington: U. S. Government Printing Office, 1983). All figures are per 100,000 population.

36. The average loss ratio for the years 1976 through 1984 are used as the dependent variable. The source is *Best's Review.* For a more elaborate analysis of this problem, see Meier (1987a).

37. Automobile ALRs are subject to an underwriting cycle. ALRs increase and, in turn, insurance companies raise prices which depress the ALR. Using a nine-year average for the dependent variable avoids any problems with the cycle. Regressions for individual years show some variations, but the results are consistently in the same direction. The percentile change for no-fault plans is 11.35 for 1976, 7.14 for 1977, .64 for 1978, 2.72 for 1979, 6.44 for 1980, 10.84 for 1981, 9.77 for 1982, 8.83 for 1983, and 4.26 for 1984 (see Meier, 1987a). Except for 1978, 1979, and 1984, each figure is statistically significant.

38. No other variable could explain any additional variation. Among the variables tried were proportion of automobiles stolen, number of automobiles per 100,000 people, rate of traffic fatalities, percent of automobiles with insurance, percent of automobiles in the involuntary market, whether the insurance commissioner was elected, the state's median education, median income, percent urban, percent non-white, and percent Democratic party control.

39. None of the relationships in Table 7–17 is statistically significant when all others in addition to whether the state had a no-fault law were controlled. The findings, therefore, must be regarded as tentative.

40. Both the proportion of individuals receiving insurance under FAIR plans and the proportion of individuals in the auto insurance shared market were standardized. These two standardized scores were then added to get the measure of access. The shared market percentages were taken from Automobile Insurance Plans Service Office, *AIPSO Insurance Facts: A Handbook of Auto Shared Market Facts and Figures.* New York: author, 1983. The FAIR plan percentages were from the Insurance Information Institute (1984).

Chapter 8

1. McConnell (1966) argues that less visible forums mean that industry interests are more likely to dominate the political process. Because each of the state and federal forums has other interests in it, the insurance industry does not get very many

easy wins. McConnell is correct when one does not consider the counter force of the bureaucracy and the intervention of political elites.

2. The author is not particularly impressed with the election of insurance commissioners, a practice in about 12 states. Analysis by the author, but not shown in this book, found that elected insurance commissioners did not make regulatory policies differently from appointed insurance commissioners. Because such selection methods appear to not influence policy, no recommendation will be made on election versus appointment.

3. Given the heavy reliance on reporting of information on standardized sorts of forms, the insurance commissioner should require reports on computer readable forms such as computer tape. This would allow the commissioner to access such information without the effort of reentering all the data. It would make such effort easier for insurance companies because they would not have to produce a hard copy of the reports.

4. Some individuals will, of course, prefer higher quality service and be willing to pay the price for it. Agents have made this claim for years. Others such as the author prefer lower prices even if this means lower levels of overall service because they are particularly good at complaining to insurance companies.

5. One might note that universal life insurance was invented by E. F. Hutton Life. Only a brokerage firm would design an insurance policy such as universal life.

Bibliography

Aaron, Henry J. 1983. *The Peculiar Problem of Taxing Life Insurance Companies.* Washington: The Brookings Institution.

Aberbach, Joel and Bert A. Rockman. "Clashing Beliefs Within the Executive Branch: The Nixon Administration Bureaucracy." *American Political Science Review* 70 (June), 456–468.

Abney, F. Glenn and Larry B. Hill. 1966. "Natural Disasters as a Political Variable: The Effect of a Hurricane on an Urban Election." *American Political Science Review* 60 (December), 974–981.

Adams, James Ring. 1986. "The Reinsurance that Wasn't." *Forbes* (September 22), 40–42.

Akers, Ronald L. 1968. "The Professional Association and the Legal Regulation of Practice." *Law and Society Review* 2 (May), 463–482.

Alexis, Marcus. 1983. "The Political Economy of Federal Regulation of Surface Transportation." In Roger G. Noll and Bruce M. Owen, *The Political Economy of Deregulation.* Washington: American Enterprise Institute, 115–131.

Alliance of American Insurers, American Insurance Association, and National Association of Independent Insurers. 1985. "Insurance Availability." (December 6). mimeo: author.

American Council for Life Insurance. 1986. *Life Insurance Fact Book: Update 1986.* Washington: author.

_____. 1985. *Life Insurance Fact Book: Update 1985.* Washington: author.

_____. 1984. *Life Insurance Fact Book.* Washington: author.

Anderson, Douglas D. 1980. "State Regulation of Electric Utilities." In James Q. Wilson, *The Politics of Regulation.* New York: Basic Books, 3–41.

Anderson, Ronald T. 1976. "The Professional Urge." *CPCU Annals* 29 (June), 116–122.

Appleton, Lynn M. 1985. "Explaining Laws' Making and Their Enforcement in the American States." *Social Science Quarterly* 66 (December), 839–853.

Ardman, Carol. 1985a. "Insurers Help Tackle N.H.'s Liability Woes." *Journal of Commerce* (October 23).

_____. 1985b. "3 States Use MAPs for Liability Lines." *Journal of Commerce* (December 6).

Armentano, Dominick T. 1982. *Antitrust and Monopoly.* New York: John Wiley & Sons.

Austin, Regina. 1983. "The Insurance Classification Controversy." *University of Pennsylvania Law Review* 131 (January), 517–584.

Bachrach, Peter and Morton S. Baratz. 1970. *Power and Poverty.* New York: Oxford University Press.

Bailey, Elizabeth E. and William J. Baumol. 1984. "Deregulation and the Theory of Contestable Markets." *Yale Journal on Regulation* 1 (Number 2), 111–138.

Barrett, Francis D. 1972. "Congress v. The Insurance Industry." *CPCU Annals* 25 (March), 63–73.

Bauer, Raymond, Ithiel de Sola Pool, and Lewis A. Dexter. 1963. *American Business and Public Policy.* New York: Atherton Press.

Beam, David R. 1983. "From Law to Rule: Exploring the Maze of Intergovernmental Regulation." *Intergovernmental Perspective* 9 (Spring), 7–22.

Beavan, Gerald F. and Colin S. Braybrooks. 1982. "The Sale of Insurance Through the Mail." *CLU Journal* 36 (April), 18–26.

Behrman, Bradley. 1980. "Civil Aeronautics Board." In James Q. Wilson, *The Politics of Regulation.* New York: Basic Books, 75–121.

Bennett, Andrea. 1986. "Setting the Unisex Pace." *Best's Review* (Life/Health Edition) 86 (January), 23ff.

Benston, George J. 1982. "The Economics of Gender Discrimination in Employee Fringe Benefits: *Manhart* Revisited." *University of Chicago Law Review* 49 (Winter), 489–542.

Bernstein, Marver H. 1955. *Regulating Business by Independent Commission.* Princeton: Princeton University Press.

Berry, Jeffrey M. 1984. *The Interest Group Society.* Boston: Little, Brown.

Berry, William D. 1984. "An Alternative to the Capture Theory of Regulation: The Case of Public Utility Commissions." *American Journal of Political Science* 28 (August), 534–558.

_____. 1979. "Utility Regulation in the States: The Policy Effects of Professionalism and Salience to the Consumer." *American Journal of Political Science* 23 (May), 263–277.

Bickelhaupt, David Lynn. 1961. *Transition to Multiple-Line Insurance Companies.* Homewood, IL: Richard D. Irwin.

Blair, Roger D. and Stephen Rubin. 1980. *Regulating the Professions.* Lexington Books.

Blodgett, Nancy. 1986. "Premium Hikes Stun Municipalities." *ABA Journal* 72 (July 1), 48–51.

Bradford, Michael. 1985a. "Citicorp VP Rebuts Arguments Against Banks in Insurance." *Business Insurance* (September 9), 50.

———. 1985b. "Is the Industry's Capacity Crisis for Real?" *Business Insurance* (February 4).

———. 1985c. " 'Unusual' Events Aid Capacity: ISO." *Business Insurance* (September 23), 1,40.

Brilmayer, Lea, Richard W. Hekeler, Douglas Laycock, and Teresa Sullivan. 1980. "Sex Discrimination in Employer-Sponsored Insurance Plans." *University of Chicago Law Review* 47 (Spring), 505–561.

Brook, Herbert C. 1950. "Public Interest and the Commissioners' All-Industry Laws." *Law and Contemporary Problems* 15 (Autumn), 606–628.

Brown, Anthony. 1973. *Hazard Unlimited.* London: Peter Davies.

Brown, Anthony E. 1985. "The Regulatory Policy Cycle and the Airline Deregulation Movement." *Social Science Quarterly* 66 (September), 552–563.

Browne, William P. 1977. "Organizational Maintenance: The Internal Operation of Interest Groups." *Public Administration Review* 37 (January/February), 48–57.

Browning, Graeme. 1986. "Doctors and Lawyers Face Off." *ABA Journal* 72 (July 1), 38–41.

Buley, R. Carlyle. 1953. *The American Life Convention.* Volume 1. New York: Appleton-Century-Crofts.

Cain, Carol. 1985. "States Take Steps to Ease Rate, Capacity Crisis." *Business Insurance* (September 10), 1,38.

Carron, Andrew S. 1983. "The Political Economy of Financial Regulation." In Roger G. Noll and Bruce M. Owen, *The Political Economy of Deregulation.* Washington: American Enterprise Institute, 69–83.

Cater, Morrow. 1982. "Trimming the Disability Roles—Changing the Rules During the Game." *National Journal* 14 (September 4), 1512–1514.

Central Arizona Chapter CPCU. 1978. "The Licensing of Property-Casualty Insurance Agents in the United States." *CPCU Journal* 31 (June), 132–138.

Cheit, Earl F. 1961. *Injury and Recovery in the Course of Employment.* New York: John Wiley & Sons.

Cicero, Anne C. 1985. "Strategies for the Elimination of Sex Discrimination in Private Insurance." *Harvard Civil Rights—Civil Liberties Law Review* 20: 211–267.

Clark, Timothy B. 1986a. "Divided They Stand." *National Journal* 18 (April 19), 928–933.

_____. 1986b. "How to Succeed Against Business." *National Journal* 18 (May 3), 1059–1061.

Clarkson, Kenneth W. and Timothy J. Muris. 1981. *The Federal Trade Commission Since 1970.* Cambridge: Cambridge University Press.

Clifford, Mark. 1985. "Sure-Thing Bloodbath." *Forbes* (September 23), 218.

Cline, Robert S. 1982. "Commercial Banks and the Distribution of Property and Liability Insurance." *CPCU Journal* 35 (June), 76–82.

Cohen, Richard E. 1985a. "Despite Misgivings, Finance Committee May be Forced to Tackle Tax Reform Bill." *National Journal* 17 (October 19), 2356–2361.

_____. 1985b. "Tax Reform, Democratic Style." *National Journal* 17 (November 30), 2717–2718.

Cohen, Jeffrey E. 1986. "The Dynamics of the 'Revolving Door' on the FCC." *American Journal of Political Science* 30 (November), 689–708.

_____. 1985. "Congressional Control: A Test of Two Theories." Paper presented at the annual meeting of the American Political Science Association, New Orleans, August.

Consumer Reports. 1986. "The Manufactured Crisis." *Consumer Reports* (August), 544–549.

Copeland, Gary W. and Kenneth J. Meier. 1986. "Helping Out the Rich: The Impact of the Medical Malpractice Insurance Reforms." Paper presented at the 1986 annual meeting of the Midwest Political Science Association. Chicago.

Couric, Emily. 1986. "The A. H. Robins Saga." *ABA Journal* 72 (July 1), 56–60.

Crane, Frederick, G. 1972. "Insurance Rate Regulation: The Reasons Why." *Journal of Risk and Insurance* 39 (December), 511–534.

Culhane, Paul J. 1981. *Public Lands Policies.* Baltimore: Johns Hopkins University Press.

Daniels, Stephen. 1986. "Punitive Damages: Storm on the Horizon." Paper presented at the American Bar Foundation Fellows Seminar, American Bar Association Midyear Meeting, Baltimore, MD. (February 8).

Danzon, Patricia Munch. 1985. *Medical Malpractice.* Cambridge: Harvard University Press.

Decker, Richard J. 1980. "Servicing the Shared Automobile Insurance Market." *CPCU Journal* 33 (December), 131–134.

Department of Transportation. 1971. *Motor Vehicle Crash Losses and Their Compensation in the United States.* Washington: author.

Derthick, Martha and Paul J. Quirk. 1985. *The Politics of Deregulation.* Washington: The Brookings Institution.

Dickerson, O. D. 1968. *Health Insurance.* Homewood, IL: Richard D. Irwin.

Downs, Anthony. 1967. *Inside Bureaucracy.* Boston: Little, Brown.

———. 1957. *A Economic Theory of Democracy.* New York: Harper and Row.

Dye, Thomas R. 1966. *Politics, Economics and the Public.* Chicago: Rand-McNally.

Edelman, Murray. 1964. *The Symbolic Uses of Politics.* Champaign, IL: University of Illinois Press.

Elmore, Franklin H., Jr. 1959. "How Insurance Became Commerce." In H. Wayne Snider, *Readings in Property and Casualty Insurance.* Homewood, IL: Richard D. Irwin, 497–522.

Etzioni, Amitai. 1986. "Does Regulation Reduce Electricity Rates?" *Policy Sciences* 19 (Winter), 349–357.

Faron, Robert S. 1985. "The Pollution Liability Dilemma." *Risk Management* (May), 20–26.

Farrell, Christopher and Elizabeth Ehrlich. 1985. "Now Even Insurers Have a Hard Time Getting Coverage." *Business Week* (December 2), 128–9.

Federal Trade Commission. 1979. *Insurance Cost Disclosure.* Washington: Bureau of Consumer Protection, author.

Feldman, Lawrence P. 1976. *Consumer Protection.* St. Paul, MN: West.

Felter, Bethany. 1985. "Insurance Alternatives Increase as Commercial Market Tightens." *Best's Insurance Management Reports* (December 9).

Fenske, Doris. 1985a. "The Year Ahead." *Best's Review* (Life and Health Edition) 85 (January), 16ff.

———. 1985b. "Adequacy of Loss Reserves Debated at Quality of Earnings Sumposium [sic]." *Best's Insurance Management Reports* (October 14).

Finsinger, Jorg. 1986. "A State Controlled Market: The German Case." In Jorg
    Finsinger and Mark V. Pauly (eds.), *The Economics of Insurance Regulation*.
    New York: St. Martin's Press, 111–160.

_____ and Mark V. Pauly. 1986. "Introduction." In Jorg Finsinger and Mark V.
    Pauly (eds.), *The Economics of Insurance Regulation*. New York: St. Martin's
    Press, 1–23.

Formisano, Roger. 1982. "Consumers, Prosumers and the Future of Insurance." In
    Nathan Weber, *Insurance Deregulation: Issues and Perspectives*. New York:
    The Conference Board, 33–36.

Franson, Robert T. 1969. "The Prior-Approval System of Property and Liability
    Insurance Rate Regulation." *Wisconsin Law Review* 1969 (December), 1104–
    1137.

Freedman, Marian. 1986. "General Liability and Medical Malpractice Insurance
    Marketing—1985." *Best's Review* (Property/Casualty Edition) 86 (October),
    32ff.

Freeman, J. Leiper. 1965. *The Political Process*. New York: Random House.

Galanter, Marc. 1983. "Reading the Landscape of Disputes: What We Know and
    Don't Know (and Think We Know) about Our Allegedly Contentious and Liti-
    gious Society." *UCLA Law Review* 31 (October), 4–70.

Garfin, Louis. 1982. "Current Issues in the Federal Taxation of Life Insurance Com-
    panies." *Journal of Insurance Issues and Practices* 5 (June), 1–13.

Geisel, Jerry. 1985. "Rate Hikes 'Gouge' Buyers: Consumer Group." *Business Insur-
    ance* (August 24).

General Accounting Office. 1986a. *Pensions: Plans with Unfunded Benefits*. Wash-
    ington: author.

_____. 1986b. *Auto Insurance: State Regulation Affects Cost and Availability*. Wash-
    ington: author.

_____. 1985a. *Tax Policy: Information on the Stock and Mutual Segments of the Life
    Insurance Industry*. Washington: author.

_____. 1985b. *Congress Should Consider Changing Federal Income Taxation of the
    Property/Casualty Insurance Industry*. Washington: author.

_____. 1985c. *Tax Administration: Information on How the Property/Casualty Insur-
    ance Industry Is Taxed*. Washington: author.

_____. 1984. *Economic Implications of the Fair Insurance Practices Act*. Washing-
    ton: author.

_____. 1983. *Survey of Investor Protection and the Regulation of Financial Interme-
    diaries*. Washington: author.

Genthner, Amy B. 1985. "*Arizona v. Norris:* Supreme Court Death Knell for Sex Segregated Mortality Tables." *Insurance Counsel Journal* 52 (April), 295–303.

Gersuny, Carl. 1981. *Work Hazards and Industrial Conflict.* Boston: University Press of New England.

Glaberson, William B. and Christopher Farrell. 1986. "The Explosion in Liability Lawsuits in Nothing But a Myth." *Business Week* (April 21), 24–25.

Goldberg, Stephanie. 1986. "Manufacturers Take Cover." *ABA Journal* 72 (July 1), 52–55.

Goldman, Eric Frederick. 1952. *Rendezvous with Destiny.* New York: Knopf.

Gormley, William T. 1986. "Regulatory Issue Networks in a Federal System." *Polity* 18 (Summer), 595–620.

_____. 1983. *The Politics of Public Utility Regulation.* Pittsburgh: University of Pittsburgh Press.

_____. 1982. "Alternative Models of the Regulatory Process: Public Utility Regulation in the States." *Western Political Quarterly* 35 (September), 297–318.

_____. 1979. "A Test of the 'Revolving Door' Hypothesis at the FCC." *American Journal of Political Science* 23 (November), 665–683.

Granelli, James. 1985. "The Attack on Joint and Several Liability." *ABA Journal* 71 (July), 61–63.

Grant, H. Roger. 1979. *Insurance Reform: Consumer Action in the Progressive Era.* Ames, IA: Iowa State University Press.

Green, Mark R. 1978. "Government Insurers." In John D. Long, ed., *Issues in Insurance* Volume I. Malvern, PA: American Institute for Property and Liability Underwriters, 303–384.

Greene, Richard. 1986. "The Tort Reform Quagmire." *Forbes* (August 11), 76–79.

Greenspan, Nancy T. and Ronald J. Vogel. 1982. "An Econometric Analysis of the Effects of Regulation in the Private Health Insurance Market." *Journal of Risk and Insurance* 49 (March), 39–58.

Haase, Robert D. 1969. "Control of Unauthorized Insurance." In Spencer Kimball and Herbert Denenberg, eds., *Insurance, Government, and Social Policy.* Homewood, IL: Richard D. Irwin, 311–341.

Hanson, Jon S. 1977. "An Overview—State Insurance Regulation." *CLU Journal* 31 (April), 20–31.

_____., Robert E. Dineen, and Michael B. Johnson. 1974. *Monitoring Competition: A Means of Regulating the Property and Liability Insurance Business.* Milwaukee, WI: National Association of Insurance Commissioners.

_____ and Thomas E. Obenberger. 1966. "Mail Order Insurers." *Marquette Law Review* 50 (November), 175–345.

Harman, William B. 1985. "The Structure of Life Insurance Company Taxation—The New Pattern under the 1984 Act—Part I." *Journal of the American Society of CLU* 38 (March), 56–66.

Harrington, Charles F. 1950. "Administration of Insurance Rate Regulatory Laws." *Law and Contemporary Problems* 15 (Autumn), 597–605.

Harrington, Scott. 1984. "The Impact of Rate Regulation on Prices and Underwriting Results in the Property-Liability Insurance Industry: A Survey." *Journal of Risk and Insurance* 51 (December), 577–623.

Hartman, Gerald R. 1972. "New Era of Insurance Rate Regulation." *CPCU Annals* 25 (June), 153–163.

_____. 1971. "A Current Look at the Fire Insurance Rate Regulatory Laws." *CPCU Annals* 24 (March, 5–61.

Hashmi, Sahjad A. 1982. "Flood Insurance—1982." *CPCU Journal* 35 (March), 20–29.

Health Care Finance Administration. 1986. *Medicare Annual Report Fiscal Year 1983.* Washington: author.

Heap, Ian R. 1985. "Capital, Capacity, and Competition." *National Underwriter* (Property and Casualty Edition). (August 23), 24.

Heclo, Hugh. 1978. "Issue Networks and the Executive Establishment." In Anthony King, *The New American Political System.* Washington: American Enterprise Institute, 87–124.

Herbert, Alan. 1985. "Tougher Insurance Rules Loom." *Journal of Commerce* (October 10), 1ff.

Herring, Pendelton. 1936. *Public Administration and the Public Interest.* New York: McGraw-Hill.

Hiebert, Timothy H. 1986. "The State Regulation Requirement Under Section 2(b) of the McCarran-Ferguson Act." *Insurance Counsel Journal* 53 (April), 234–243.

Hilder, David B. 1986. "Tort Wars." *Wall Street Journal* (August 1), 1,14.

_____. 1985. "Changes in Liability Insurance Spur Confusion Among Business Clients." *Wall Street Journal* (November 20), 33.

Hira, Labh S. and Norman W. Sivertsen. 1986. "Life Insurance as a Perquisite after the 1984 Act." *Journal of the American Society of CLU* 40 (March), 66–70.

Hofferbert, Richard I. 1969. *The Study of Public Policy.* Indianapolis, IN: The Bobbs-Merrill Company.

Hofstadter, Richard. 1955. *The Age of Reform.* New York: Alfred Knopf.

Huebner, S. S. and Kenneth Black. 1974. *Life Insurance.* 9th ed. Englewood Cliffs, NJ: Prentice-Hall.

Hunter, J. Robert. 1986. "Taming the Latest Insurance 'Crisis'." *New York Times* (April 13), 3.

_____. 1985a. "Banks in Insurance: A Consumer Viewpoint." *Banks in Insurance Report* 1 (April), 6–8.

Hunter, J. Robert. 1985b. "Testimony Before the Commissioner's Special Task Force on Property/Casualty Insurance." Eau Claire, WI (December 18).

Huntington, Samuel P. 1952. "The Marasmus of the ICC." *Yale Law Journal* 61 (April), 467–509.

Hurtz, Rebecca M. 1984. "Ratemaking and Investment Income." *Best's Review* (Property and Casualty Edition) 85 (December), 16–18.

Indiana Chapter CPCU. 1984. "Success or Failure: A Case Study of Federal Flood Insurance." *CPCU Journal* 37 (December), 204–214.

Innes, James J. 1972. "American Marine Insurance." *CPCU Annals* 25 (March), 53–61.

Insurance Information Institute. 1986. *Insurance Facts: 1986–87 Property/Casualty Fact Book.* New York: author.

_____. 1985. *Insurance Facts: 1985–86 Property/Casualty Fact Book.* New York: author.

_____. 1984. *Insurance Facts: 1984–85 Property/Casualty Fact Book.* New York: author.

Ippolito, Richard A. 1979. "The Effects of Price Regulation in the Automobile Insurance Industry." *Journal of Law and Economics* 22 (March), 55–89.

Jackson, Bartlett A. 1960. "Comment: The Extraterritorial Effect of Insurance Regulation." *Michigan Law Review* 58 (February), 558–570.

Johnson, Glendon E. 1969. "The Direct and Indirect Effect of Federal Programs and Regulations on Insurance Operations and Markets." In Spencer Kimball and Herbert S. Denenberg, eds., *Insurance, Government and Social Policy.* Homewood, IL: Richard D. Irwin, 365–388.

Jones, Charles O. 1975. *Clean Air.* Pittsburgh: Pittsburgh University Press.

Joskow, Paul L. 1973. "Cartels, Competition and Regulation in the Property-Liability Insurance Industry." *Bell Journal of Economics* 4 (Autumn), 375–427.

Kahn, Alfred E. 1983. "Deregulation and Vested Interests: The Case of Airlines." In

Roger D. Noll and Bruce M. Owen, 1983. *The Political Economy of Deregulation*. Washington: American Enterprise Institute, 132–154.

Kasouf, Deborah. 1986. "Insurance Reform Bill Mandates Lower Rates." *Public Administration Times* 9 (July 1), 1,8.

Keeton, Robert E. and Jeffrey O'Connell. 1965. *Basic Protection for the Accident Victim*. Boston: Little, Brown.

Keiser, K. R. 1980. "The New Regulation of Health and Safety." *Political Science Quarterly* 95 (Fall), 479–491.

Kelman, Steven. 1981. *Regulating Sweden, Regulating America*. Cambridge, MA: MIT Press.

_____. 1980. "Occupational Safety and Health Administration." In James Q. Wilson, ed., *The Politics of Regulation*. New York: Basic Books, 236–266.

Kemp, Kathleen A. 1984. "Accidents, Scandals, and Political Support for Regulatory Agencies." *Journal of Politics* 46 (May), 401–427.

_____. 1981. "Symbolic and Strict Regulation in the American States." *Social Science Quarterly* 62 (September), 516–526.

Kettl, Donald F. 1986. *Leadership at the Fed*. New Haven, CT: Yale University Press.

Key, V. O. 1951. *Southern Politics in State and Nation*. New York: Knopf.

Kimball, Spencer L. 1969a. "The Regulation of Insurance." In Spencer L. Kimball and Herbert S. Denenberg, eds., *Insurance, Government and Social Policy: Studies in Insurance Regulation*. Homewood, IL: Richard D. Irwin, 3–16.

_____. 1969b. "The Case for State Regulation of Insurance." In Spencer L. Kimball and Herbert S. Denenberg, eds., *Insurance, Government and Social Policy: Studies in Insurance Regulation*. Homewood, IL: Richard D. Irwin, 411–434.

_____. 1969c. "Unfinished Business in Insurance Regulation." *Wisconsin Law Review* 1969 (December), 1019–1025.

_____. 1960. *Insurance and Public Policy*. Madison: University of Wisconsin Press.

_____ and Ronald N. Boyce. 1958. "The Adequacy of State Insurance Rate Regulation." *Michigan Law Review* 56: 545–578.

_____ and Herbert S. Denenberg. 1969. "The Regulation of Investments: A Wisconsin Viewpoint." In Spencer L. Kimball and Herbert S. Denenberg, eds., *Insurance, Government, and Social Policy*. Homewood, IL: Richard D. Irwin, 126–136.

King, Rosa W. 1985. "The Coverage Crisis at Town Hall." *Business Week* (August 26), 72–75.

Kingdon, John W. 1981. *Congressmen's Voting Decisions*. New York: Harper and Row.

Kintner, Earl W., Joseph P. Bauer, and Michael J. Allen. 1985. "Application of the Antitrust Laws to the Activities of Insurance Companies." *North Carolina Law Review* 63: 431–491.

Kocolowski, Linda. 1985. "300–500% Premium Hikes Are Reported in the Tightening Daycare Liability Market." *National Underwriter* (Property and Casualty Edition (May 24), 2,45.

Kohlmeier, Louis. 1969. *The Regulators*. New York: Harper and Row.

Kolko, Gabriel. 1965. *Railroads and Regulation*. Princeton: Princeton University Press.

Kosterlitz, Julie. 1985. "Broad Coalition Prepares to Do Battle on Taxing Employee Fringe Benefits." *National Journal* 17 (May 4), 956–960.

Krooss, Herman E. and Martin R. Blyn. 1971. *A History of Financial Intermediaries*. New York: Random House.

Kulp, C. A. 1950. "The Rate Making Process in Property and Casualty Insurance— Goals, Technics, and Limits." *Law and Contemporary Problems* 15 (Autumn), 493–522.

Lease, Stephen L. and James W. Ruddy. 1985. "Bankers' Hopes and Fears: An Insurer's View." *Banks in Insurance Report* 1 (March), 7–9.

Lent, Linda M. 1981. "McCarran-Ferguson in Perspective." *Insurance Counsel Journal* 48 (July), 411–433.

Lester, James P., James L. Franke, Ann O'M. Bowman, and Kenneth W. Kramer. 1983. "Hazardous Wastes, Politics, and Public Policy: A Comparative State Analysis." *Western Political Quarterly* 36 (June), 257–285.

Lewis, Albert B. 1981. "Winning the Rehabilitation Battle: A Lesson for the Industry and the Regulators." *Best's Review* (Property and Casualty Edition), 81 (March), 10ff.

Life Insurance Association of America. 1962. *Life Insurance Companies as Financial Institutions*. Englewood Cliffs, NJ: Prentice-Hall.

Light, Paul. 1985. *Artful Work: The Politics of Social Security Reform*. New York: Random House.

Lilly, Claude C. 1976. "A History of Insurance Regulation in the United States." *CPCU Annals* 29 (June), 99–115.

Litan, Robert E. and William D. Nordhaus. 1983. *Reforming Federal Regulation*. New Haven, CT: Yale University Press.

212   The Political Economy of Regulation

Little, I. M. D. 1957. *A Critique of Welfare Economics*. 2nd ed. London: Oxford University Press.

Long, John D. 1977. "Should Punitive Damages Be Insured?" *Journal of Risk and Insurance* 44 (May), 78–87.

Long, Norton. 1962. *The Polity*. Chicago: Rand McNally.

Lowi, Theodore. 1969. *The End of Liberalism*. New York: W. W. Norton and Company.

Lusk, William B. and Douglas T. Hibbard. 1981. "The Independent Property-Casualty Agent Distribution System." *CLU Journal* 35 (January), 10–19.

MacAvoy, Paul W. 1979. *The Regulated Industries and the Economy*. New York: Norton.

_____. 1975. *Federal-State Regulation of the Pricing and Marketing of Insurance*. Washington: American Enterprise Institute.

MacDonald, Robert. 1985. "Bankers and Insurers: Logical Allies." *The Bankers Magazine* (January-February), 11–16.

Marcotte, Paul. 1986. "Media Blitz: Insurers Claim Lawsuit Crisis." *The ABA Journal* 72 (June 1), 19.

Marcus, Alfred. 1980. "Environmental Protection Agency." In James Q. Wilson, ed., *The Politics of Regulation*. New York: Basic Books, 267–303.

Markham, Jesse W. 1965. "Mergers and the Adequacy of the New Section 7." In Almarin Phillips, ed., *Perspectives on Antitrust Policy*. Princeton: Princeton University Press.

Marryott, Franklin J. 1950. "Mutual Insurance Under Rate Regulation." *Law and Contemporary Problems* 15 (Autumn), 540–562.

Mashaw, Jerry L. 1983. *Bureaucratic Justice: Managing Social Security Disability Claims*. New Haven, CT: Yale University Press.

Mayerson, Allen L. 1965. "An Inside Look at Insurance Regulation." *Journal of Risk and Insurance* 32 (March), 51–76.

Mazmanian, Daniel A. and Paul A. Sabatier. 1980. "A Multivariate Model of Public Policy-Making." *American Journal of Political Science* 24 (August), 439–468.

McConnell, Grant. 1966. *Private Power and American Democracy*. New York: Knopf.

McHugh, Donald P. 1969. "The Real Issue: State Versus Federal or Regulation Versus Competition?" In Spencer Kimball and Herbert S. Denenberg, eds. *Insurance, Government, and Social Policy*. Homewood, IL: Richard D. Irwin, 193–208.

McNamara, Daniel J. 1985. "The Capacity Crunch." *Banks in Insurance* 1 (April), 1–5.

Meier, Kenneth J. 1987a. "The Policy Impact of No-Fault Automobile Insurance." *Policy Studies Review* 7 (February), 497–506.

_____. 1987b. "The Political Economy of Consumer Protection." *Western Political Quarterly* 30 (June), 343–367.

_____. 1985a. "Little Groups of Actuaries: The Politics of Insurance Regulation." Paper presented at the annual meeting of the American Political Science Association, New Orleans, August.

_____. 1985b. *Regulation: Politics, Bureaucracy and Economics.* New York: St. Martin's Press.

_____ and Gary W. Copeland. 1986. "The Politics of Injury: Explaining State Legislative Responses to the Medical Malpractice Insurance Crisis." Paper presented at the annual meeting of the Southwest Political Science Association, San Antonio, March.

_____ and Lloyd G. Nigro. 1976. "Representative Bureaucracy and Policy Preferences: A Study in the Attitudes of Federal Executives." *Public Administration Review* 36 (July/August), 458–469.

Melnick, R. Shep. 1983. *Regulation and the Courts.* Washington: The Brookings Institution.

Michelbacher, G. L. and Nestor R. Roos. 1970. *Multiple-Line Insurers.* New York: McGraw-Hill.

Milbourne, Walter R. 1985. "Sex Discrimination by Insurers in the Rating of Policies: A Post-Norris Examination." *Insurance Counsel Journal* 52 (April), 264–273.

Miles, Rufus E. 1978. "The Origin and Meaning of Miles' Law." *Public Administration Review* 38 (September/October), 399–403.

Miles, Robert H. and Arvind Bhambri. 1983. *The Regulatory Executives.* Beverly Hills, CA: Sage Publications.

Miller, John W. 1982. "Faded History: The 1905 Armstrong Investigation. *CLU Journal* 36 (October), 78–84.

Millus, Albert J. 1985. "Too Little, Too Late?" *Best's Review* (Property and Casualty Edition), 85 (August), 32–40.

Mitnick, Barry M. 1980. *The Political Economy of Regulation.* New York: Columbia University Press.

Moe, Terry M. 1985. "Congressional Control of the Bureaucracy: An Assessment of the Positive Theory of 'Congressional Dominance.' " Paper presented at the annual meeting of the American Political Science Association, New Orleans, August.

_____. 1984. "Control and Feedback in Economic Regulation: The Case of the NLRB." Paper presented at the American Political Science Association meetings, Washington, August.

_____. 1982. "Regulatory Performance and Presidential Administration." *American Journal of Political Science* 26 (May), 197–225.

_____. 1980. *The Organization of Interests.* Chicago: University of Chicago Press.

Moore, Robert H. 1985. "Insurance-Availability Crisis Will Get Worse." *Journal of Commerce* (October 18).

Morais, Richard. 1985. "Faulting the Fortune Tellers." *Forbes* (October 21), 102–104.

Moser, Henry S. 1950. "Operation of Independents Under the Rate Regulatory Pattern." *Law and Contemporary Problems* 15 (Autumn), 523–539.

Munnell, Alicia H. 1982. *The Economics of Private Pensions.* Washington: The Brookings Institution.

Myers, Robert J. 1985. *Social Security* (3rd ed.) Homewood, IL: Richard D. Irwin.

"N. Y. Municipal Liability: Corcoran Outlines Plan for State to Sell Coverage." 1985. *Journal of Commerce* (October 18), 8A.

Nadel, Mark V. 1971. *The Politics of Consumer Protection.* Indianapolis, IN: Bobbs-Merrill.

National Center for State Courts. 1986. *A Preliminary Examination of Civil and Criminal Trend Data in State Trial Courts for 1978, 1981, and 1984.* Williamsburg, VA: author.

Newton, Blake T. 1979. "The Misleading Report on Life Insurance Cost Disclosure of the Federal Trade Commission Staff." *CLU Journal* 33 (October), 12–22.

Nice, David C. 1985. "State Party Ideology and Policy Making." *Policy Studies Journal* 13 (June), 780–796.

Nichols, G. Buddy and Kenneth W. Smith. 1985. "Who's Really to Blame for the Current Insurance Crisis?" *Risk Management* (July), 44–46.

Niskanen, William. 1971. *Bureaucracy and Representative Government.* Chicago: Aldine, Atherton.

Nolan, James. 1985. "Trial Lawyers vs. Tort Reform Drive." *Journal of Commerce* (December 10).

Noll, Roger G. and Bruce M. Owen. 1983. *The Political Economy of Deregulation.* Washington: American Enterprise Institute.

Nordlinger, Eric A. 1981. *On the Autonomy of the Democratic State.* Cambridge, MA: Harvard University Press.

Norton, Paul A. 1973. "A Brief History." In Davis W. Gregg and Vane B. Lucas, eds., *Life and Health Insurance Handbook.* Homewood, IL: Dow Jones-Irwin, 1089–1102.

Nutter, Franklin W. 1985a. *Ten Proposals for Civil Justice Reform.* New York: Alliance of American Insurers.

———. 1985b. "Search for Stability: Industry Must Solve Problems that Undermine a Stable Market." *Business Insurance* (June 17), 21–23.

O'Leary, James J. 1953. "The Influence of Government." In David McCahan, ed., *Investment of Life Insurance Funds.* Philadelphia: University of Pennsylvania Press, 227–245.

Olson, Mancur. 1965. *The Logic of Collective Action.* Cambridge, MA: Harvard University Press.

Orren, Karen. 1974. *Corporate Power and Social Change.* Baltimore: Johns Hopkins University Press.

Oster, Sharon M. 1980. "An Analysis of Some Causes of Interstate Differences in Consumer Regulations." *Economic Inquiry* 18 (January), 39–54.

Pashigian, B. Peter. 1983. "How Large and Small Plants Fare Under Environmental Regulation." *Regulation* 7 (September/October), 19–23.

Pateman, Carole. 1970. *Participation and Democratic Theory.* London: Cambridge University Press.

Patterson, Edwin W. 1927. *The Insurance Commissioner in the United States.* Cambridge, MA: Harvard University Press.

Pauly, Mark, Howard Kunreuther, and Paul Kleindorfer. 1986. "Regulation and Quality Competition in the U. S. Insurance Industry." In Jorg Finsinger and Mark V. Pauly, eds., *The Economics of Insurance Regulation.* New York: St. Martin's Press, 65–107.

Pave, Irene. 1985. "The Insurance Crisis that Could Cripple Day Care." *Business Week* (June 17), 114–115.

Peltzman, Sam. 1976. "Toward a More General Theory of Regulation." *Journal of Law and Economics* 19 (August), 211–240.

Pertschuk, Michael. 1982. *Revolt Against Regulation.* Berkeley: University of California Press.

Pine, Sidney. 1985. "Tight Market Fosters Captives, Despite Tax Changes." *Business Insurance* (March 11), 19.

Plumlee, John P. and Kenneth J. Meier. 1978. "Capture and Rigidity in Regulatory Administration." In Aaron Wildavsky and Judith May, eds., *The Policy Cycle*. Beverly Hills, CA: Sage Publications, 215–236.

Posner, Richard A. 1974. "Theories of Economic Regulation." *Bell Journal of Economics and Management Science* 5 (Autumn), 337–352.

Post, James E. 1976. *Risk and Response*. Lexington, MA: Lexington Books.

Price, David E. 1972. *Who Makes the Laws?* Cambridge, MA: Schenkman.

Prybutok, Benn. 1982. "Federalism Without Washington: The Insurance Regulatory Environment in the United States." *Publius* 12 (Spring), 79–98.

Pugh, William B. 1969. "Multiple Line Insurance Regulation." In Spencer Kimball and Herbert Denenberg, eds., *Insurance, Government, and Social Policy*.

Homewood, IL: Richard D. Irwin, 243–259.

Quirk, Paul J. 1981. *Industry Influence in Federal Regulatory Agencies*. Princeton: Princeton University Press.

_____. 1980. "The Food and Drug Administration." In James Q. Wilson, ed., *The Politics of Regulation*. New York: Basic Books, 191–234.

Reagan, Michael D. 1987. *Regulation: The Politics of Policy*. Boston: Little, Brown.

_____. 1985. "Intergovernmental Implementation of Partial Preemption Regulatory Programs." Paper presented at the annual meeting of the American Political Science Association, New Orleans, August.

Robinson, Jill D. 1986. "Insurance Premium Distribution—1985." *Best's Review* (Property and Casualty Edition), 86 (August), 14ff.

Rodino, Peter W. 1986. "Property/Casualty Industry Has Positive Cash Flow in Underwriting." Press release by author, June 9.

Rose, Michael D. 1967. "State Regulation of Property and Casualty Insurance Rates." *Ohio State Law Journal* 28: 669–733.

Rosenbaum, Walter A. 1984. *Environmental Politics and Policy*. Washington: Congressional Quarterly Press.

Ross, Nancy L. 1987. "Remember the Crisis in Liability Insurance?" *Washington Post National Weekly Edition* (January 5), 18.

Rothenberg, Lawrence S. 1985. "Reassessing Capture Theory: The Politics of Trucking Regulation." Paper presented at the annual meeting of the American Political Science Association, New Orleans, August.

Rottenberg, Simon. 1980. *Occupational Licensing and Regulation*. Washington: American Enterprise Institute.

Rourke, Francis E. 1984. First edition, 1969. *Bureaucracy, Politics and Public Policy.* Boston: Little, Brown.

Roussel, H. Lee and Moses K. Rosenberg. 1981. "The High Price of 'Reform': Title Insurance Rates and the Benefits of Rating Bureaus." *Journal of Risk and Insurance* 48 (December), 638–648.

Sabatier, Paul A. 1983. "Toward a Strategic Interaction Framework of Policy Evaluation and Learning." Paper presented at the annual meeting of the Western Political Science Association, March.

_____. 1977. "Regulatory Policy Making: Toward a Framework for Analysis." *Natural Resources Journal* 17 (July), 415–460.

_____. 1975. "Social Movements and Regulatory Agencies." *Policy Sciences* 6 (September), 301–342.

Schattschneider, E. E. 1960. *The Semi-Sovereign People.* New York: Holt, Reinhart, and Winston.

Schwartz, William B. and Neil K. Komisar. 1978. *Doctors, Damages, and Deterrence: An Economic View of Medical Malpractice.* Santa Monica, CA: The Rand Corporation.

Scotch, Richard K. 1984. *From Good Will to Civil Rights: Transforming Federal Disability Policy.* Philadelphia: Temple University Press.

Sharp, Anne A. 1976. "Insolvency Funds: Problems and Perspectives." *CPCU Annuals* 29 (December), 259–262.

Shenefield, John H. 1982. "Competition and the Insurance Industry: the New Frontier of Deregulation." In Nathan Weber, ed., *Insurance Deregulation: Issues and Perspectives.* New York: The Conference Board, 14–19.

Sherrill, Robert. 1986. "One Paper That Wouldn't Shut Up." *The Nation* (May 17), 688–691.

Sherwood, Steve. 1984. "Cancellation Hikes Cities' Coverage Costs." *Business Insurance* (December 17), 1,30.

Sichel, Werner. 1966. "Fire Insurance: Imperfectly Regulated Collusion." *Journal of Risk and Insurance* 33 (March), 95–114.

Sigelman, Lee and Roland E. Smith. 1980. "Consumer Regulation in the American States." *Social Science Quarterly* 61 (June), 58–76.

Skogh, Goran. 1986. "The Regulation of the Swedish Insurance Industry." In Jorg Finsinger and Mark V. Pauly, eds., *The Economics of Insurance Regulation.* New York: St. Martin's Press, 163–186.

Sloan, Frank A. 1985. "State Responses to the Malpractice Insurance Crisis of the 1970s: An Empirical Assessment." *Journal of Health Politics, Policy and Law* 9 (Winter), 629–646.

Smith, Janet Koholm. 1982. "An Analysis of State Regulations Governing Liquor State Licenses." *Journal of Law and Economics* 25 (October), 301–319.

Smith, Roland E. and Sidney E. Young. 1974. "Correlates of Policy Output: The Case of No-Fault Insurance." Paper presented at the annual meeting of the Southwestern Political Science Association, March.

Stelzer, Irwin M. and Geraldine Alpert. 1982. "Benefits and Costs of Insurance Deregulation." In Nathan Weber, ed., *Insurance Deregulation: Issues and Perspectives*. New York: The Conference Board, 6–13.

Stewart, Richard E. 1972. "Insurance Regulation: Current Issues and Problems." *The Annals of the American Academy of Political and Social Science* 400 (March), 59–68.

———. 1969. "Ritual and Reality in Insurance Regulation." In Spencer L. Kimball and Herbert S. Denenberg, eds., *Insurance, Government and Social Policy: Studies in Insurance Regulation*. Homewood, IL: Richard D. Irwin, 22–32.

Stigler, George J. 1971. "The Theory of Economic Regulation." *Bell Journal of Economics and Management Science* 2 (Spring), 3–21.

——— and Claire Friedlander. 1962. "What Can Regulators Regulate?: The Case of Electricity." *Journal of Law and Economics* 5 (October), 1–16.

Stokey, Edith and Richard Zeckhauser. 1978. *A Primer for Policy Analysis*. New York: Norton.

Stone, Alan. 1982. *Regulation and Its Alternatives*. Washington: Congressional Quarterly Press.

Stone, Deborah A. 1984. *The Disabled State*. Philadelphia: Temple University Press.

Tapp, Julian. 1986. "Regulation of the UK Insurance Industry." In Jorg Finsinger and Mark V. Pauly, eds., *The Economics of Insurance Regulation*. New York: St. Martin's Press, 27–61.

The Economist. 1986. "The Guilty Parties in the Great Liability Insurance Crisis." *The Economist* (March 22), 23–24.

Thomas, Rich and David Pauly. 1986. "Who's Killing the Thrifts?" *Newsweek* (November 10), 51–54.

Thompson, Lawrence H. 1986. "Statement Before the Senate Committee on Commerce, Science and Technology." (March 4). Washington: General Accounting Office.

Tobias, Andrew. 1982. *The Invisible Bankers*. New York: Simon and Schuster.

Trenerry, C. F. 1926. *The Origin and Early History of Insurance.* London: P. S. King and Son.

Truman, David. 1951. *The Governmental Process.* New York: Knopf.

Trupin, Aaron. 1978. "Open Rating in Insurance." In John D. Long, ed., *Issues in Insurance* Volume I. Malvern, PA: American Institute for Property and Liability Underwriters, 219–302.

U. S. Commission on Civil Rights. 1978. *Discrimination Against Minorities and Women in Pensions and Health, Life and Disability Insurance.* Washington: author.

Vaughn, Emmett J. 1982. *Fundamentals of Risk and Insurance.* New York: John Wiley and Sons.

van Aartrijk, Peter. 1985. "1985: The Battles Ahead." *Best's Review* (Property and Casualty Edition), 85 (January), 24ff.

Vig, Norman J. and Michael E. Kraft. 1984. *Environmental Policy in the 1980s.* Washington: Congressional Quarterly Press.

Viscusi, W. Kip. 1983. *Risk By Choice.* Cambridge, MA.: Harvard University Press.

Washington Correspondent. 1986. "Nader, Hunter Continue Anti-Insurance Offensive." *Best's Insurance Management Reports.* (January 20), 1.

Wasilewski, Charles. 1986a. "Tort Reform: Courting Public Opinion." *Best's Review* (Property and Casualty Edition), 86 (June), 14ff.

Wasilewski, Charles. 1986b. "Auto Insurance—1985." *Best's Review* (Property and Casualty Edition), 86 (September), 14ff.

Webb, Bernard L. 1979. "Investment Income and Ratemaking." *CPCU Journal* 32 (September), 128–136.

Weese, Samuel H. and J. Wesley Ooms. 1978. "The National Flood Insurance Program—Did The Insurance Industry Drop Out?" *CPCU Journal* 31 (June), 186–203.

Weingast, Barry R. and Mark J. Moran. 1983. "Bureaucratic Discretion or Congressional Control? Regulatory Policymaking by the Federal Trade Commission." *Journal of Political Economy* 91 (Number 5), 765–800.

Weisbart, Steven N. 1975. *Extraterritorial Regulation of Life Insurance.* Homewood, IL: Richard D. Irwin.

Welborn, David and Anthony Brown. 1980. *Regulatory Policy and Process: The Public Service Commissions in Tennessee.* Knoxville: Bureau of Public Administration, University of Tennessee.

Weller, Charles D. 1978. "The McCarran-Ferguson Act's Antitrust Exemption for Insurance." *Duke Law Journal* 1978: 587–641.

220   The Political Economy of Regulation

Wenck, Thomas L. 1983. "Insurance Company Insolvencies—A Prescription of Anti-
dotes." *CPCU Journal* 36 (December), 223–231.

Wiebe, Robert H. 1967. *The Search for Order, 1877–1920.* New York: Hill and
Wang.

Williams, C. Arthur. 1983. "Regulating Property and Liability Insurance Rates
Through Excess Profits Statues." *Journal of Risk and Insurance* 50 (September), 445–472.

_____. 1969. "Insurance Rate Regulation—A New Era?" *CPCU Annals* 22 (Septem-
ber), 203–219.

Williams, Nieman A. 1981. "Workers Compensation: Perspective for the Eighties."
Special Issue of *CPCU Journal* (Fall).

Wilson, James Q. 1980a. *The Politics of Regulation.* New York: Basic Books.

_____. 1980b. "The Politics of Regulation." In James Q. Wilson, *The Politics of
Regulation.* New York: Basic Books, 357–394.

_____. 1973. *Political Organizations.* New York: Basic Books.

Wish, Paul E. 1986. "Apples and Oranges—and Lemons, Too." *Best's Insurance
Management Reports* (January 20), 1.

Witt, Robert C. and Harry Miller. 1981. "Rate Regulation, Competition, and Underwriting Risk in Automobile Insurance Markets." *CPCU Journal* 34 (December), 202–220.

_____. and Jorge Urrutia. 1984a. "An Overview and Assessment of No-Fault
Plans." *CPCU Journal* 37 (March), 10–24.

_____ and Jorge Urrutia. 1984b. "No-Fault Versus Tort Liability Compensation."
CPCU Journal 37 (September), 181–191.

_____ and Jorge Urrutia. 1983. "A Comparative Economic Analysis of Tort Liability and No-Fault Compensation Systems in Automobile Insurance." *Journal of
Risk and Insurance* 50 (December), 631–669.

Wolman, Harold. 1971. *The Politics of Federal Housing.* New York: Dodd, Mead.

Work, Clemens P., Jeannye Thorton, and Micheline Maynard. 1985. "As Liability-
Insurance Squeeze Hits Everyone." *U. S. News and World Report.* (October 7),
56–57.

Zeigler, Harmon. 1964. *Interest Groups in American Society.* Englewood Cliffs, NJ:
Prentice-Hall.

Index

Shenefield, John H., 66
Sherman Antitrust Act, 67, 68, 69
short-tail line of insurance, definition of, 10
Sichel, Werner, 80
Sierra Club, 195n
Sigelman, Lee, 139
Simon, Paul, 101
Sivertsen, Norman. *See* Hira, Labh
Skogh, Goran, 34
Sloan, Frank, 177, 190n
Small Business Administration, 43
Smith, Janet, 26
Smith, Kenneth. *See* Nichols, Buddy
Smith, Roland, 119
social investment, as regulatory goal, 47
Social Security, 38
solvency, 51, 61, 72, 143, 144, 156, 172; as regulatory goal, 46
South-Eastern Underwriters, 64-68, 73, 85, 111
sovereign immunity, 93
Sporkin, Stanley, 182n
St. Paul Fire and Marine Insurance, 72
Stark, Fortney, 131, 134
State Department, 43
State Farm Insurance, 9, 80, 121, 159
Stelzer, Irwin, 46
Stewart, Richard, 47, 83
Stigler, George, 18-23, 25, 27, 28, 29, 31, 138, 140, 142, 148, 154, 156, 166, 170, 181n
Stokey, Edith, 181n
Stone, Alan, 181n
Stone, Deborah, 38
Street, Charles R., 65
strict liability, 93
Supreme Court, U.S., 51, 53, 64, 66, 67, 68, 71, 100, 113, 124-126, 135, 147
swine flu vacine, 35

tax discrimination, 147, 149
Tax Equity and Fiscal Responsibility Act of 1982, 130
Tax Reform Act of 1984, 99
tax refunds, 16
taxes, insurance company, 46, 51, 68, 70, 109; federal, 126-130, 136, 170; corporate income, 127; property and casualty insurance, 130-131; life insurance, 127-130;

premium, 46, 147-149; federal recommendation, 175-6. *See also* premium taxes
Teachers Insurance and Annuity Association, 113
Teamsters, 121
Thomas, Rich, 40
title insurance, 43
Tobias, Andrew, 47
tontine, 55, 56, 58
topping up provision, unisex insurance, 123
tort cases, 158
tort liability, 118, 159
tort reform, 95, 101, 177
Travelers Health Association, 71, 112, 135
Travelers Health Association v. *Virginia,* 112
Treasury Department, 133, 137
Truman, David, 22, 140
Truman, Harry S., 114, 135
Trupin, Aaron, 77, 78, 79

underwriters, 144, 148
underwriting expenses, 103
underwriting loss, 88
Unfair Competition Act, 76
uniform model insurance laws, 45, 111, 140, 169
unisex insurance laws, 31, 109, 122-126, 135, 170, 171
United Airlines, 29
United Auto Workers, 121
universal life insurance, 132-3, 200n; definition of, 179n
urbanization, 21, 140
Urrutia, Jorge, 118, 119, 150, 158, 159, 160
Utica, Mutual, 94

van Aartrijk, Peter, 131
Veterans Administration, 40, 42, 62
Vig, Norman J., 29
Viscusi, W. Kip, 27
Vogel, Ronald J., 45, 46
Volcker, Paul, 34, 90

Wall Street Journal, 101
Walter-Hancock Bill, 68, 85
War Risk Insurance Fund, 43